*Emotional Care of the Facially
Burned and Disfigured*

Emotional Care of the Facially Burned and Disfigured

Norman R. Bernstein, M. D.

Assistant Professor of Psychiatry, Harvard Medical School;
Acting Director, Child Psychiatry Unit,
Massachusetts General Hospital;
Director of Psychiatry, Shriners Burns Institute, Boston

With a Foreword by

Oliver Cope, M. D.

Emeritus Professor of Surgery,
Harvard Medical School.
Formerly Chief of Surgery,
Massachusetts General Hospital

Little, Brown and Company · *Boston*

Library of Congress catalog card No. 75-30277

ISBN 0-316-09193-6

Printed in the United States of America

For Marilyn

Contents

Foreword

One reads Dr. Bernstein's warm and erudite book with troubled wonder. What is wrong with a world in which people must be taught how to care psychologically for their injured fellowman?

Any disfigurement is a source of embarrassment, but burn accidents are particularly traumatic and mutilating because they so often involve the unprotected face and hands. People stare, comment thoughtlessly, ask rude personal questions, are embarrassed into silence, or are unable to converse easily. Without intending to, strangers and friends in one way or another repeatedly make the disfigured person feel abnormal, our of place, unwelcome, and unwanted.

Dr. Bernstein has elucidated in straightforward language the desperate needs of disfigured people. He has given us, in the health professions, realistic guidelines for the long-term care essential to a disfigured person's psychological recovery and his ability to come to terms with his burden.

This book explains the importance of facial expression in relating to other people and the disastrous effect of having this expressive ability diminished or, in the most severe cases, destroyed altogether, leaving a frightening "mask" of scar tissue. How does his irrevocably altered visage affect the self-image and the psychological integrity of the victim? How do the people around him react to the mask? No matter how the disfigured person may have regarded himself before the accident, the descent upon him of a wholly unexpected and sudden change in body image and life prospects leaves him vulnerable, seriously depressed, and self-conscious in the extreme. Dr. Bernstein shows how everyone with whom he comes into contact—family, hospital personnel, social workers, nurses, and physicians—can and should be helping him develop defenses appropriate to coping with his appearance.

Most readers will be aware of the tremendous amount of time and variety of skills needed just to keep a severely burned person alive. Dr. Bernstein challenges us to shift our emphasis, after the acute emergency, to the patient's need for integrated medical, surgical, and psychiatric care over the long hospital recovery period and in the establishment of a new life thereafter. Utilizing a unique opportunity at a new treatment center, the author shows how a coordinated hospital staff was developed to accept the responsibility of being a continuous bridge to life for the patient.

This is a very difficult goal to achieve for many reasons. At first, the need for intensive care takes precedence over all else. At all stages there are involved a number of specialists, who will understandably take a narrow view. In addition, the stamina of those giving daily care is easily drained by the effort to cope with their own emotional reactions as they try to meet the patient's inexhaustible need for loving care. It is most important that the core medical staff explicitly assume responsibility for overseeing the entire care program as long as the patient is in the hospital and later as long as he maintains contact with it. Otherwise it is too easy for each specialist to attend only to his area of interest while the patient withdraws into "social death."

Dr. Bernstein is most interested in exploring in this book the psychiatric aspect of burn patient care, specifically of the patient with a severely damaged face. Any long-term hospital patient has difficulty accepting his helplessness and dependency. And any severely burned person also has to cope with the isolation and alienation inherent in his technical care. A fascinating aspect of this book is Dr. Bernstein's exploration of the effects of disfigurement at various ages and in various life circumstances. The fact that certain circumstances were found to be favorable should lead us to develop treatment programs and personnel that will provide such a favorable environment.

Most important is Dr. Bernstein's description of the development and functioning of the burn care team, in which the physicians, nurses, social workers, physiotherapists, secretaries, and other hospital personnel form a therapeutic milieu for the patient and his family.

Everyone connected with the care of injured and disfigured people should read this book. It is a magnificent start toward dissolving psychological scars, dissipating our primitive fear of the disfigured, and showing us the real people remaining behind the masks. It will be a medical classic.

Oliver Cope

Preface

At the present time, there is a rapid expansion in the number of intensive care units being developed around the country, and new, extraordinarily complex burn centers are being planned and opened all over the world. The descriptions of these centers, and much of the newer literature on burn care, form a litany extolling the superb facilities available for the physical care of burned people. For example, according to a new burn center plan recounted in the *New York Times* (August 1975), there will be superb professional medical care, plastic surgery, helicopter access, and complete support from other nearby medical facilities, making the center capable of serving large numbers of people. Only in the very last sentence of the article was it noted that provisions would be made for rehabilitation services, psychiatric care, and occupational therapy.

All of us working in large medical centers recognize the steady advance of costs, the encroachment of stultifying bureaucracies, and the increasing medical specialization, which carry with them the threats of dehumanized patient care, diminished confidence in the physician, and increased fear of hospitals. It has therefore been a particularly heartening experience to see that even with all the inevitable struggles and frictions a burn care unit could be conceived and constructed that would actually provide fine patient care, a chance to teach others how to give such care, and a chance to pursue clinical and laboratory investigation for the direct benefit of people, rather than as a public relations triumph. Travelers from around the country and around the world have visited and asked how our center works—how we prepare people to face life with the handicaps of their disfigurement with minimum dislocation.

As one visiting burn surgeon described our efforts at rehabilitation and the combined use of psychiatric and social service personnel, "Everybody talks about it, but here you seem to make it work." It is not a miracle but an achievement to be proud of that we have converted some of the rhetoric into the best comprehensive care for patients and their families and have devised ways to teach others to do the same thing. This is the best reason for putting down in writing what we have been about. We have emphasized taking a broad view of the life course of people who have been burned and of some of the basic defense mechanisms that make it difficult for facially disfigured people to resume normal lives. Every opportunity we have had to share information and techniques with workers in the United States and abroad has reinforced the conviction that we are on the right road.

This is not intended as a book to scan quickly so that the reader can then turn to a score of more specialized works on how to approach these problems. It is intended to be a self-contained focal work on the nonsurgical aspects of rehabilitating burned children and adults. It was written with a great deal of assistance from many humane and superbly skilled surgeons and other specialists, whom I thank.

N. R. B.

Acknowledgments

No aspect of this work has been carried out alone. A dozen years ago Dr. William Sharpe and I first tried to hypnotize burn patients. Subsequently, he and Dr. Jack O. Rice became consultants to the Shriners Burns Institute when it opened in Boston in 1969, and I became the psychiatrist for the Burns Institute.

Dr. Oliver Cope, who had worked with the Cocoanut Grove fire victims over 30 years ago and was Chief of Surgery at the Massachusetts General Hospital, became the first Chief of Staff at the Shriners Burns Institute when it was planned and built alongside Massachusetts General to serve as its burn ward for children. He originated the idea of having a chief of psychiatry at the Burns Institute because of his experiences with the emotional problems of these sufferers. He invited me to take this position and has supported me generously ever since. Under the leadership of his successor, Dr. John Francis Burke, the psychological services have grown, and awareness of the psychosocial aspects of burn care has increased.

Mrs. Elizabeth Sheehy, chief of nursing, has consistently advocated good, comprehensive patient care and the in-service psychological training of her staff; along with this she has provided prompt emotional buttressing for her nurses, burn technicians, aides, and clerical staff whenever needed. Miss Maureen Doran, clinical leader on the reconstructive ward, has worked steadily to develop the nurse interviewing project and has cooperated in individual patient planning, social, psychological, or surgical.

Dr. John Crawford, chief of pediatrics, with his encyclopedic knowledge of pediatrics and human nature, offered unstinting support. He also helped to develop the drug protocol with Dr. Nathaniel Hollister, the neurosurgeon and psychiatrist who consulted on burned children. Dr. Alia Antoon, senior staff pediatrician, helped in all aspects of patient management. Drs. Bradford Cannon, John Constable, and John Remensnyder, the plastic surgeons, all gave me access to their case reports, as well as the opportunity to work in collaboration with them. Dr. Robert Goldwyn, a plastic surgeon at Beth Israel Hospital, Boston, also gave wise counsel and recounted clinical experience very generously.

Mrs. Katherine O'Malley and her assisting recreation therapists provided a lot of information about the patients and their behavior; Miss Nancy Newton, chief physical therapist, cooperated actively in individual patient care and also took part in the group work with the patients.

Dr. David Chedekel, principal psychologist, helped with in-service training, meeting with groups of nurses and nursing assistants, but he also contributed greatly in tracing patients for follow-ups and did many of the follow-up interviews. He continues to provide psychotherapy for burned children on our service, supervise trainees, and lead the teenage group.

Miss Joan Murphy, former assistant director of nursing, helped with the interviewing and coding of interviews with adolescents. Miss Roberta Crosby helped with the follow-ups while working as a technologist in Dr. Constable's research laboratory at the Burns Institute.

Dr. Richard Goldberg, research psychologist of the Massachusetts Rehabilitation Commission, gave generously of his time and effort in helping us to develop questionnaires and to think out comparisons of different types of handicaps and of the ways individuals respond to them in terms of rehabilitation.

Dr. Richard Schmitt, a psychologist at the Galveston Shriners Burns Institute and the University of Texas Medical Branch at Galveston, shared ideas, research data, and encouragement as our work evolved. His ideas have been gratefully included and cannot be sufficiently acknowledged.

Dr. Barry Pless, at the University of Rochester School of Medicine, provided a wealth of information about chronic illness in children and shared his thoughts about the difficulties of assessing these problems.

With great industry and psychological sensitivity, Mrs. Nancy Hart made home visits and provided reports on the reactions of families.

Mrs. Shirley Moscow was very helpful in editing, while Mrs. Lin Richter, Medical Editor for Little, Brown, helped formulate the original idea and kept after me with the right blend of encouragement, criticism, and exhortation—all executed with a matchless sense of the pressures on a practicing physician and a precise sensitivity to the tolerable moment to push.

Mrs. Mildred Leavitt typed, delivered, and tirelessly retyped the manuscript, while Ms. Paulette Nippet added late afterthoughts, sought references, and photocopied bibliographies—both working without complaint and with consummate good cheer. Mrs. Celia Kutz proofread and transmitted the manuscript and helped scour the libraries for references. My thanks go to all of them.

N. R. B.

Emotional Care of the Facially Burned and Disfigured

Prologue

This book grew out of work with patients and is intended to be helpful in clinical care and social rehabilitation. This direction was prefigured when Dr. Stanley Cobb founded the Department of Psychiatry at the Massachusetts General Hospital 40 years ago. He gathered together a group of people who were intensely interested in working on the psychological problems of patients in a general hospital setting and focused on what he considered a psychosomatic approach, which he was fond of interpreting as a specialty dedicated to the removal of a hyphen, the one separating psyche and soma. In time, the work with physically ill patients resulted in major involvement with the hundreds of burn victims of the disastrous Cocoanut Grove fire that occurred in a Boston nightclub over 30 years ago. From that time on, the psychological aspects of burns and burn care have had an important role in Massachusett General's Department of Psychiatry.

When the Division of Child Psychiatry was opened, it continued the direction of giving attention to biomedical problems in psychiatry. In 1963 Dr. William Sharpe and I studied hypnosis in order to deal with our first burn patients who were having serious pain problems during dressing changes, and since that time I have worked with adult and child patients with severe burn lesions. In 1968 the Shriners Burns Institute (Figure 1) was opened, affiliated with the Massachusetts General Hospital and staffed by it in association with Harvard Medical School.

Figure 1.   Shriners Burns Institute, Boston, opened in 1968 for the acute and long-term treatment of burned children.

Dr. Oliver Cope, Professor of Surgery at Harvard and Chief of Staff of the new Burns Institute, actively promoted the participation of psychiatrists in the care of burn patients in the Burns Institute, implementing the humanizing care he had taught over many years in many places and delineated in his book *Man, Mind and Medicine* [1].

The work developed along several different lines. First, there were problems of dealing with acute burns, deliria, agitation, extreme fright, and responses to loss and bereavement. Later, psychiatric help was requested for difficulties with eating, dressing changes, and obtaining compliance with treatment regimens and for aiding the dejection, despair, and loss of hope attendant on being in the hospital under such severe stresses. As time passed, we became more involved in the care of long-term patients and the difficulties they posed for the nurses, doctors, and physical therapists. Our view was broadened by our dealing with relatives and close friends. Many problems persisted in the maintenance of hope for patients and their families, as well as for the staff, who commonly experienced periods of discouragement in dealing with severe burns. Over the course of time, the different stages of care became associated with special problems—encouraging patients to be more active and to get up and walk, and preparing them to participate in groups or to go home and to come back for future care.

Whether the patients returned home, to work, or to school, numerous issues arose that widened our concerns. At first we were impressed by the mixed attitudes of professionals toward this work and how people (most people) tended to be either repelled or tremendously absorbed by this work. We came to see that the general community attitudes were negative and that the more obvious the deformity or disfigurement with which a patient was left, the greater was the social handicap. The sociology of stigma and deviance began to seem important, and we eagerly turned to works in medical sociology for aid in conceptualizing and dealing with the altered roles of the burn victims. This in turn proved to be helpful in many branching directions. One fork led to the question of classification of burns and an unsuccessful attempt to grade or categorize levels and degrees of disfigurement. From this effort it quickly became obvious that no simple classification was feasible, and that each of the different types of lesions, whether distorting, discoloring, or immobilizing, involved a complex description, as well as delineation of the areas burned and their special meanings and importance.

When the effort to assemble the many variables in a unified system failed, we turned to considerations of the psychology of individual and group perception and made some excursions into aesthetics in an effort to get at the basic issues in disfigurement and tried to determine how psychosocial forces alter the manner in which a visible lesion is viewed and how the personal perceptions of relatives and the community accept or reject these lesions in multifarious ways that alter the patient's adaptation following burn injuries.

Another logical direction for investigation and study was in the area of body image and self-image and the ways in which personality development is altered by conspicuous congenital and acquired deformities. In this book, we have tried to give examples of what forms adaptations take when disfigurement is acquired at different points in the life cycle and of what we have found in our attempts to follow up on what happened to these patients over the years. As we sought out the patients, it became clear that many had disappeared from public view and that society had helped force this disappearance. It also seemed evident that some aspect of the medical care system furthered this exclusion of the deviant and the nonhelpable. When the technical procedures were accomplished, the medical specialists felt they had little to add, and they discontinued working with the disfigured, thus adding to the patients' isolation. For the facially disfigured, it was the worst—as described by MacGregor et al., their fate had been "social death" [2].

However, as we worked more and more with the children at the Shriners Burns Institute, and a thousand children were treated, we came to see that not all patients followed this course. We became obsessed with a number of questions: Which patients made successful adaptations? Which were the crucial points and ways in which we might intervene or have members of the caretaking teams intervene? When should we intervene, either in terms of the age of the patient or the stage of reconstructive care? The overall effort became a continuing clinical investigation of the psychology of desperate situations. This yielded broader meanings to our work. We shared the problems of death and dying with our co-workers in the emergency room, with the coronary care staff, and with those who worked with cancer patients and problems of terminal care. These patients' need for repeated surgery led us to deal with anesthesiologists, who were eager to help minimize the traumatic effects of surgery and anesthesia and who kept asking for opportunities to discuss the reactions of adults and children undergoing anesthesia and for ways of improving the human aspects in spite of the pressures of busy hospital routines. There were many conferences on pain, its significance and its management, and the ways in which the staff dealt with having to cause pain and to observe pain being endured by the patients, especially the children.

These efforts went on over a decade, and in that period there have been some significant changes in the care of burn victims. One of the uniformly appalling features of burn care was once the dreadful smell that attended it, a fact not often mentioned, but generally endured. With the coming of silver nitrate dressings and sulfonamide creams this disappeared, making the atmosphere more tolerable. Advances in antibiotics and in the struggle against the universal threat of infection made their appearance.

The ways in which sterile precautions were maintained at one time made parents and relatives almost unrecognizable when they visited the isolated patient, since they had to come swathed in masks and gowns. In planning the Burns Institute, special bacteria control units were designed to deal with both the problems of isolation and infection. In these units, air flows downward, carrying dust and bacterially contaminated particles with it. They have proved to be very successful in diminishing contamination and wound infection. Figure 2 shows one of these units, with the plastic walls that make access to the patients more feasible, utilizing slits in the partition through which care can be given

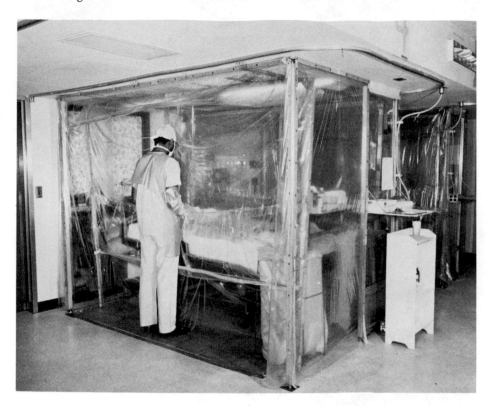

Figure 2.   Bacteria control unit at Shriners Burns Institute.

and objects handled. In Figure 3, a nurse is seen making crayon drawings with a child, demonstrating both the improvement over having a solid isolation room around the child and the remaining disadvantage of a definite separation and a mask and gown that dehumanize the visitor or staff person. Figure 4 is a photograph taken from the position of the patient, showing the restricting sense of space patterning produced by the bacteria control unit, as well as the reflections and distortions of perception that are also introduced. The television set provided for the distraction of the patients from their miseries can be seen. But fever, toxicity, and distance often interfere with the children's ability to keep their attention focused on the screen. Figure 5 is a photograph of the open ward, and Figure 6 shows the physical therapy room, with a child walking in the hydrotherapy tank, which is a regular part of the care of the burned child.

The same surgeons often care for both adult and child burn patients. However, the adult burn patients are cared for in Massachusetts General Hospital's burn ward, across the street from the children at the Shriners

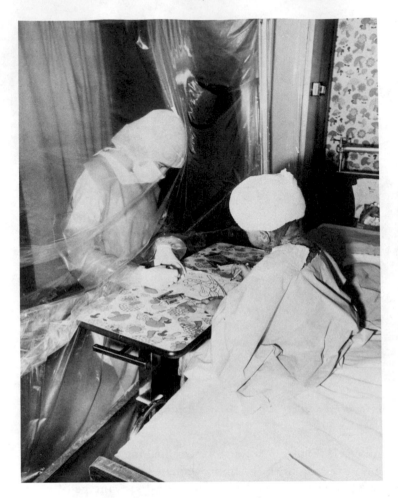

Figure 3. Nurse and patient playing through plastic wall of bacteria control unit.

Burns Institute. The institutions are connected by a tunnel, and the journey is often referred to as going from the "Shrine to Mecca" as the doctors hurry back and forth. The adult burn ward keeps severely burned patients in single rooms, as shown in Figure 7. They may later be shifted to shared rooms, but in early treatment of the burn wound, isolation techniques are applied to the entire single room. The burn ward is on the twelfth floor of a busy, 1000-bed hospital with 7000 employees and has a different design and a vastly different atmosphere from that in the 30-bed Shriner's unit with its generally separate staff of 200. However, the principles of care are similar, and many of the routines and programs are identical. In both, the staff uses psychiatric

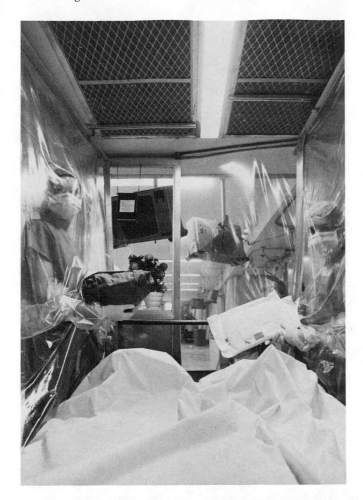

Figure 4. Patient's view from within bacteria control unit. Two nurses are shown holding objects inside the unit through the openings.

consultation freely and involves the patients in talking in groups as soon as it is feasible. The surgeons have a generally similar philosophy of active treatment and, as noted, often work with both adults and children. There is some visiting and sharing of conferences by the professional staff, but the inevitable time pressure severely limits this kind of interaction.

Because the structure of a well-established and heavily staffed hospital is familiar, it might, in contrast, be useful to describe the smaller and newer children's unit. It is housed in a separate three-story building with its own dining room, offices, physiotherapy facilities, conference room, and chapel on the first floor. Laboratories for research into many

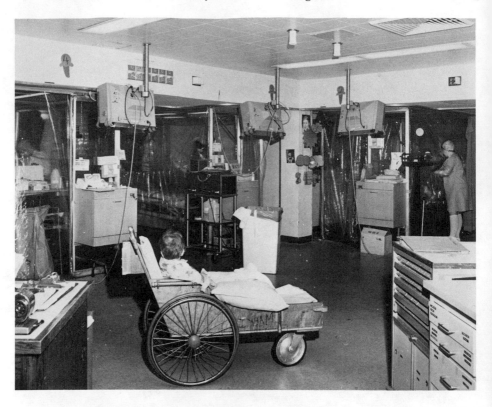

Figure 5. Acute Burn Ward, showing deployment of bacteria control units.

aspects of tissue growth, repair, bacteriology, and plastic surgery are located on the second floor. On the third floor, there are 30 beds, which are placed in several types of areas. One group is the acute care section, which is shown in Figures 2–5. Some beds are in separate rooms or on the open part of the ward. The less acutely ill patients, or those who have come in for elective and reconstructive surgery, are placed in side rooms or on the open ward of the reconstructive side of the floor.

The hospital was planned so that it would involve all the staff in comprehensive care, especially the nurses. However, for nearly two years staff development was so focused on surgical techniques and the stabilization and maturation of a core group of experienced senior nurses that little attention could be given to psychological and social issues. As experience with difficult patients and their families accumulated, the nurses began to deal more and more with the social workers in planning. Psychiatric consultation led to setting up nursing groups for staff development and also as a vehicle for handling the severe tensions and overall reactions to this specialized type of work. These groups continue

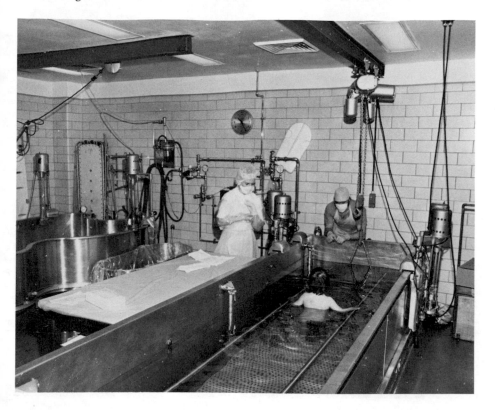

Figure 6.   Attendants walking child in hydrotherapy tank.

in operation and are led by the psychiatrist or the psychologist at different times. The four pediatricians attend social service rounds at different times in their duties. The staff now has two half-time social workers who participate in caring for individual families and also take part in the nurse interviewing project described in Chapter 8. The head physical therapist helps run the therapy group with adolescents held weekly by a staff psychiatrist.

The recreational therapists have shared information freely with the clinical staff and the schoolteachers provided by the city of Boston have regularly attended conferences and coordinated their work with the staff and also participated in the discharge planning. This has involved varied approaches. Teachers have come to the hospital to see what the children look like. Nurses and social workers have gone to local schools to talk about the needs of the children, as well as to talk about fire prevention. There is now a director of fire prevention who coordinates these efforts and who also participates in videotaping of the interviews with children that are becoming more and more a part of in-service

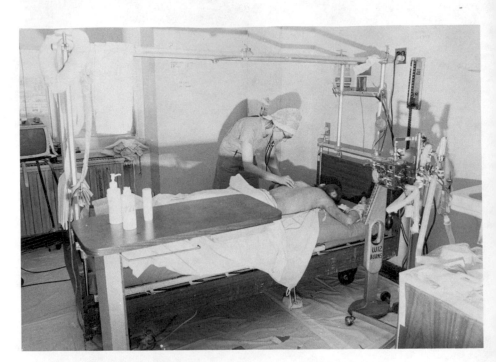

Figure 7. At the Massachusetts General Hospital a severely burned adult patient stays in a single room, where isolation techniques are used. As he recovers, he may be transferred to a shared room.

training. In addition, psychology trainees and child psychiatry fellows see patients in consultation for the Burns Institute.

The configuration of surgical training rotates residents in surgery from the Massachusetts General and Beth Israel hospitals to the Burns Institute. There is also a Massachusetts General surgical intern and a pediatric resident. The surgical involvement is heavily restricted to the technical training, though the residents have generally tried to cooperate with plans for rescheduling operations and transporting patients from different cities. The pediatricians generally become more involved with the families in the traditional pediatric roles and work in coordination with the social service, physical therapy, and psychological staff in their handling of the children.

The competition and pressures from each service for the time of its trainees in the larger institution across the street have sometimes created difficulties. There are advantages to a small unit, in that the personal contacts help one to bridge the communications problems common to all active academic and research hospitals with their intrinsic conflicting pressures for patient care and for achievement in research and teaching. However, the largest single hazard from this small social system is the absence of a critically needed teacher or nurse who is ill or has gone on vacation or resigned. Friction between staff members is much more disrupting in the small unit than in the large institution, where there is some pressure from the overall milieu to dilute or randomize some of these stresses and conflicts.

Communication, while better in the small institution, is never easy, and the range of communication problems has covered the whole spectrum, from families who could not or would not hear what they were being told, to inept ways of telling people what was going on or the slight differences in phrasing that can be misheard and mistranslated as they are passed along. Conflicts over whether or not to operate, what to hint about prognosis, when to say a child is definitely dying are, of course, common in all areas of clinical care. With the parents of burned children, the timing and tact with which they are told about the future medical needs of the children and how much scarring, incapacitation, and disfigurement are expected are part of the communication problem.

Plastic and reconstructive surgeons, collaborating with the general surgeons in the work of the hospital, have provided the most precise information available about disfigurement and patients' future needs. Further, these surgical specialists have a particular interest in psychological factors in patient care and have longer-term contacts with patients than any of the other specialists. Residents may come and go, but the plastic surgeons are most likely to have contacts with severely burned patients for at least a decade, repeatedly revising scars as children grow and trying to maintain hope and psychological growth by continual efforts to improve appearance. These efforts sometimes involve the assistance of cosmeticians and wigmakers.

The hospital is special in several other ways. It is one of 20 hospitals funded by the Shriners, a group of some 900,000 thirty-second-degree Masons, who, with their affiliated ladies' and young people's groups, pay for all the care given in their hospitals, which include three burns institutes, as well as children's orthopedic institutions. All three burns institutes are university-affiliated: the Cincinnati Shriners Burns Institute with the University of Cincinnati Medical School, which is next door; the Galveston Shriners Burns Institute with the University of Texas Medical Branch at Galveston and its teaching hospital; and the Boston unit, affiliated with Harvard Medical School. These three institutions keep informal clinical contacts with each other, and staff members in each specialty have had some opportunities to share information on patient care, through either direct meetings or specialty conferences such as those of the American Burn Association and The International Burn Society meetings, and through various physical therapy, social work, psychological, psychiatric, and plastic surgery conferences, which are now giving more attention to the problems of trauma, particularly of burns, and the operation of intensive care units.

A special boost to staff morale is the publicity the Shriners give to patients who come to the hospital. These children are described on television, radio, and in the local newspapers. There have been fund drives, blood drives, and articles about the staff, as well as burn prevention shows and efforts by the staff to appeal for legislation for flame-retardant clothing for children. This adds a sense of mission to the group; and however sophisticated the staff, pleasant public attention is appreciated. These fillips to morale are needed (even the special buttons now worn by members of the burn team).

The work of the Burns Institute is arduous, with many stresses and strains for all. The rewards are long-term and not immediate, but the work yields steadily more opportunities for study and for ever-enlarging challenges. The organization of the material presented here will, it is hoped, give some coherent sense of the avenues traveled by this burn group and provide ideas for others who are helping burn patients and the people around them.

REFERENCES

1. Cope, Oliver. *Man, Mind and Medicine: The Doctor's Education.* Lippincott, Philadelphia, 1968.
2. MacGregor, Frances C., et al. (Eds.). *Facial Deformities and Plastic Surgery: A Psychosocial Study.* Thomas, Springfield, Ill., 1953.

1

Appearance: Concepts of Perception and Disfigurement

Seeing is believing.
Farquhar [1]

Art is the lie that makes us realize truth.
Picasso [2]

Physical handicaps afflict millions of people in this country. The handicaps that seem most socially destructive to individuals are the most visible ones. Here, we will be focusing on the disfigurements that burn patients suffer and on the facial scars that impair their social and personal functioning. The details covered herein have both particular and general applications, as many of the factors influence all disabilities that can be noticed in normal work or school or family life. The ways in which visible handicaps alter social and psychological functioning are so powerful and important that a fuller understanding of them is important for the care of these large numbers of people and, one hopes, for changing social attitudes and the reactions of people around them.

Fires occur in larger numbers in the United States than in any other country, to a large extent owing to the predominance of wood home construction. Fires are an index of poverty, and, more than other groups, the poor suffer the horrors accompanying home fires and the agonies of burn injuries. Several hundred thousand persons are injured by fire yearly; one-third of these are children [3]. Most of these patients survive, to bear their scars throughout their lives. This book is a review of how some people with facial disfigurement from burns have fared, and what factors interact to determine their adaptation to their disfigurement.

All disfigurement is judged by implied public standards of how people should look and what is normal. This chapter will examine some features of these limiting standards.

THE IMPORTANCE OF APPEARANCE

We should not underrate the importance of actual beauty and ugliness in human life. Beauty can be a promise of complete satisfaction and can lead up to this complete satisfaction. Our own beauty or ugliness will also figure in the image others build up about us, which will be taken back into ourselves.

Most people want to see things with their own eyes to confirm reality. Though science warns us that this is not reliable, all experience impresses on us an automatic acceptance of what we see as truth. Most of the stimuli in our lives are visual. Trevor-Roper pointed out that half the fibers "that convey sensation to our brains are sent from the optic nerves. We live in a world almost wholly orientated by sight, and we seek our food, sex, and shelter through information provided by our retinal images" [4, p. 9]. Obvious cultural confirmation exists in the cosmetic industry, which daily provides advertisements on television, film, radio, newspaper, billboards, and books on the need to control appearance and to be aware of it. From the first cave paintings of Cro-Magnon man to the present, all cultures have been involved with representing and interpreting the human form and trying to separate what we appear to be from what we are in essence.

While inner values have consistently spoken in a quiet and spiritual voice, the louder and more insistent focus on surfaces can nowhere better be seen than in our current society, with its preoccupation with beauty culture. The creams, lotions, diets, exercises, and rituals keep changing, but the din in the salons and the supermarkets is a steady one, demanding increasing effort and expense, presuming that attractiveness enhances basic worth. While health and good looks are assumed to be related, the work ethic has been enlisted in the quest for youth and beauty. For example, in 1974 Jessica Krane [5], the self-styled inventor of Face-O-Metrics, published *The Sensuous Approach to Looking Younger,* a guide to *remaking* face and body without surgery. Diligence is assumed to be the main requisite for accomplishing a good appearance, and the concept of "beauty you can buy" is spreading. Cosmetic surgery is booming. Orthodontics in the suburbs has long been an accepted procedure, largely done to enhance the acceptability of our children. Ear piercing to anchor earrings is routine. For more and more people, rhinoplasty is as acceptable as dieting. Contact lenses and rapidly changing styles in eyeglasses, sunglasses, and eyeshades are de-

signed to enhance the allure of the eyes. Today surgeons are beseiged
with requests to enlarge, trim, and shape breasts. Operations to remove
fat, erase scars, lift sagging chins, remove pouches under the eyes, and
fill in cavernous cheeks are all common; and the details of applying eye
shadow, powdering, coloring the lips, and lining and plucking the eyebrows, and the limits of naturalness in appearance, all rapidly fluctuate.
More men than ever are having their faces lifted [6]. Each season has a
new "look," whether decreed by Paris or by the chemistry laboratory,
from which new tanning lotions, skin softeners, or rapid hair dyes flood
into the public's consciousness through the media [7, 8]. The goal is to
make people more aesthetically and sexually attractive, through diligent
work on their appearance.

When we think of deviance we mean permanent differences that are
never fashionable. Crandell, in "The genesis and modification of attitudes toward the child who is different" [9], indicated that children
with physical or behavior deviations aroused upsetting feelings. Although one's reactions to these elements may be changed through
learning, they are fundamentally reflexive and are more difficult to
change than cognitive or behavioral elements.

Wright [10] traced sources of attitudes toward persons with atypical
physiques to reactions to physical deviance among lower animals. Her
data showed a scatter of reactions, from animals that ignore differences
to such animals as baboons who behave ruthlessly toward their physical
inferiors. She reviewed cross-cultural comparisons that show the great
variations in attitudes among different cultures and noted that negative
attitudes are more common than positive ones.

In presenting cross-cultural and animal data as evidence, there is always a danger of selecting data that will reinforce a particular thesis,
and of having critics descend on one another with opposing data, as in
Ardrey, Lorenz, or Desmond Morris.

Wright [10] noted that the Hindu idea of *dharma,* which explains a
person's existing personal condition as the inevitable result of past behavior in previous incarnations, precludes sympathy for persons with
defects, since they have brought their affliction on themselves.

Charles DeGaulle refused to wear his eyeglasses in public in spite of
poor vision because of his desire to maintain a vigorous and imposing
public image. The teams that prepare politicians' faces for public view
are becoming eligible for subcabinet positions. Lyndon Johnson's curling his hair and using makeup has been commented on at great length,
as have Mrs. Richard Nixon's conflicts over whether to bring her hairdresser with her to China, Gerald Ford's contact lenses, and Senator
William Proxmire's hair transplants.

Obvious defects, like Moshe Dayan's need for an eye patch, can be turned into an asset only occasionally. Goffman [11], in discussing the problem of aggrandizing a stigma instead of being mortified by it, pointed out the pain involved. In the case of former Israeli Defense Minister Dayan, the loss of the eye occurred during military combat and heightens his martial image, and also serves as a clearly distinguishing mark in caricatures and photographs, which are useful to a politician as long as he augments this with signs of virility and vigorous activity. When Indira Gandhi's nose was broken by a rock thrown from a crowd she was quick to have it cosmetically repaired and did not choose to bear it as a sign of sacrifice for her country, and when Eleanor Roosevelt had her prominent front teeth damaged in an auto accident, she did not hesitate to have them replaced to achieve a more aligned profile.

When Elizabeth Taylor tries to cover a tracheotomy scar or have an operation done on her eye without scarring, it is considered congruent with her role as a film actress. Similarly, when actor Rod Steiger has a face lift to look young or when the newspapers describe performers who wear toupees, it is all received with intricate patronizing interest (seeing how "phony" they are), and a secret hope that the individual might be justified in similar efforts to improve appearance.

Allport [12] introduced the term *Bezugvorstellungen* to refer to ideas of the relations between the self and the object to which the self is responding. He attempted to explicate the concept of attitude:

1. It must have definite orientation in the world of objects (or values) and in this respect differ from simple and conditioned reflexes;
2. It must not be an altogether automatic and routine type of conduct, but must display some tension even when latent;
3. It varies in intensity, sometimes being regnant, sometimes relatively ineffective;
4. It is rooted in experience, and therefore is not simply a social instinct.

Attitude can be generally defined as the specific mental disposition toward an incoming or arising experience, whereby that experience is modified, or a condition of readiness for a certain type of activity. Allport defined attitude as a mental and neural state of readiness organized through experience, exerting a directive or dynamic influence on the individual's response to all objects and situations in which it is related. Attitudes obviously figure in the responses that individuals have in the presence of ugliness, disfigurement, or mutilation, and produce some of the intricate neural, experiential, and organized patterns that show in complex observable behavior. Social status is determined in this way through rank, clothes, color, or physical handicaps.

Perceptions and beliefs about inferior status may exist side-by-side with those that bring about salutory status. Hughes [13] cited an example of status clash in the question of whether to regard a black physician as a black or a professional. A crippled social worker, a scarred lawyer, and a one-eyed psychiatrist would all produce attitude conflicts. Condon [14] carried out careful examinations of interaction patterns by the method of slowed films of segments of human interaction, and executed microanalysis of two- to five-second behavior sequences. He underscored the intertwining of both speech and body motion within the flow of behavior, reinforcing and counterpointing one another. The body motion and facial patterns of individuals who are emotionally disturbed lack the variability and rhythmic mobility observed in normal people. This limited freedom occurs with a parallel lack of variability in the speech stream, both giving rise to a sense of monotony or flatness in the patient's total behavior presentation. People note this automatically, and respond unconsciously in a number of ways.

The asynchronic lack of smooth integration of pattern, voice, and communication is observable in the physically handicapped as well as the facially disfigured, whether they are scarred, blotched, or discolored, whether or not their faces have altered shapes, and whether or not they are inhibited from using hand, arm, and shoulder movements to aid in communication. The individual with an unfavorable physical trait, therefore, may be the object of an immediate negative reaction even though this may be followed by the recognition that sympathy should have been the feeling awakened by his condition. It is not unusual to see horror or disgust reflected in the expression of one who suddenly looks upon a grossly disfigured person and to hear seconds later such a remark as, "Oh, that poor man."

Although a disfigured face may not necessarily be unsightly or difficult for others to look at, it may serve as a misleading mask that blinds others, in spite of their efforts to make impartial and rational judgment, not only to the play of subtle and meaningful expressions but to the real self behind the mask. A facial paralysis or ptosis of the eye, either of which alters normal expression, may preclude objective judgments of the real personality or result in a distorted image of it. Such is the mechanism frequently found in the perceptual processes whereby one feature unduly claims attention, like a scar. It becomes what Allport termed an *anchorage point,* and from it no judgment is allowed to drift.

Since, then, the disfigured person cannot disguise his harelip or twisted face or mutilated ear, but must bear the deformity others see, his face is a visual stimulus to impressions and affective attitudes he is helpless to prevent. To further complicate his situation, there are the prevailing prejudices and misunderstandings in our society concerning those who physically deviate from the "norm." More often than not such individuals discover that they are regarded as social inferiors, and in some instances, they are assigned a marginal or minority status, or both. Opportunities available to the nondisfigured are often denied them; social participation, matters of employment, prestige, role and status, interpersonal relationships, personality organization, and a variety of cultural activities are affected or altered as well.

PHENOMENOLOGY OF DISFIGUREMENT
The sudden uprush of feelings about a disfigured person seems related to the threat of repressed affects and images returning—as powerful and realistically threatening—to consciousness, where our immediate thoughts about him are more pressing than the objective disfigurement before us.

Many of the terrified reactions to marked disfigurement seem to resemble the traditional terror and revulsion that people manifest toward lepers. There is, of course, a historical tradition, involving an aura of misinformation about the leper, both as an outcast and as an example of communicable and infectious misfortune. While the disfigured do not seem automatically infectious, there is dread of touching them and coming near them, as if some of the damage can be caught or spread. The tactile image is exaggerated; touching a scar is hardly a strange feeling. But it is dreaded, like touching a snake viewed as slimy though snakes are quite dry. Confrontation with a damaged face disrupts the sense of inner security and the confident self-system of daily life. Our feeling that we are getting on all right is momentarily sundered by a sight we treat as a physical threat.

Psychosomatics and Physiognomics
Adler [15] noted that people have always disliked individuals who had physical peculiarities, and such unfortunates become victimized by popular superstitions about handicaps.

MacGregor et al. reported that the strong tendency to ". . . impute deformity to the sins of the fathers, punishment for some wrongdoing, incestuous parentage, or maternal impression . . . go[es] back to the beginning of history when 'evil spirits' or 'the wrath of the gods' was believed responsible for physical anomalies." [16, p. 63].

Castration Anxiety

In Sigmund Freud's view the basic human apprehension is related to the threat of loss of the male organ, and according to Fenichel [17] it represents the culmination of the fantasied fears of bodily damage. The term *castration anxiety* has come to be used more generally to refer to threats and fears of bodily damage. Anna Freud wrote of responses of children with the "activation, reactivation, grouping, and rationalization of ideas of being attacked, overwhelmed and/or castrated" [18, p. 74] and referred to the different ways a child will react to threats to his bodily integrity in terms of his stage of personality development, stressing that in the phallic phases whatever part is threatened will take over by displacement the role of the genital part. While symbolically the threats are related to the loss of penis, more general psychological usage covers broad anxieties about loss of power, mutilation, and removal of parts.

There appears to be a continuum of anxiety about the body [19]; some people apparently are always afraid of bodily damage, while others seem to be only slightly bothered about the possibility. In the hypochondriac the fear of harm to the person is strongly developed, and it is best stated by Wright: "The psychoanalytic viewpoint, insofar as it posits universal and far-reaching castration anxieties leads to the conclusion that negative attitudes toward persons with disabilities are inevitable though, to be sure, they may be ameliorated" [10, p. 272]. The argument continues about how general is the Oedipus complex in society, or how narrowly to define castration threat. However, it is evident that in the broader formulation of threat of damage, in all human cultures the presence of disfigured persons produces threatening emotional responses, though the nature of these responses varies enormously according to personal experience and cultural and social settings.

SUMMARY

The appearance and perception of the human face is neither a simple picture nor a passive event. It is a series of interventions that can be placed only roughly on a scale. On one end there is the aesthetic pole, with beauty, contemplation, sexual appeal and arousal, and the socially learned attractions and value systems that go with looking at intact faces. Nearby on the scale are acceptability, healthy appearance, unremarkable appearance, and the more or less unconscious interpersonal use of the face for communication, employing the repertoire of expressions of conventional communication.

Central to this concept of a standard or scale is a need to "find" persons, to locate a human relationship, to reach out in the most conventional human way. As we begin to observe features in people that draw unflattering attention to the face itself, the whole nature of communication is altered. The relatedness between people is disrupted, mobilizing a whole range of unpleasant and disconcerting emotions. The ugly, the unattractive, and the deviant begin to be viewed apart from ordinary interactions, because comfortable responses to other people require that we view them in reasonable and non-anxiety-provoking ways, and be able to ignore or minimize their differences in nonthreatening ways. (Within this "manageable" context fall the attractive flirt, the poor old man, and the not too visibly handicapped.) The scale cannot be made too simple, because in each situation the context is a complex one, socially, culturally, and in terms of both individual experiences and special defects that draw attention. It also involves all of the innate and learned intricacies of perception. When one moves from the ugly toward the disfigured and frightening, all the dysphoric factors load the experience; a new set of affects has become operative as well, including shock, horror, loathing, repulsion, castration anxiety, incomprehension, inability to complete a tolerable gestalt, and threat. These all enter with sudden disruptive force into the mental set. The equilibrium of the viewer with his self, his external world, his figure-ground perception, and his standard controlled scanning of the environment are all abruptly disrupted when the eyes are arrested by a disfigured face. The individual feels endangered and under risk of being flooded by uncontrolled feelings.

Phenomenologically, a face is an *interhuman event;* in Merleau-Ponty's terms [20] this means that it is something that is being expressed but is at the same time an indistinguishable thing, like a novel, a poem, a picture, or a musical work, whose meaning is accessible only through direct sensory contact. In this sense the face is comparable to a work of art. It is a focal point of living meanings.

REFERENCES

1. Farquhar, G. In B. Evans (Ed.), *Dictionary of Quotations.* Delacorte, New York, 1968. P. 613.
2. Picasso, P. In G. Seldes (Ed.), *The Great Quotations.* Lyle Stewart, New York, 1960. P. 562.
3. *America Burning.* Final report of the National Commission on Fire Prevention and Control. U.S. Government Printing Office, Washington, D.C., May 1973.
4. Trevor-Roper, P. D. *The World Through Blunted Sight.* Bobbs-Merrill, New York, 1970.
5. Krane, J. *The Sensuous Approach to Looking Younger.* McKay, New York, 1974.
6. Goldwyn, R., and Goin, J. Personal communication, 1975.
7. Brown, J. A. C. *Techniques of Persuasion.* Penguin, Baltimore, 1963.

8. Rudofsky, B. *The Unfashionable Human Body.* Doubleday, Garden City, N.Y., 1971.
9. Crandell, J. The genesis and modification of attitudes toward the child who is different. *Training School Bull.* (Vineland). 66:72–79, August 1969.
10. Wright, B. A. *Physical Disability: A Psychological Approach.* Harper & Row, New York, 1960.
11. Goffman, E. Studies in adjustment to visible injuries: Evaluation of curiosity by the injured. *Jl. Abnorm. Soc. Psychol.* 43:13–28, 1948.
12. Allport, G. *Pattern and Growth in Personality.* Holt, Rinehart & Winston, New York, 1961.
13. Hughes, E. Dilemmas and contractions of status. *Am. J. Sociol.* 50:353, 1945.
14. Condon, W. Sound film analysis of normal and pathological behavior patterns. *J. Nerv. Ment. Dis.* 143:338–347, 1966.
15. Adler, A. *What Life Should Mean to You.* Putnam, New York, 1958.
16. MacGregor, F. C., et al. *Facial Deformities and Plastic Surgery: A Psychosocial Study.* Thomas, Springfield, Ill., 1953.
17. Fenichel, O. *The Psychoanalytical Theory of Neurosis.* Norton, New York, 1945.
18. Freud, A. The Role of Bodily Illness in the Mental Life of Children. In R. S. Eissler, et al. (Eds.), *Psychoanalytic Study of the Child.* International Universities Press, New York, 7:69–81, 1952.
19. Fisher. S. Experiencing your body: You are what you feel. *Saturday Review,* July 8, 1972. P. 27.
20. Merleau-Ponty, M. *Phenomenology of Perception.* Humanities Press, New York, 1962.

2

Body and Face Images:
Personality and Self-Representation

This chapter is an attempt to sketch out some of the varied conceptions, data, and problems of designating the personality equipment and physical apparatus with which an individual manages his life, and the styles and strategies of coping with major changes in his body image and his interpersonal relations. It is not yet feasible to bridge the various clinical examples and the multiplicity of conceptual formulations, but bringing them together may prefigure directions in which we can seek new formulations and new knowledge.

The face is the part of the body most often looked at not only because, whatever else may be concealed by clothes, the face is left exposed, but because it is a symbol, a visible index to what is by nature invisible, and the most convincing of all proofs of identity. (Fingerprints are not so readily accessible.) It is the face, even more than the voice, the words we speak, or the emotions we keep in or let out, more even than the mannerisms and tics we produce involuntarily and unawares, that presents each one of us to the world. "If we really had modesty," says Raymond Mortimer in his "Essay on Clothes," "it is our faces we should conceal. By comparison our legs are anonymous, our bellies uneventful" [1, p. i]. Without their faces, human beings would hardly be human at all.

In the face are gathered together many of the most important instruments needed for the task of staying alive. The face includes the chief organs of four of the traditional five senses, the sense of touch being distributed over the entire surface of the body with varying degrees of sensitivity. The eyes and the ears are directly connected to the brain. The sense of smell works through the nose as a subordinate function to breathing. The mouth is used for breathing, tasting, ingesting, and speaking.

In dealing with people whose faces have been mutilated or with those asking for cosmetic surgery, the focus is on the particular organ or scar to be repaired. The patient will tell what he wants done to his nose or the skin under his eyes or chin and this will evoke an image of what he would like to resemble, but it is unlikely to give a formal description of his appearance or the special appearance he would like to assume. The momentary and continued emphasis is on improving a defect in order to enhance overall appearance, and it is clear that the patient usually wants to change his role in life as a major part of the surgical outcome, to look younger, more attractive, more sexy, more aesthetically appealing. As most plastic surgeons comment, badly disfigured patients focus on one particular deformity [2–4] and will sooner or later begin to tell what they want done on themselves in terms of a subjective schedule and not in terms of functional need. A patient may ignore a marked mouth distortion, which might interfere with eating, while asking to have his ears, a nostril, or a particular scar repaired. This, too, is carried out without a general description of the self, or even of the ultimate goals. Such patients make general statements about "the way I look" that suggest distinct and precise imagery, but this is not directly explicated. The attitude is very much the one that Wright [5] reported of somehow separating the body or the externals from what is being worked on. This involves a series of images: (1) the practical image of what I look like, how my appearance will affect people, and also how it will function, (2) a picture of what others see as acceptable overall, and (3) the images of what I would like to look like and what things I would secretly or publicly like to alter.

THE BODY IMAGE

In his classic work, Schilder [6] wrote of the schema of the body, the *Körperschema,* as the spatial image that everyone has surrounding him, defining it as a combination of perception, action, impression, and expression, a unit in which subjective feeling and action are interrelated. As the complexity of the concept evolved it has been stressed that the body image is a hypothetical construct of images, both conscious and unconscious, as Horowitz stated, "in constant transactional relationship with current perception, memory, emotions, drives, thoughts and actions" [7, p. 24]. It is a tridimensional image which includes the part of our bodies we see, the sensations we receive from other modalities, including position sense and the relationship of the body to its surroundings, and the significant people and events in our surroundings. While Schilder made clear that the body image involves a conglomeration of the mental representations of the body and its organs, it does not coincide with the objective body. The body schema has both physical features as in the "postural model" and secondary emotional values associated with this physical image. Qualities of the person's appearance are included. Clothes, eyeglasses, and prostheses may be included. Kolb [8] stressed that the various and multiple sensory experiences and impressions are conveyed by pain, visual, temperature, tactile, and kinesthetic systems to the cortex of the brain, and that additional attitudes about these percepts become ingrained through verbal remarks as well as non-verbal communications and indications of importance about individual physical traits and types of body behavior.

The study of the body image is a constantly changing field, and it is full of terms and concepts that are difficult to segregate out or to relate to specific anatomical regions or explicit psychological functions. These terms include *body image, body concept, body schema, self-concept, self-representation, self-reliance, body ego, ego boundary, self-system,* and *self-boundary.* Each term is complex in itself and involves clusters of associated concepts so that it is not feasible to unify these many ideas about the body under one or two categories; but it is clear that the nodal concept of Schilder remains both current and historically valuable. As Rubins [9] indicated, the generally accepted functions of the ego—its defensive, synthesizing, cognitive, perceptive, reality-testing, and regulative activities—do not seem to apply to this function, except perhaps tangentially. These terms refer to aspects of what is essentially a holistic process and, in fact, may be applicable to the phenomena involved. We need to make groupings of body image phenomena in order to handle some of these complexities. "The body image is, however, only part of a larger functional entity, the self-concept (or self-image) in which it is inextricably linked" [9, p. 61].

When we have built up our own body image we spread it again all over the world and melt it into others. Everybody builds his own body image in contrast with others. There is, however, a constant giving and taking so that it is true that many parts of body images are common to persons who see each other, meet each other, and are in an emotional relation to each other. Psychic life is experienced as shifting around an imaginary ego center.

If we follow carefully the way in which body images communicate between various persons, there can be no doubt that there exists not a collective image of the body, but a collection of the various images of bodies. This collection is not in the full light of consciousness.

Shadows form swiftly changing aspects of the self-image. We build up also in the dead person the body image of a living person. The body of a fellow being is built up and constructed like a picture of a dream. The continuation of the body image in dream and fantasy retains as important, therefore, part of what we actually perceive in fellow human beings.

Theoretically there may be a series of body images, the most current one being added onto and developed out of a series of body images and concepts of personal space extending backward in time to the earliest body images of childhood. Some of these body images may be preconscious; in a psychoanalytical sense they can be raised into consciousness with volitional effort. Other body images are unconscious, cannot be deliberately raised to conscious representation, and emerge only under unusual circumstances.

When body image experiences gain consciousness, the degree of vividness will determine whether the image is a thought image, a pseudohallucination, or a hallucination. Thought images of the body commonly occur when a person anticipates performing an unusual, nonautomatic physical act. Pseudohallucinatory body image experiences may occur in states of unusual body sensations or when injuries change the physical structure of the body. For example, after a disfiguring facial burn or plastic surgery some patients experience vivid images of the body as it was and as it is. In altered states of consciousness, whether induced by drugs or other processes, strange body experiences are common; these include a feeling of leaving the body, of seeing it from a distance, of shrinkage or expansion, and of specific changes in a given body part.

Horowitz [7] tried to categorize types of mental images, but while he listed body image in one category it is clear it actually relates to all his categories. His classification, somewhat modified, is given here:

1. Images categorized by vividness
   a. Hallucination
   b. Pseudohallucination
   c. Thought image
   d. Unconscious image
2. Images categorized by context
   a. Hypnagogic image
   b. Dream image; nightmare
   c. Psychedelic image
   d. Flashbacks
   e. Dream scintillations

3. Images categorized by interaction with perceptions
   a. Illusion
   b. Perceptual distortion
   c. Déjà vu
   d. Negative hallucination
   e. Afterimage
4. Images categorized by content
   a. Memory image; eidetic image
   b. Imaginary image
   c. Body image; body schema experience
   d. Phantom limb
   e. Hallucination
   f. Imaginary companion
   g. Number and diagram forms

One could conceivably correlate almost all cognition and imagery with body image phenomena. Several analysts have focused on the inclusion of particular body parts, e.g., the mouth, the hand and arm, the genitals and anus, and the skin, into the total body image. Various psychosomatic conditions have been explained by the incomplete inclusion or detachment of such libidinized body parts from the total image. Schilder [6] used a combination of libidinal, developmental, and social factors to explain the origin and importance of body image.

In fact, the organization and development of the body image is a complex psychophysiological process depending on many factors, such as immediate contact with others, self-touching as a dual sensation (compared with touching others as a single sensation), spatial organization, resolution of inner tensions, the openness for exploration of parts of the body, and cultural or parental taboos.

The discrepancy between the conscious and unconscious forms may sometimes come into awareness momentarily, as when we hear our recorded voice, look in a mirror, or see a photograph of ourself, or with sudden changes in the body, as with new glasses, false teeth, or following a mutilating operation. The alien feeling may disappear as the changed part is absorbed into the body image. At times the discrepancy may be most striking, as in the person who experiences himself as taller or shorter, younger or older, prettier or uglier, or even of a different color or sex than he really is.

The Mind-Body Problem

In dealing with the psychosomatic unity of the body image, the problems of conceptualizing mind and body recur. Langer [10] noted that in spite of the scientific efforts toward monism, psychical entities lie outside the realm of physiological psychology. She explicated that many writers allege that causes and effects could not possibly belong to the same system, and consequently could not be what they are supposed to be with respect to each other. Therefore, they must belong to different systems, but these systems might bear some relation to each other. The orientation that philosophical thinking developed from Cassirer, Russell, Whitehead, and Wittgenstein presented another view: The two systems contain equivalent statements of the same natural facts, but in different "logical languages." The system couched in physical terms is greater than that which can be constructed in psychical terms, but the latter is equivalent to a subtest of the former.

This notion of two scientific systems, differently formulated but referring to the same objects and facts, namely, mental phenomena, and equally capable of describing them, actually antedates the semantic studies that occupy much of the limelight today. William James [11] attempted the first application of that logical finding to the mind-body problem in his famous essay "Does Consciousness Exist?". The same objects, he held, namely, physical things, may function either as things in what he called "objective history" or as percepts in "subjective" (personal) history; and concepts, similarly, may function as "abstract" entities in science or as "real" relations in perception and concrete imaginative thought.

Development of the Body Image

Two factors play a special part in the creation of the body image. The one is pain, the other the motor control over our limbs. Our body image is built up according to the needs of the personality.

The discovery of the objective world is made by the infant in connection with the discovery of his own body, which is distinguished from all other parts of the universe by the remarkable fact that it is perceived through two types of sensation simultaneously: through external tactile sensations and through internal sensations of depth sensibility. Freud stated that the ego is primarily a bodily thing, that is, the perception of one's own body. Numerous authors, including Piaget and Gesell, have shown that the infant begins to become aware of himself as a bounded entity, as an experiencing "I," or self, very early in life.

Piaget and Inhelder [12] have documented the degree to which early spatial relationships are egocentrically perceived in terms of the child's own body. It takes years before the child learns to make judgments based on internalized verbal standards, because the force of certain types of body arousal continues to influence a child in his decision making. The early trust in body experience as a guide is never given up and, indeed, continues to play an important role throughout life via an elaborate system based on the assignment of meaning to body areas and the monitoring of sensations from these areas.

Piaget distinguishes three psychological stages in growing up: egocentrism, socialization, and complete objectivity. He feels these stages also contribute to the body image. According to Ernest Kafka [13], a child may not recognize the picture of an ear, mouth, or a finger though he is able to recognize these parts on the complete body. At any rate, we gain the impression that from the point of view of sensory motor development the child brings more or less isolated and uncorrelated experiences into a complete form by continual effort. Even then the parts are not in such a close relation to the whole as they are in the adult.

Gallup [14] demonstrated that after prolonged exposure to their reflected images in mirrors chimpanzees marked with red dye showed evidence of being able to recognize their own reflection. Monkeys did not appear to have this capacity, which at bottom appears to be the capacity for forming a self-concept. Babies usually give signs of recognizing themselves in mirrors when they are about 10 months old. Children with little exposure to mirrors or other reflecting surfaces may take longer. Retarded persons may never reach this stage of self-recognition, though as the majority of retardates are mildly retarded, the greatest defects in their self-recognition appear to be attitudes they were taught about themselves.

Most animals react as though mirror images were other animals. Put a baby chick alone in a box and it will start to chirp loudly, with up to a hundred or more high-pitched distress calls per minute, and make fluttery attempts to escape; put in another chick, or a mirror, and the distress calls and flutters dwindle almost to zero. A chicken will eat more in the presence of another chicken or a mirror than in isolation. Similarly, a female pigeon will lay more eggs in the company of another pigeon or a mirror than in isolation.

Mirrors can reinforce instrumental learning. Some fish can learn to navigate a simple maze when the only reward is exposure to a mirror. And a monkey will learn to open a door to get a brief look at his reflection. Goldfish, too, favor the mirror three to one. Some birds and primates also react more strongly to mirrors than to other members of their species. A parakeet will look at a mirror four times as long as it will look at another parakeet. An adult male patas monkey confronted with an unfamiliar male will make threatening yawnlike facial expressions; faced with a mirror, it will double its hostile display. In more advanced primates, social experience can influence the preference for mirrors. A wild-born preadolescent rhesus monkey will spend more time watching a live peer than it will watching its own reflection in a mirror. However, a monkey raised in isolation with an artificial mother (made of cloth) seems to prefer viewing its own reflection.

Pritchard, Heron, and Hebb [15] studied the importance of eye movements and reported on the tendency of visual patterns to break down into smaller units when the gaze is maintained. They demonstrated that the normal continuous movement and tremor of the eye at rest maintains an excitation of the retina that is very necessary for normal perception, leading to the striking conclusion that in order for the eye to maintain a fixed, stable image there must be continuous small variations in the image.

Gregory [16] wrote that the early preference for facelike patterns is not truly innate but is learned extremely rapidly. He suggested that the perceptual system does not always agree with the rational thinking cortex. To the cortex the distance of the moon is a quarter of a million miles; to the visual part of the brain it is a mere few hundred yards. Though in this instance the cortical view is the correct one, the striate area is never informed, and we still see the moon as though it lay almost within our grasp.

Gregory believes that the visual system has developed the ability to use nonvisual information and to go beyond the immediate evidence of the senses. He sees the brain as a probability computer, and our actions are based on the best bet in a given situation. The human brain makes efficient use of its rather limited sensory information in the same way that astronomers discover the distance and constitution of the stars by inference.

Greenacre [17] emphasized the important *emergence of vision* in the functioning of the infant after 6 months of age. Infants touch, finger, and mouth according to what they see as part of the establishment of the body image. Vision is prehensile, but because of its increasing scope in range and distance, it can take in the surroundings with extraordinary discrimination, better than touch and extensor motion. Feeling one part of the body with another is a special situation. In the case of those parts of the body that are not visible to the child himself, the endogenous and contact sensations are supplemented by visual impressions of the bodies of others. Consequently, the body image is not based just on the perception of one's own body but to some extent on visual perception of the bodies of others. Greenacre suggested the possibility that the force of visual incorporation of others may be one of the reasons why people who live together through the years often come to look alike or have similar facial expressions.

The anal area, the genital area, the back, and the face are the parts of one's body that cannot be taken in thoroughly through visual perception—the face even less than the genitals. The awareness of these and their location in the body image must be supplemented by the observation of these parts in others.

Piaget and Inhelder, in examining mental imagery in children, commented:

According to the empiricist's view the copy is merely a tracing of perceptible physical objects. Now Platonism, which is still very much alive amongst mathematicians and logicians, also sees knowledge as a copy—but as a copy of ideal or abstract entities, not of perceptible reality. . . .

In another view, knowing the object means acting upon it in order to transform it, and discovering its properties through its transformations. The aim is always to get at the object. Cognition is not, however, based only on the object, but also on the exchange or interaction between subject and object resulting from the action and reaction of the two. . . .

The combination of deduction and experiment proves that the operational mechanisms and empirical verification are in fact interdependent [12, p. 384].

Ernest Kafka [13] described the general pattern of body image development, saying a parallel development sequence of body-self experience might be (1) primal state of indifferentiation, (2) container and the thing contained, (3) orifice and some organ awareness, with differentiated surface and interior separate from waste products and secretions and with some sense of control over the liquid contents, (4) mind awareness, with mind differentiated as a psychic organ controlling differentiated body organs and their contained materials, and (5) self-conscious awareness of mind.

This sequence is consistent with Mahler's views [18]. She described two subphases within the phase of primary narcissism, absolute primary narcissism followed in the third month by the symbiotic state.

Fisher noted that body constancy is a learned aspect of the self-image:

As quickly as possible the culture tries to conventionalize body experience: . . . certain body zones are defined as publicly touchable and others are "off limits". . . . By and large, the culture enjoins one to keep one's body feelings out of descriptions, judgments, and communications. The socialization process attempts to render body experience a constant controlled variable [19, p. 27].

Our body, and with it our body image, is a necessary part in every life experience. One sees that the body image can shrink or expand. As one example of this, Goffman [20] pointed out that the upper classes are commonly considered to have a great deal of poise, and that this may be due to conventional social situations in which the upper-class person outranks the other participants and feels independent of the opinions of the others. For most of us some importance is given to the valuation others give us; we try to appear fair and acceptable, and we abide by unspoken rules of interaction and support others in their roles as the mark of our courtesy. With a change in clothes we change our attitude. When we take off our clothes in the evening we change our set of attitudes, partly because the body image as such is in the closest relation to our libidinous strivings and tendencies. Schilder [6] believed the desire to be seen, to be looked at, is as inborn as the desire to see.

In the army the relationship between officers and men has certain elements that require distance and impersonality. Different ranks have formalized ways of relating to each other. Hall [21] pointed out that in reporting to a superior officer the inferior officer proceeds to a point three paces in front of the officer's desk, stops, salutes, and states his rank, his name, and his business. This is not the way people relate in civilian life, where Hall found that the normal speaking distance for business matters, at the beginning of the conversation, is five and a half to eight feet, or something less than three paces.

There appear to be measurable distances for types of relationships. For Americans, Hall [21] listed the following voices associated with specific ranges of distances:*

Very close (3 to 6 in.)	Soft whisper; secrets
Close (8 to 12 in.)	Audible whisper; confidential
Near (12 to 20 in.)	Indoors, soft voice; outdoors, full voice; confidential
Neutral (20 to 36 in.)	Soft voice, low volume; personal subject matter
Neutral (4½ to 5 ft.)	Full voice; nonpersonal subject matter
Public distance (5½ to 8 ft.)	Full voice with slight overloudness; public information
Across the room (8 to 20 ft.)	Loud voice; talking to a group

In Latin America the interaction distance is much less than in the United States. Indeed, Latin Americans cannot talk comfortably with one another unless they are very close to the distance that evokes either sexual or hostile feelings in the North American. The result is that when they move close, Americans tend to back away. As a consequence, they think we are distant or cold, withdrawn, and unfriendly. We, on the

*From E. T. Hall, *The Silent Language*. New York: Doubleday, 1959. Pp. 163–164. Copyright © 1959 by Edward T. Hall. Reprinted by permission of Doubleday & Company, Inc.

other hand, are constantly accusing them of breathing in our faces, crowding us, and spraying our faces.

For the disfigured person, there is a strong tendency to evade very close, close, or near distances, and to choose *at best* what Hall calls neutral distance, though public distance is preferred, with all the demeaning and isolation that result in damaged self-esteem for the disfigured and his thirst for intimacy.

Landis [22] has explicated part of the body schema problem. The ego boundary is used as a conception that delimits in varying degrees the phenomenal self (1) from those aspects of the personality not represented in consciousness and (2) from the world of reality external to the person, as psychologically experienced. While *self-boundaries* would be a more accurate term, it is not employed since the term *ego boundary* is already established in the literature.

Psychoanalysts emphasize interest in the vital function of *reality testing,* which involves the capacity to tell whether something refers to the self or to the nonself. Psychoanalytical thinking has also seen the ego boundary as representing the demarcation between the ego and the rest of the personality. Ego boundaries are viewed as having a variable cathectic quantity. These various metapsychological points of view, however, are frequently not clearly separated in the literature.

The name most closely associated with the concept of ego boundaries is Federn [23], who was the first to view the ego boundary as a complex construct that, he insisted, was indispensable to an understanding of many psychological phenomena, especially psychotic conditions. Considering the ego as the "continuous experience of the psyche" and referring to this experience as "ego feeling," Federn conceptualized the ego boundary as the periphery of the ego feeling at any given time. He referred to the expansion and contraction of ego boundaries and, in general, depicted boundary qualities as influencing, and varying with, different states of consciousness.

Self-Confrontation and Self-Perception

It has long been known that a person is stirred to special response when he views his own image. Even the very young react with special excitement and gestures when seeing themselves in the mirror [24].

Deno [25] attacked a problem that concerned the question of self-recognition. Individual rearview photographs were taken of 40 nude male subjects ranging in age from 14 to 16 years. The subjects were all members of a school group and were well acquainted with each other. The 40 photographs, with the heads masked, were shown to each individual and he was asked not only to identify them but also to rate them for goodness of physique. One of the pictures was, of course, of himself. A second presentation of the photographs was then made with the heads unmasked. Efforts were also made to measure the social standing or popularity of each subject in the group by means of a socio-metric technique.

It turned out that only 30 percent of the boys could correctly identify themselves if the heads of the photographs were covered. When the heads were uncovered, correct self-identification rose to 37.5 percent. Those who were able to identify themselves correctly not only were better in their ability to identify others but were in turn easier to identify by others. There was no relation between ability to detect one's own photograph and one's popularity in the group, but there was a positive correlation between popularity and the rate at which one was correctly identified by all other group members. Finally, it is noteworthy that there was a trend for those who were most easily identified by themselves and others to have been rated as especially good or poor in physique. This raised the possibility that their higher rate of identification was due to physical characteristics that made them conspicuous. Perhaps one of the most important findings in this study was the fact that only a third of the subjects could correctly designate their own photograph when the head was masked. This is of special import because it corroborates Wolff's [26] earlier discovery that it is difficult for an individual to recognize representations of aspects of his own body (e.g., hands, facial profile).

Shontz felt that "body schemata, body values, and body concepts are something like cooperating partners co-managing the unified enterprise of ongoing behavior [27, p. 206]. He felt these different aspects were not primarily visual, and did not correlate reliably with overall personality.

FACE AND HEAD PARTS IN THE BODY IMAGE

Hoffer [28] quoted Gesell on the hand-to-mouth response in intra-uterine development, and others have noted the ways in which the fetus introduces its fingers into its mouth. He went on to describe how the infant places everything that is within reach in his mouth, and the accumulated experience of the hand and mouth relationship is an important and rich developmental one. In later writings he discussed the development of the *mouth ego,* stressing interplay of perceptual activity, motor control, memory, reality testing, and the synthetic function of the ego. The discussion enlarged on the idea that the differentiation of the ego from the id shows itself on the infant's body surface, when in the service of the oral partial instinct and for the sake of autoerotic pleasure, two sensations, an oral one and a tactile one, are aroused simultaneously by finger sucking. The hand and mouth convey the first personal sensation of self. Later in adult life the hands and touching, sucking, oral behavior, and the intricate, flowing imageries of the self continue to be major adaptive and experiential qualities. Each area of the face has a network of body memories, incoming stimuli, and shifts in awareness. The cheeks come and go in importance in shaving or growing a mustache or beard, but rapidly come back to attention when a man thinks he is blushing. Spiegel spoke of *Ich-Gefühl,* which he translated as "self-feeling," and declared that for individuals who do not have a disturbed feeling about self, the "feeling of personal identity, the I-feeling, is a silent one, carried around so to speak, like one's clothes or one's name . . . in moments of triumph and exaltation a positive sense of self may emerge spontaneously into consciousness" [29, p. 83].

Arnheim [30] quoted Darwin: ". . . when a child cries or laughs, he knows in a general manner what he is doing and what he feels; so that a very small exertion of reason would tell him what crying or laughing meant in others."

In *Seven Psychologies,* Heidbreder [31] postulated a basic tendency for experience to be formed and patterned to maintain an equilibrium. Along this line is the view that the neurotic will plunge himself back into the reliable old feeling of dejection or of feeling ugly or undesirable, partly because it accomplishes a stabilization of tensions, and partly because it may also evade the unpleasant anxieties of more active adaptive behavior. The shifting of attitudes about the face is seen and shows some regular points of stabilization.

As Ashley Montague [32] pointed out, chucking under the chin and hair patting are in the Western world forms of behavior indicating affection, and all are tactile, while for many individuals pseudocontacts often take the form of words. From weeping eyes, crinkling around the eyes, flaring nostrils, flushing and blanching, frowning, Birdwhistel [33] has classified and categorized a hundred thousand expressions. These are all part of a mask we show to the world. Television, photos, and newspapers make us more aware of these externals, but do not touch the inner self.

There remains a feeling of this self peeping out of the facial mask through the eyes. The ears may be scratched, the tongue and teeth touched, and lips employed in sex play, but the self that walks behind the face is somehow a focal point for personal experience. We might talk of a *face ego* or a *head ego* just as well as a *body ego* to convey the idea of depth, of things that really "get through to us" or ideas we carry deeply buried. Culturally we carry our faces bared to the world, but we may hide behind eyeglasses, a beard, mascara, or a frozen expression. We are concerned with "losing face," or with "losing our cool," the fear of losing emotional control and the suspected accompanying dangers of being caught out, or *seen* to be vulnerable. For example, an articulate professor who speaks genially and humorously to large groups, can be tense, anxious, and fractious in a tête-à-tête, where his self-confidence is threatened by close emotional penetration. His public facade has been removed and his particular control method lost. On the other hand, the physician who feels secure and comfortable talking to one patient, where he is in control, may develop severe anxiety in public lectures.

Following Schilder, we might talk of a social *facial schema,* or *facial body image,* and in another context we might speak of the *postural model,* the way the head is held, and the *kinesthetic feelings* of the head. The most exquisite distinctions of self-consciousness can be seen in the ways people experience their facial parts. Twisted lips, squinting eyes, flared nostrils, flushing, and glaring are used as primary instruments for adaptation throughout life. Bellak [34] described the rapid and enormous shifts in body and face-mouth perception we undergo, giving the example of the common experience in the dental chair, in which we suddenly feel that our person is "all mouth" when under assault from the dental probe, and how rapidly this shifts when a different part of the body becomes central in life adaptation. The face in flushing is a sudden repository of all the feelings of shame, embarrassment, and inadequacy. The winking eye and subtle, varied eye movements seem to be a part of cross-cultural flirting in *Homo sapiens;* following Hewes: "Ocular expression depends not only on the action of the orbicularis or on movements of the eyeball but on pupil size, ordinarily simply a matter of illumination but also an indicator of emotional interest" [35, p. 81]. Expressiveness may be enhanced by using eyeshadow or increasing the thickness, color, or length of the eyelashes. Eye movements also appear to be important in higher primate communication. Other features, like the mouth, may be focused on, and hiding the mouth behind the hand when giggling is a very common young female gesture, no doubt related to the concern over showing what is inside or to the Victorian and polite attitudes about not chewing with an open mouth and not making visible bodily functions, as if the composed, controlled, well-groomed face were something that transcended animality in all forms. The dilated nostril, the furrowed brow, or tight lips are all part of the signaling system that focuses attention on the face. Cosmetic surgeons commonly speak of the facial triangle made by imaginary lines between the outer angles of the eyes and the point of the chin; this is the most important area of the face for reconstructive work, it includes much of the sensory apparatus other than that for hearing, and it is the most subtle area in communication. The use of the head is complex—cocking it, bowing it, and shaking it. The gestures of the hands are facile and varied, and they seem more subtle than a flirtatious walk, a sad manner of leaning, or an aggressive posturing. Subjectively using the "good side" of one's profile, flashing a smile known to be engaging, covering protruding teeth with the upper lip, and stiffening the lip stoically are all intricate amalgams of gestalt, symbolism, and particular facial anatomy. The face comes to be the most socially critical instrument of interpersonal communication, and the most complex area of the body image.

Schilder [6] put this in more psychodynamic terms. He said that "body images are on principle social. Our own body image is never isolated but is always accompanied by the body images of others . . . there is a continuous interchange between parts of our own body image and the body images of others" [p. 265]. This is especially true of the facial images when we talk, or remember, or relish contacts with other people; and the relations between our memories of tense bitter expressions when we recall humiliating or infuriating exchanges we had the day before. In matters of aesthetics, of art and love, Schilder also has some interesting wisdom to impart. He speaks of beauty not provoking desires immediately, " . . . but it contains in itself the germ of the development of desires. When we remain purely in the field of aesthetics we repress the immediate urge. The individual feels that he can command his desires . . ." [p. 265].

Murstein reported a study on what makes people sexually appealing:

Considering sex appeal prior to interaction, it seems that men tend to focus primarily on physiognomy and physique, the latter including chiefly three areas: breast, buttocks, and legs. Women seem less centered on the body and more on the face and overall masculinity. First contacts, therefore, often work to the woman's disadvantage because highly desirable men do not often approach unattractive women, whereas attractive women are not as ready to immediately reject homely men [36, p. 76].

Physical characteristics serve chiefly to determine who are eligible sexual partners. When a man and a woman get to know each other, sexual attraction subsequently depends heavily on social and psychological factors. Knowing that someone is of low status often makes him less desirable, because we associate undesirable qualities with low status and our own vanity is not served by association with the devalued and unattractive; following Murstein, a hobo is less attractive than a physically similar professor. Style and manner increase appeal, but Murstein feels that in dating people are not approached as a function of their sex appeal, but generally only to the degree that the approacher feels confident that he has a fair chance of success; couples are commonly composed of individuals of generally equivalent physical attractiveness. A sexually attractive woman may be unapproached because no man believes himself sufficiently attractive to interest her. An unattractive woman may not seem a worthy challenge. People speak of couples who "look good together"; yet we are increasingly aware of how little this relates to sexual and personal compatability in the long run.

Berscheid, Walster, and Bohrnstedt [37] described research findings that indicate that we are trained to assume the best about beautiful people beginning in kindergarten. They found that students thought people who shared their political views were more attractive (indeed, a fascinating finding). In terms of evaluating good looks and self-esteem, they reported that in both sexes individuals who are satisfied with the appearance of their faces have more confidence generally.

They found that unattractive teenagers were more likely to be unhappy with their body images and with their lives as adults than were attractive teenagers. They also found that persons who had experienced a sudden, dramatic change in appearance, through either rapid gain or loss of weight, cosmetic surgery, war injuries, or accidents, were less happy than persons with more stable appearance; and a surprisingly high percentage (38 percent) had had these experiences. They assessed the social interactions of people in terms of "market considerations," assembling data to show how people who are more *desirable* socially will tend to be matched against others who have equally desirable qualities; while the factors may shift with the culture, good looks seems to remain an important one.

Within all the fluctuations of conscious and nonconscious imagery, the social distance, and the developmental problems of self-esteem, there appear to be regularly recurrent attitudes about the self and the ways in which people deal with each other. These involve an evolving concept of worth and self-esteem. The face is an anatomical part, a functional instrument, a mask, and an instrument; it is also a crucial measurement of value, through its good looks and its expressiveness. Balikov [38] described the way in which the facial image develops, going through the phases of individualization of the child, with the on-layering of attitudes from mother's smiles to being considered cute, freckled, plump, or agile, through the establishment of a school-age network of facial concepts. The repertoire of expressions is expanded, and the schoolteacher and one's peers all establish a scale of appearance;

the teasing or praise of this era is internalized. In adolescence the acne and social positioning all seem terribly vital to establishing a stable self-image. Balikov feels that around age 16 or 17 in middle-class white children there is a partially stabilized self-concept, a combination of definitely achieved attitudes about the self as well as idealized concepts about how one ought to appear, a mixture of pictures of aspiration as well as percepts of the self. He feels that this is stabilized in the early twenties. He conceptualizes the self-concept as moving through the life course developmentally between object relationships and systems of defenses. In a particular situation that has meaning for the individual, his facial self-image will shift in terms of his defensive system and the object toward which he is reacting. "Facing it" indeed turns out to be a very intricate process.

REFERENCES

1. Mortimer, R.   Essay on Clothes. In J. Brophy, *The Human Face Reconsidered.* Harrap, London, 1962.
2. Cannon, B.   Personal communication, 1974.
3. Constable, J.   Personal communication, 1975.
4. Goldwyn, R.   Personal communication, 1975.
5. Wright, B. A.   *Physical Disability: A Psychological Approach.* Harper & Row, New York, 1960.
6. Schilder, P.   *The Image and Appearance of the Human Body.* International Universities Press, New York, 1950.
7. Horowitz, M. J.   *Image Formation and Cognition.* Appleton-Century-Crofts, New York, 1970.
8. Kolb, L. C.   Disturbances of the Body Image. In S. Arieti (Ed.), *American Handbook of Psychiatry.* New York, Basic Books, 1959. Vol. 7.
9. Rubins, J. L.   Self-awareness and body image, self-concept and identity. In J. H. Masserman (Ed.), *The Ego.* Grune & Stratton, New York, 1967.
10. Langer, S.   *Mind, An Essay on Human Feeling.* Johns Hopkins Press, Baltimore, 1973. Vol. I.
11. James, W.   Does Consciousness Exist? In *Essays in Radical Empiricism.* Longmans, Green, New York, 1912.
12. Piaget, J., and Inhelder, B.   *Mental Imagery in the Child.* Basic Books, New York, 1956.
13. Kafka, E.   On the Development of the Experience of Mental Self, the Bodily Self and Self-Consciousness. In A. Freud et al. (Eds.), *Psychoanalytic Study of the Child.* Quadrangle, New York, 1971. 26:236.
14. Gallup, G.   It's done with mirrors—chimps and self-concept. *Psychol. Today* 4:58–61, 1971.
15. Pritchard, R. M., Heron, W., and Hebb, D. O.   Visual perception approached by the method of stabilized images. *Can. J. Psychol.* 14(2):67–77, 1960.
16. Gregory, R. L.   *Eye and Brain: The Psychology of Seeing.* McGraw-Hill, New York, 1966.
17. Greenacre, P.   Fetishism and Body Image. In R. S. Eissler et al. (Eds.),

Psychoanalytic Study of the Child. International Universities Press, New York, 1953. Vol. 8, p. 91.

18. Mahler, M. S. *On Human Symbiosis and the Vicissitudes of Individuation.* International Universities Press, New York, 1968.
19. Fisher, S. Experiencing your body: You are what you feel. *Saturday Review,* July 8, 1972. P. 27.
20. Goffman, E. Studies in adjustment to visible injuries: Evaluation of curiosity by the injured. *J. Abnorm. Soc. Psychol.* 43:13–28, 1948.
21. Hall, E. T. *The Silent Language.* Doubleday, New York, 1959.
22. Landis, B. *Ego Boundaries (Psychological Issues,* Vol. VI, No. 4, Monograph 24). International Universities Press, New York, 1970.
23. Federn, P. *Ego Psychology and the Psychoses.* Basic Books, New York, 1952.
24. Fisher, S. *Body Experience in Fantasy and Behavior.* Appleton-Century-Crofts, New York, 1970.
25. Deno, E. Self-identification among adolescent boys. *Child Dev.* 24:269, 1953.
26. Wolff, W. *The Expression of Personality.* Harper & Row, New York, 1943.
27. Shontz, F. C. *Perceptual and Cognitive Aspects of Body Experience.* Academic, New York, 1969.
28. Hoffer, W. Mouth, Hand and Ego Integration. In R. S. Eissler et al. (Eds.), *Psychoanalytic Study of the Child.* International Universities Press, New York, 4:49–56, 1949.
29. Spiegel, L. The Self, the Senses of Self and Perception. In R. S. Eissler et al. (Eds.), *Psychoanalytic Study of the Child.* International Universities Press, New York, 14:83, 1959.
30. Arnheim, R. *Art and Visual Perception.* University of California, Berkeley, Calif., 1969.
31. Heidbreder, E. *Seven Psychologies.* Appleton-Century-Crofts, New York, 1933.
32. Montague, F. M. A. *Touching, The Human Significance of the Skin.* Columbia University Press, New York, 1971.
33. Birdwhistel, R. *Kinesics and Context.* University of Pennsylvania Press, Philadelphia, 1970.
34. Bellak, L. Ego functions. *J. Nerv. Ment. Dis.* 148:569–585, 1969.
35. Hewes, G. W. Communication of sexual interest, an anthropological view. *Med. Aspects Hum. Sexuality* 7:66–92, 1973.
36. Murstein, B., Gadpaille, W., and Byrne, D. What makes people sexually appealing. *Sexual Behav.* 76, June 1971.
37. Berscheid, E., Walster, E., and Bohrnstedt, G. Beauty and the best. *Psychol. Today* 5(10):42, March 1972.
38. Balikov, P. Personal communication, 1975.

3

Disfigurement and Personality Development

In conventional designations of sickness and the social role of the sick, most authors have been influenced by Parsons's [1] categorization of the "sick role." He stressed that the incapacitation of the patient is thought to be beyond the choice of the person, and the person is not viewed as responsible for the trouble, and is not expected to be able to cure the matter on his own. The disability of the individual exempts him from some of the normal obligations of social behavior. Parsons further noted that in being sick the person is able to deviate legitimately from conventional social behavior, but this legitimization depends on the sufferer's recognition that to be ill is undesirable, seeing in the situation something that should be overcome if possible. The sufferer is expected to seek help for his illness and to cooperate with attempts to get him well. This means an adoption of the "patient role," a set of conditions that move a sick person into the care of a physician. The physician in his turn helps to define further the conditions of this aspect of life and to tell both the patient and his family, and essentially the community, what is right in terms of treatment and role behavior.

Unquestionably this concept conflicts with some of the designations of emotional disorder, and who shapes and patterns the visible manifestations of psychological malfunction, but in the physical realm it is generally clear, as Freidson [2] has schematized. The person with a heart attack is freed from most ordinary obligations, and he is obligated

41

to seek help and cooperate with treatment. In physical medicine, the disease is commonly treated as a thing imposed on a person, and while man *is* in one sense a body, it may also be distinguished that man *has* a body and that he believes himself to be an entity that is not identical with his body, but has the body at his disposal. "In other words, man's experience of himself hovers between being and having a body, a very special type of equilibrium, and deviance may be viewed in sociological perspective, both as a set of circumstances and also as a special way of viewing these circumstances" [2, p. 277]. Thus, a person who stammers may be relieved of some responsibilities such as lecturing to groups, or a person with epilepsy may lose the privilege of driving a car. The patient with meningitis is released from his normal duties and treatment is imperative for his problem, while the patient with a cold has a temporary surcease from work or at least work at the highest level; and cancer makes for a permanent suspension of duties and may put the person in a permanently privileged position.

Most of the time, labeling persons as sick or deviant heavily defines their lack of privileges. Society and the professions require labeling in order to make predictions about behavior, and in order to pursue their goals. These predictions may involve labeling, diagnosing, and stigmatizing a person in inimical ways that go beyond their helpfulness to society and may be harmful to him. The poor may be labeled as inadequate, the retarded may be unfairly restricted, and people who look different in terms of race or social class may be stigmatized on this basis—and all may be treated and forced to act in a devalued way without the sympathetic or supportive aids of the sick role. Furthermore, to put the problem in a different way, a facially unattractive person with pockmarks or a scar may be treated in a stigmatized way without the logical assumptions of being sick, and with some of the unconscious assumptions that he is deviant and unacceptable. Similarly (Goffman [3]), we see seedy, shamefaced people losing face, being in the wrong face, or assuming lower status other than in the sick role.

THE CHRONICALLY ILL OR DISABLED CHILD

Pless [4] and others who have studied the relationships between behavior and physical status in developing children feel that there are some generalizations to be drawn even though specific correlations are difficult to make. There is consensus that children who experience rapid physical development are socially enhanced in their relations with children their own age and with adults around them, and that they tend to respond with social confidence and try to achieve along the lines indicated by their surrounding culture. The personality patterns appear to develop largely through changes in the expectations of the people around the child, and therefore alter his self-perception and confidence [5–8]. For the handicapped child the attitudes he has about his disability may be the greatest determinant in whether or not he can cope with his problems and make a successful adaptation in the community.

Although chronically ill or handicapped children as a whole are more likely to experience emotional difficulties than are normal children, it has not been possible to relate either the nature of a disability or its severity to particular emotional problems; however, the ways in which children are cast in deviant or sick roles appear to be important in their personality development. A number of investigations, especially those of Richardson [7], have confirmed the view that there is a hierarchy of preferences for different types of disabilities. People prefer the normal to the handicapped, and with considerable uniformity find facial disfigurement the least desirable. Normal individuals feel uncomfortable with the handicapped, they tend to be more formal in reaction, wishing to cover up their negative feelings, and hence they appear more anxious, inhibited, and contained in their behavior [8]. As part of this interaction handicapped people frequently do not receive full or spontaneous responses from others with whom they deal socially. According to Kleck [9], they are subjected to more rigid and more distorted opinions from respondents, who tend to answer their questions more briefly. Kleck went on to say that schoolwork remained one of the least distorted areas.

Davis [10] described three characteristic stages in the development of social behavior between handicapped and normal individuals. The first is one of "fictional acceptance" in which the handicapped person is offered a chance to interact as if there were no problems, even though the public may be unconsciously stiff in responding. Then there is a second phase in which the nonhandicapped person forgets the handicap and responds to the person as an individual. In the final stage, the speaker takes note of the disability and does not allow it to interfere with the interaction, but qualifies the relationship with this knowledge. Large numbers of disabled children are shy and sensitive, and in comparison with their normal peers, appear to be less socially involved and to have less social experience as a result of their more limited contacts. Kriegel, in a sensitive and bitter article describing his own experiences with disability, wrote of the handicapped person as a "social fugitive, a prisoner of expectations molded by a society that he makes uncomfortable by his very presence" [11, p. 416]. He discussed the feelings of the crippled person who is irrelevant to ordinary living and who is tolerated by a society that makes it clear that if he wishes to be accepted in spite of his stigma, he does best to keep his distance. "He can be challenged in his illusions of self-sufficiency by the most haphazard event" [11, p. 428]. This continuing discomfort is seen in the obsessive concern of the obese with weight and eating and, said Mayer [12], is similar to the heightened sensitivity and constant preoccupation with status found among members of ethnic and racial minorities, who rarely forget discrimination and never seem entirely free of a dim sense of vaguely impending doom. Interwoven with this is a general finding that children who are sick are bothered by feelings of guilt and self-blame [13], which confirms Pless's conclusion that chronically ill and handicapped children are more likely to have emotional problems. However, Fisher [13] found that comparing the body image reorganization in people with visible disabilities to that in people with concealed problems such as heart disease did not give clear differences with regard to self-evaluation.

From a number of sources there is evidence suggesting that concern over physical appearance and physical disability increases with adolescence and decreases after the twenties [14]. There are also indications that physical disability has somewhat different meaning and consequences for boys than for girls. Boys uniformly show more concern than girls for the functional consequences of disability, whereas girls show more concern for the cosmetic consequences.

It is estimated that about 30 million people in the world have highly visible deformation, which, though this is less than one in a thousand of the world population, is a huge figure. These defects cause difficulties not only for the handicapped but also for the people with whom they come in contact. In a recent German study of thousands of adults and children, Jansen and Esser [15] reported that few of their respondents wanted to be friends with a deformed person, much less marry or adopt one, and almost two-thirds felt that the disfigured should be kept out of sight. Children seemed more definitely rejecting. And 9 percent of the people studied did not know how to approach the victim. Jansen and Esser felt that the normal person's aversion was due to a fear of being struck by a similar fate. The weight of this societal reaction falls on the handicapped person. Children grow up and learn to have more pity, but still it is the disfigured person who must show others how he functions and how he needs or wants to be treated. He must direct attention away from his deformed body and toward the self within. A disfigured young person strains to remain a "sharer" in conventional life and to evade the passive sick role. But he may fall between the beds or gradually surrender to a more constricted sick role, with all its accompanying social deprivations.

Children with congenital defects are often viewed by their parents as unfinished, and their mothers tend to implicate their own imperfections in the problem. They want to work at treatment to "complete" their child. Tizard and Grad [16], who noted this, also pointed out that these mothers have combined their love and investment in their children with intense sadness, guilt, and pain, which they dare not express. This leads these children to hide their own anxiety and pain and to present themselves with less overt feeling in order to fend off loss of love.

A wealthy San Francisco friend of Gertrude Stein's, Annette Rosenshine [17], whose life struggles for self-realization in social life and art were dominated by her harelip, wrote in 1920 of the "inner scar of my disfigurement" and of the "grotesque morphology of our emotions," showing graphically the interweaving of inner and outer self-perceptions.

The problems of acquired disability are somewhat different from those of congenital deformity. There is a period of presumably normal development and interaction with parents; of course, it is becoming clearer that many of the children who sustain burn injuries come from poor homes, with depressed and angry mothers, where supervision is poor, where affection is stunted, and the self-esteem of the child is precarious. The wide range and multiplicity of these factors are difficult to segregate from the specifics of the burn or trauma situation. High levels of emotional disturbance and social disorders have been noted by investigators working with burned children at a number of institutions. Woodward [18] surveyed children who had been burned several years prior to her investigation at the Birmingham Accident Hospital in England, and found that 81 percent showed signs of emotional disturbance according to their mothers. This level of disturbance was in striking contrast to that noted in 600 siblings of these same patients and in a random control group, where 7 and 14 percent, respectively, were considered disturbed according to their parents.

At the same time that burned children attempt to cope with the chronic turmoil and conflict of their home life and the many stresses of their injuries, they are particularly burdened if they are facially disfigured. In her studies of facially disfigured individuals, Abel [19] found that whether their defects were of a mild or severe nature their disfigurement was a deterrent to successful living; many complained that they were in some way discriminated against either at work or in social situations. She found these difficulties in adaptation reflected in the projective material of psychological tests, except that the more severely disfigured were somewhat less disturbed than the mildly disfigured, and they had better control over their feelings and impulses and accepted themselves somewhat better. She believed the less disfigured people were insistent that others should perceive their actual or supposed deformity in the same way that they did, that they were projecting personality problems into this issue, and that they were making the face the focal point for their subjective difficulties. Because society ambivalently offers the visibly disabled or marred a superficial acceptance with admixtures of inferior or deviant status and some of the special privilege of the sick role, the disfigured person may combine any of these patterns of interaction with his own distorted self-concepts and perceptions.

Special conditions and personality states dominate the traffic patterns in interpersonal relations. A particular experience, said Tauber [20], may encourage friendliness or enlarge intimacy in a person ordinarily guarded or remote, as when people get together to gossip, or an individual may be "focused on" as people react to his large nose or facial scar, as if there were particular regions for interactions and particular dangers. The handicap is a threat to social interaction as well as a focus for interaction. There is what Davis [10] called an "inundating potential," referring to the way the particular stigma can overwhelm all other aspects of the relationship. Under the general rubric of the "sociology of the body image," Schilder [21] described the body experience a person has in the presence of others who are unusually small or large, graceful or awkward, beautiful or ugly, and noted that the information about body feelings and attitudes is constantly shifting in social relationships. The individual with a fixed scar or facial deformity can be contrasted to the patient who seeks elective cosmetic surgery. The cosmetic patient is generally not deformed in the public's view and is seeking to alter his external appearance in order to resolve some internal personality problem. Therefore, the standards for satisfactory results are also much more subjective. A number of investigators have confirmed what Abel [20] suggested, that more severe defects or deformities are likely to be handled more realistically and to result in well-accepted surgical outcomes, while the minor defects are more likely to be distorted by elaborate subjective elaborations.

Schmitt [22] studied burned children at the Galveston Shriners Hospital, and from his sample felt that the life experience of these facially disfigured patients in the community was not overwhelming compared with that of other school children. He felt this was a hopeful sign for preadolescents, but not conclusive. My own experience is totally in disagreement—disfigured children find life adjustment totally engulfing and frequently crushing. Remensnyder and Constable [23] described "cosmetic surgical patients who sought repeated surgery to correct minor or absent defects, because they felt they lived lives distorted by deformities, which were actually neurotic dislike of their appearance."

Gifford [24] found that nearly all patients seeking reconstructive rather than cosmetic surgery for congenital or traumatic defects are satisfied with the operative results, even limited ones, and that even among cosmetic patients the majority obtain satisfying long-term results even though they come for the resolution of unrealistic motivations. He concluded that whatever the neurotic or symbolic underpinnings, the patients feel the surgery provides an "augmentation." Thus, one can compare the cosmetic patient who sees the defect as a *psychological* reality that is altered with the disfigured patient who views his disfigurement an *objective* reality that is improved. He also wrote that "unlike general surgery, cosmetic surgery does not confer the special status of being ill. The patient concerned about his appearance usually thinks of himself as 'ugly' or 'defective' rather than sick, a state equated with being morally 'bad' or incapable of inspiring love" [p. 29]. The configuration of forces for the disfigured patient may be seen as analogous but different; the subjectively neurotic feelings of guilt, badness, and being unloveable are also very strong, but they are imprinted by the ways described earlier that other people have actually responded to the patient's appearance. Where the cosmetic patient may have trouble defining the anatomical change desired, the posttraumatic patient does not usually have this problem, though many times he will have an unusual preference about which part of his disfigurement should be worked on first, whether an eyelid, a lip, an ear, or a minor scar.

Transsexual patients typify the complexity of themes that enter into the attempts to deal with life and with oneself by visible surgical change of the body, as exemplified by Jan Morris in the book *Conundrum,* an autobiography of a transsexual [25]. Here, a man who found himself sexually wrong, in spite of being considered masculine, a husband, a father, and a professional success, seemed to want to flee from the sadistic and cruel aspects of masculinity as part of his wish to become a woman. This is one pole of an extremely complex reaction.

After 30 years of war in Vietnam, with hordes of burned and maimed people, the plastic surgery most requested by the Vietnamese middle class is change of Oriental eyes to look more Western. Many want their noses made more Caucasian. This is striking evidence of the cultural values and lack of personal esteem imposed by the colonial heritage.

Sensory deprivation appears to produce similar body image changes in the deformed and patients of normal habitus. However, his actual disfigurement remains a nodal point in his relations with the world and others will not let him evade this, even if he were subjectively capable of effective, blanket denial.

Chronic Strain—The Deviant Role

The handicapped individual has to deal with a series of blows that pattern his development and relations with others. They are developmental interferences in the sense of being alterations of the conventional patterns; and they are also a series of traumata and, in another sense of the word, provide chronic trauma in the interpersonal relations of the growing child.

Freud [26] defined as traumatic those excitations or stimuli from within or without that are powerful enough to break through the protective shield. In trauma the ego is unable to cope with a stimulus within a given span of time; it temporarily loses its mediating capacity. Of the two kinds of stimuli operative in trauma, the internal ones are invariably instinctual in origin and have a common characteristic, namely, they involve a separation from, or loss of, a loved object, or loss of its love.

A traumatic occurrence is characterized by the intrusion into the psyche of a stimulus or series of stimuli that set off an unconscious train of intrapsychic events beyond the capacity of the ego to master at that particular time. The ego's barrier, or defensive capacities against stimuli, is breached, without a corresponding subsequent ability of the ego adequately to repair the damage in sufficient time to maintain mastery and a state of security. The resulting traumatic state is a feeling of psychic helplessness, which may be temporary, intermittent, or lasting. There is a feeling of lack of control and vulnerability without the expectation of adequate containment, mastery, and adaptation. In a relatively mild or transitory degree, this state is a part of the human condition. In a moderate or severe degree, either in quantity or in duration, it is a pathological state, comparable to an anxiety state that is substantial or long-lasting. In almost all traumatic events, both internal and external stimuli are present. Together they constitute a complementary series. Of utmost significance is whether the stimulus, or the combination of stimuli, is strong enough to pierce the stimulus barrier, and how long it lasts or how often it is repeated. The intensity of the stimulus, however, cannot be measured by any single criterion. Rather, its traumatic potential will depend on a number of factors, including constitutional predisposition, the state of the psychic apparatus, and the relatedness of the stimulus itself to prevailing drive-cathected wishes and conflicts. Thus, a given stimulus may be traumatic for one individual but not for another. Further, for a given individual, a stimulus that is traumatic at one time may be assimilated without being overwhelming at another.

As Anna Freud [27] suggested, neither symptoms nor life tasks can be used to assess mental health or illness in children; the most significant determinants of the child's mental future are the capacity to develop progressively and the damage to that capacity. She designated the following criteria for evaluating a child's developmental progress:

1. Whether the current behavior disturbances are within the wide range of variations of normal.
2. Whether symptoms are essentially transitory in nature and represent by-products of developmental strain.
3. Whether there are important fixation points or massive regressions, or both, on the side of the drives, which have an impoverishing effect on drive progression, involving the ego in conflict and initiating character disorders or neurotic symptomatology.
4. Whether fixation and regression of drives are accompanied by arrests and regressions of ego and superego development, with crippling effects on personality growth and symptom formation of a borderline, delinquent, or psychotic nature.
5. Whether primary organic deficiencies or earliest deprivations have distorted development and structuralization, producing a defective, retarded, nontypical personality.
6. Whether destructive organic, toxic, or psychological processes have disrupted mental growth.

Overall, her interest has been in examining the complex psychic systems, their rigidity, tolerances, and predispositions, in the context of both external and internal pressures.

Stress
The concept of trauma shades over to include stress, the corrosive influence of prolonged tension of lower intensity. We may ask, Of what does psychological stress consist? We speak, for instance, of the stress of the busy physician. What, in psychological terms, do we mean?

The physician or lawyer has to make decisions, the results of which he will be *responsible* for; that is, unfavorable consequences of these decisions will be brought home to him personally. Today insurance claims and costs are driving some physicians out of practice, and the pattern of practicing "defensive medicine" is rapidly evolving, especially in reconstructive work. He may suffer through loss of position, prestige, or possessions. At the least, he will be blamed for the consequences or he may be tormented by his conscience. Sometimes the decision may be clear-cut, with all advantages on one side and none on the other; in such cases, responsibility is easy to bear. But often there will be assets and liabilities on both sides, and the decision-maker cannot escape anxiety. Sometimes, the decision will be what is called "difficult," i.e., assets and liabilities are more or less evenly distributed, with no preponderance on either side. In such cases the decision-maker will have to bear heavy tension and pressure; there is no possibility of complete discharge or even of sizable relief.

Thus, psychological stress seems to be a condition of permanent exposure to danger without the possibility of escape. For practical purposes, we may speak of medium- or low-level tension, for high-level tension is likely to be traumatic rather than merely stressful. The level of tension must, of course, be evaluated in terms of existing tolerance.

Greenacre [28] stated that no truly traumatic event is ever wholly digested, that increased vulnerability inevitably remains, and that the individual concerned is prone to break down at some later date. The facially burned child has to cope with a continuing, mammoth series of traumata in his development. He is continually confronted with the difficulties of his healing scars, their contractures, and repeated surgical efforts to alter them, along with the reactions of his parents to this stress and the incursions of other people's responses to him.

Case History: Robert A.
Robert was a 7-year-old boy who, in a house fire, was burned over 40 percent of his body, including the chest, front and right side of the neck, and face and right ear. He remained scarred by contractures of the neck, a crumpled ear, rubbery, raised scars of the cheeks and chin, and a ropy scar that pulled his lower lip down on the right side.

Hospitalized for intensive care, he was subsequently transferred to the Shriners Burns Institute when the family discovered that he could be given treatment in a specialized burn unit without cost. He was in an isolation unit, and had a period of delirium, a long series of skin grafts, and physical therapy for scar contractures under his arms. While in the first hospital, he had had a period of moderate depression, with eating problems and fear of getting up and walking. For some months his parents felt guilt over their responsibility for the fire because they had not undertaken rewiring of the home, which had been recommended. The home was shadowed by parental guilt, financial problems, medical and surgical assaults, school absence, loss of friends, isolation, orthopedic problems, and the fear of the patient and his parents that he would become a pariah. Most children faced with similar problems use ego restriction or personality constriction to protect themselves, while forcibly focusing on the enormous reality problems immediately involving them.

There were problems of planning further surgery, of getting to and from the hospital, of rearranging the household to manage Robert, and of the mother's learning to change dressings (a frightening prospect for her). Robert had been wetting the bed in the hospital and this gradually ended in the first weeks at home. His sleep patterns took two months to return to normal, with episodes of waking during the night, nightmares, and restlessness marking this period. His eating habits had changed while he was in the hospital, and he had become fussy, after developing a style of using the refusal of food to show anger to the nurses. The massive investment of psychical energies in the physical problems of his recuperation seemed to mask any other symptomatology, but the attention of the family was also turned elsewhere. The traumatic event became part of the continuing stresses of adjustment to rehabilitation.

SHAME

A silent, steady, chronic, and disturbing feature of the life of the disfigured is the need to deal with feelings of shame and self-consciousness.

Self-consciousness is a proneness to regard oneself as the object of observation of others, failure to forget oneself in society. Self-consciousness describes an accentuated state of awareness of the own self and also indicates the assumption that the same exaggerated amount of attention is paid to one's person by others.

Seeking attention may be a means to undo feelings of insufficiency, but the imagined fulfillment of this wish can be experienced as extremely unpleasant. The attention desired from others is contained in and replaced by the ego's concentration on the self. The ego thus plays a double role: it is the observer and simultaneously the object of observation. What is relevant in cases of disfigurement is that cathexis has been shifted to the self not only from objects but also from normally neutralized ego activities, to a degree that is intolerable. Self-conscious persons seek to undo feelings of inadequacy by forcing everyone's attention and admiration on themselves, but they fail in this defensive attempt. They feel that attention is indeed focused on them in a *negative* way, as though others, instead of being dazzled, were discerning the warded off "inferiority" behind the false front. The Russian term *dysmorphobia,* meaning the belief that some part of the body is ugly or unpleasant, fits many adolescent ideas. Occasionally the symptom of self-consciousness becomes further complicated by a deficiency of the self-evaluating functions. It is as though such persons were unable to form any independent moral judgment about themselves, but needed public opinion as a yardstick. This is especially enforced on the patient with visible handicaps.

The most significant external factors in the arousal of shame are criticism, ridicule, scorn, and abandonment. During the process of development these precipitate various defenses that include the following: (1) the limiting of self-exposure, (2) repression of certain internalized thoughts, feelings, and impulses that evoke shame in the absence of self-exposure, (3) the wish to perform in such a manner as to protect oneself from being shamed by others, (4) the limiting of libidinal invest-ment, and (5) the discharge of aggression, e.g., the blaming of others for one's own failures.

Case History: Dwayne S.

Dwayne S., 9 years old, has burn scars on both hands and on his neck and chin, and without any apparent limitation of movements. He said he can do anything except high tree climbing. His ambition is to become a magician. He bites his nails, has scary dreams, and still wets the bed two years after his injury. His parents are sepa-rated. He talked about being able to lift up his big brother, whom he described as large and fat, and he told of a girlfriend who is about 10 years old, but with whom he has practically no contact. He described several fights at school, saying he won them; he does not want to tell the teacher why he is crying when he has a fight, and he does not want his mother to know, so instead he tells them that he stumbled. "All we do in school is fight, fight, fight. They call me monkey, french fries, burnt fingers, and all that. They are always saying those things and they won't leave me alone. It makes me mad and we get into fights." He told of a dream of climbing up a trapeze in which he fell and died, and another in which "I was dead and came alive and I met a tiger and he ate my head off." Dwayne drew deformed and primi-tive pictures for me and signed his name. He was described as somewhat hyper-active. But in the school yard and after school hours he hangs back fearfully from contact with children and dreads teasing. While he does win fights he is still a scapegoat of his classmates.

Shame begins to appear in early childhood and may undergo major reinforcement or accentuation during the oedipal phase or latency. As development proceeds, shame tends to concentrate on aspects of the self that are exposed to others and may therefore be manifested through obsessive preoccupation with certain parts of the body, e.g., an obsessive concern with size or shape. The obsessions to which shame gives rise may readily undergo displacement onto external objects, parents, friends, and so forth. In an attempt to counteract these feelings such patients may deny their sensitivity or deny their inhibitions, and present a facade of happy indifference to these problems.

Case History: Scottie R.

Scottie was first seen at 7½ years of age. He had been severely burned when a camp stove exploded, and his injury had left his face looking mummified (Figure 8). Until his accident his development had been described as normal, and he had been in good physical health, charming, outgoing, and easy-tempered. Afterward, with remnants of blond hair and a dehumanized, immobile mask for a face, his appear-ance frightened most bystanders, yet his manner seemed a model of unself-conscious good nature. He was seen by a psychiatrist who remarked, "this youngster has an amazing quality of cheerfulness. He relates especially well to stories he likes. There

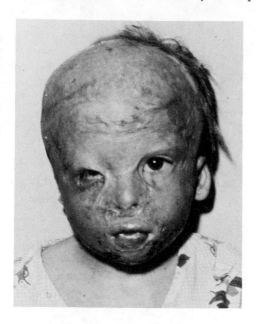

Figure 8. Scottie R. showed striking denial of his massive deformity, but testing revealed deep underlying depression.

seems to be no self-consciousness in his face and his smile continued throughout the meeting. I don't understand why this youngster is so unaware of himself, and so many other children are."

A month later he was reported to be playing more aggressively and was competing for attention with a girl of his own age, and longing to go home. His parents' only expressed concern at that time was whether he liked the hospital as much as the first one he had been in. After Scottie returned home, they tended to live in isolation, with few social contacts.

Four years later he continued to be viewed by the hospital staff as a model child who seemed to a striking degree to be unaware of his appearance. Psychological testing done at that time showed a different picture, a child desperately anxious to get along, and bitterly fighting off his feelings of depression.

DEPRESSION, APATHY, AND EGO RESTRICTION
Although past and present experiences have been shown to be related to self-esteem, the role of a person's future outlook in determining his sense of worth has not been systematically investigated, even though we know it is important. Ongoing actualization and growth are integral to positive self-regard. By contrast, individuals with low self-esteem often express considerable hopelessness about achieving personal and inter-personal goals. Thus, attitudes toward the future, which often govern how a person interprets his past and present experiences, may be funda-mentally related to an individual's perception of his worth. Attitudes of

handicapped persons shift dramatically with their hopes and expectations of future surgery and their realistic and unrealistic hopes for improvement or cure.

For many burn-disfigured individuals the body is focused on relentlessly by multiple operations and treatments. Because they do not see a future without handicaps and suffering, many find the treatment exhausting and are depleted of hope. They frequently are seen to be apathetic, grim, and inward looking.

Bibring [29] explained that in *depression there is usually an emotional loss due to disappointment.* He stressed that the individuals he studied felt either helplessly exposed to superior powers, fatal organic disease, or recurrent neurosis or to the seemingly inescapable fate of being lonely, isolated, or unloved, or unavoidably confronted with the apparent evidence of being weak, inferior, or a failure. In all instances, the depression accompanied a feeling of being doomed, irrespective of the conscious or unconscious background of this feeling. In all of them a blow was dealt to the person's self-esteem, on whatever grounds such self-esteem may have been founded.

The feelings of helplessness are not the only characteristic of depression. Irrespective of their unconscious implications, one may roughly distinguish between three groups of persisting aspirations of the person: (1) the wish to be worthy, loved, and appreciated, not to be inferior and unworthy, (2) the wish to be strong, superior, great, and secure, not to be weak and insecure, and (3) the wish to be good and loving, not to be aggressive, hateful, and destructive. It is exactly from the tension between these highly charged narcissistic aspirations on the one hand, and the ego's acute awareness of its (real and imaginary) helplessness and incapacity to live up to them on the other hand, that depression results.

Case History: Brenda L.
Brenda, 10 years old, was desperately frightened about coming to the hospital for surgery on her chin. She had rough, red scarring from her lower lip downward to her neck that was the result of an attempt to drink out of a lye bottle when she was 2½ years old. The family was taciturn, but dejected about her future. She did not want to return to school, where they called her Monster. She was sure that nothing further could be done to help her, and was progressively becoming more shy and dreaded any social contact even though she had a few friends. Her parents' efforts to encourage her were unconvincing and ineffective. She had changed schools and made efforts to stay at home whenever possible. Her work had been meager so that she had been held back twice. Though she responded to the friendly overtures of nurses and women doctors, she exuded fearful dejection and cringed from the surgeons or male strangers. She refused to be drawn into any discussion of her wishes for the future or for cosmetic surgery, saying that nothing did any good. Once her mother remarked, "Brenda's life is destroyed." The patient said to the nurses who knew her, "I'll never be pretty or get married. That's destroyed."

Adolescent growth is powerfully facilitated by a new inner awareness of biological parity, physically and even intellectually, with adults. New confidence is facilitated by the adolescent's seeing himself accepted by people around him, and it is inhibited by rejections. The middle adolescent must play out his sexual and aggressive fantasies with the body of a child, in effect, at least as compared with the larger, complete body of an adult. In late adolescence the individual is biologically, and in some cases socially, on a par with adults, if not, in fact, in a superior position. If he is able to incorporate perceptions of this in his body image, there results intrapsychically something like the closing of the epiphyses. The achievement of a stable body image is both a *consequence* of the complex changes going on and an *organizer* of psychological development. The burn patient cannot complete a stable body image. Too much physical pain, damage, and scarring persist, and too much medical therapy intrudes.

Physical maturity is the biological landmark of the beginning of late adolescence. In most persons the corresponding psychological events involve a rapid restructuring within the ego of a new, more unified body image, of more mature self-representation and object representations, along with the deployment of more stable patterns of drives and defenses. These events tend to occur whether the individual is essentially normal or neurotic. The Oedipus complex is revived, but in a new context of body image parity with adults. The handicapped adolescent cannot objectively function as an equal. Many of the normal developmental events occur, but with more tentativeness and muted external expression. The psychical energies continue to be heavily tied to managing the physical problems and their social concomitants. People surrounding handicapped teenagers don't expect or accept them in quite normal roles.

THE ALTERED SELF

Just as the philosophers have struggled to decide whether or not consciousness and subjectivity really exist, so have individuals continued trying to escape the emotional agonies of the split between "what I look like" and "what I am." Imbedded in the concept of identity are to be found the three qualities explicated by Erikson [30]: a sense of individual uniqueness, a striving for continuity of experience that is automatic and unconscious, and solidarity with a group. Each of these is influenced by deformity, so that the person feels unique in a negative sense and the striving for continuity of experience is frequently interrupted by the intrusion of negative self-consciousness, surgical and medical interference, and social pressures to accept deviance. The wish for solidarity with an acceptable group is constantly skewed in the direction of association with a devalued group, the sick, the halt, the handicapped, the unattractive, and the unacceptable. Organizations asking us to "hire the handicapped" tell us that the successfully adapted person with a handicap is likely to be more conscientious, well-organized, reliable, and clear in goal direction [9] than the average worker. It is not clear how exceptional this style may be. A number of personality variables are involved. The handicapped, like very beautiful people, tend to be responded to initially more as things than people, and both groups have to respond to this phenomenon. A handicapped or stigmatized individual must thrust ahead socially and vocationally, often using obsessional mechanisms, accompanied by the earnestness and humorlessness of the obsessive, to reach his goal [9, 31].

Usually, the more a child has seen and heard, the more he wants to see and hear; the more monotonous and restricted the environment that surrounds a child, the more likely there is to be apathy. In a general way, this can be directly applied to disfigured children and their families. They are restricted in their intake of stimuli because of the medical treatment limitations. One can argue that even the best hospital does not in any way approximate the experiences of a normal child in his natural home and school situation. They miss out on conventional rhythms of social interaction, they probably see hours and hours more of television during the interminable periods at home and in the hospital, and they are even more passive in watching than other children, tending to stare into space a good deal of the time the television set is on.

In the experience of burn centers, their patients come overwhelmingly from lower class and disturbed families. The children seen at the Shriners Burns Institute in Boston seem to come from poor, disrupted families or middle-class disturbed families, with only a small group from normal-appearing households. In our experience approximately 80 percent of burned children come from troubled homes.

Many themes flow together, but fundamentally the disfigured person has to grow up with added problems in the balance between forces; he has more trouble meeting his needs and more difficulty being autonomous. This leads to conflicts between the individual and his environment as well as internalized conflicts about the individual's guilt and unworthiness. Wright [32] describes the process of "spread," which refers to the tendency of a person perceiving one characteristic in another person, such as a scar, to develop a generalized perception about that person based on the initial impact of the scar. People are likely to make negative interpretations of a whole person with a single handicap on such a basis, and disfigured individuals are likely to face this mechanism in working out their own self-images, particularly when so much energy is taken up by the problems of management of the disfigurement in social situations. This can be oversimplified in terms of the sick role, because there are numerous roles and role-related problems for the disfigured (e.g., handicapped, sick, jester, devalued, stupid, or shocking) that may produce conflicts in the definitions of roles, and conflicts about the roles assigned to the disfigured. Added to these features are attributes of the individual person that might be called a *behavioral style or temperament,* a phenomenological term used by Thomas, Chess, and Birch [33] to describe the characteristic tempo, rhythmicity, adaptability, energy expenditure, mood, and focus of attention of a person, which are independent of specific behavior. In a more general format, Waelder [34] pointed out that individual psychical phenomena have many determinants and are not simply the sum of these determinants. Each behavior serves several functions, at once responsive to many pressures. When one facet of the personality is altered, the other aspects are shifted. When Wright [32] described shifts in a patient's value system that enable him to overcome feelings of inferiority caused by his seeing his disability as a devaluation, she touched on this problem. A person who feels a loss of personal and social satisfaction and skewed peer relations may develop intellectual and other compensatory activities, but these reorganizations require sustained emotional effort to produce a successful compensatory personality pattern. It is obvious that there are individuals who can and do accomplish this, and later chapters of this book are devoted to descriptions of the ways in which some burn-disfigured children and adults have managed their lives, surmounting handicaps.

Yuker [31] asserted that disabled persons who accept themselves and their disabilities tend to be relatively well adjusted, highly motivated, and hardworking, regardless of the extent of their disabilities. In Rogers's view [35], self-acceptance refers to the extent to which self-concept is congruent with the individual's description of his ideal self, and the common denominator in most approaches to the measurement of self-acceptance is some assessment of self-satisfaction. Rogers said that a well-adjusted person is able to accept all perceptions, including those about self, into his personality organization. He went on to suggest that these are organized into the conscious concept of the self associated with feelings of freedom from tension and a sense of comfort, which he designated as *psychological adjustment.*

This view, stressing the ability to take in unflattering and threatening facts and attitudes toward the self, is an important aspect of personality adjustment. But for people who are treated in an aberrant way by those around them, the issue of acceptance of the self may not follow the lines Rogers set forth. The body image changes of the disfigured make this too difficult. Alternative mechanisms for coping are required to support self-esteem. There is too heavy a burden of rejection and stigmatization from the people around them. As Kardiner and Ovesey [36] pointed out about oppressed American blacks, the psychosocial expressions of the oppression cannot be eradicated by educating the victims. The same is true for the scarred child. He cannot flee his problems except by withdrawing into isolation; his self-esteem must be fought for against the devaluation of the public. The possibilities for self-hate, apathy, and depression will continue to be great for these children.

LIFE IN A MINOR CHORD

Case History: Robin G.
Robin is a 16-year-old girl with burn scars on her right cheek, ear, chin, and neck, as well as on her wrist and both thighs, caused by the ignition of a flammable nightgown when she climbed onto a stove 10 years ago. She combines low-normal intelligence with the stigma of disfigurement. In an interview at the outpatient clinic, she stated that she had repeated the second grade and is now a sophomore in high school. She is getting Cs in most subjects in a business course, which she describes vaguely as a college business course. She is failing biology. Robin was a neatly dressed adolescent who looked about her age. She showed no evidence of major psychiatric disease but acted anxious. She moved around a lot during the interview, but was well coordinated. She related easily and was polite, responsive, and appropriate in her manner. She was cooperative and trusting and took the role of a much younger girl dealing with authority. At first she laughed and said, "I'm sick. I ought to see a psychiatrist," but what she turned out actually to have in mind was her frustration about school. "I'm not smart enough. My brother can do it easily all the time, while I try my best, but fail in biology. I can't even understand what the teacher is talking about." Her manner became more forward and more serious when she talked about this.

Robin watches television a lot, reads very little, but was currently reading a book about a girl recovering from cerebral palsy—"how she came out of it." She has no trouble eating or with her bowels or bladder, and her periods do not trouble her. She denied any difficulty with sex, and no evidence of psychiatric disease was noted. She has some fear of fire, being locked in, or walking down a dark street. She gave babysitting as her hobby and said she gave up collecting things that had been of interest to her. She does not go to one church anymore, but visits a number of different churches. She does not smoke or drink and does not take any medications other than aspirin.

She is going with a 16-year-old boy who has dropped out of high school and whom she plans to marry next year. Her 19-year-old sister is married; her parents say there was no point in stopping the sister's marriage because she would have run off and married anyway. However, Robin said this was not the case, and that they really like her boyfriend. When I asked her about him, she said he is used to her scars, but then added, "He's not perfect either. He has a heart condition and a bad shoulder."

Her friends tell her that as a child she was always warned not to be too active because it might open up her scars. Now she is a bit bothered by a scar on her right wrist that pulls and she fears it may open. She said people sometimes stare at her; she does not like this, but "it just doesn't bother me." She does not go to the beach anymore and feels that this is the biggest thing she has had to give up because of her injury.

When asked about her vomiting episodes in the hospital, she said she had a tendency to vomit after operations and when she got headaches. She alleged that doctors have called them migraine, and she described frontal headaches on either side that are not associated with any visual symptoms but require her to lie down, often make her feel nauseated, and sometimes cause vomiting. Aspirins and lying down will sometimes abort these headaches. She was vague about their frequency. The staff felt they actually were tension headaches related to her terror over surgery.

Robin appears to see herself as deformed physically and has attached herself with a damaged boyfriend with whom she hopes to find happiness and marriage. There is a marked passivity in her that makes it unlikely that she will rush into marriage in spite of her statements. The significance of the boyfriend's interest is also doubtful. But Robin tries desperately hard for a normal life-style.

No attempt to schematize all the variables involved in adaptation to disfigurement is likely to do justice to all the interrelated factors. However, in our experience in working with the coping patterns of facially disfigured burn victims, a diagram for some axes on which to grade adjustment to the overall situation (Table 1) has been useful.

Our pursuit of adjustment patterns for burn disfigured individuals has not confirmed the concept advanced by Wright [32] that some handicapped persons develop a broader tolerance and more altruistic form of adjustment than normal persons. Vaillant [37] also reviewed altruism and altruistic surrender as mature defense mechanisms. We have placed these mechanisms on the axis of passive surrender, representing a path toward what we view as poor coping patterns and poor outcomes. This may be prejudicing outcome in terms of personal value systems, but all through life the people who have the available energy to move ahead and thrust forward seem to have more fun and are able also to get more done. The philosophical pose of passively, wisely, and tolerantly observing the world appears to be much more acceptable to people who have already achieved and are adapting to the aging process, rather than to growing adolescents or people in active middle adult life.

DEVALUED STATUS

Case History: Charlene C.
Charlene, nearly 13, was burned in a house fire at the age of 10. Her face is markedly disfigured from the nose and cheeks down, which limits her facial expressions (Figure 9). Her initial position is to keep her head down, to put her hand up to her

Table 1. Some major axes for adjustment to disfigurement. The diagram is an ►
attempt to visualize the important variables that are critical in coping with the
catastrophe of burn disfigurement. Simply designating active versus passive mental
mechanisms is inadequate because of the complex and interweaving emotional patterns involved in actively coping. The more active, assertive pole of each axis is seen
in the upper part of the diagram. Clearly, some of the mechanisms, such as denial
versus over-awareness, and flexibility versus rigidity are not suited to the same spatial
distribution and therefore are shown as diagonal axes. All of these reactions occur
within a social matrix of factors that cannot be charted in the same way, such as
money, education, extended family support, loyal friends, religious help, and
rehabilitation services, and that importantly influence outcome.

face, or to hold her index finger in front of her mouth. Her speech is thick and her
movements generally slow. She wears her hair cropped short and appears more like
a girl of 9 than one who is almost 13 years old. She was clearly oriented with
respect to time and place, and she related in an inhibited manner. Her eyes showed
most of the expression for her face as she widened her eyes and raised her eyebrows.

   She has had over fifteen surgical procedures. Each time she comes to the hospital
she violently fights against anesthesia. She shows her panic in one of the few ways
she can express her rage, struggling with the nurses, whom she trusts, and other
patients in the hospital, which she finds a refuge and a home.

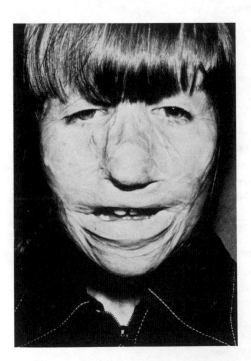

*Figure 9. Charlene C. exemplified passive surrender to her disfigurement, showing
regression, social withdrawal, and apprehension.*

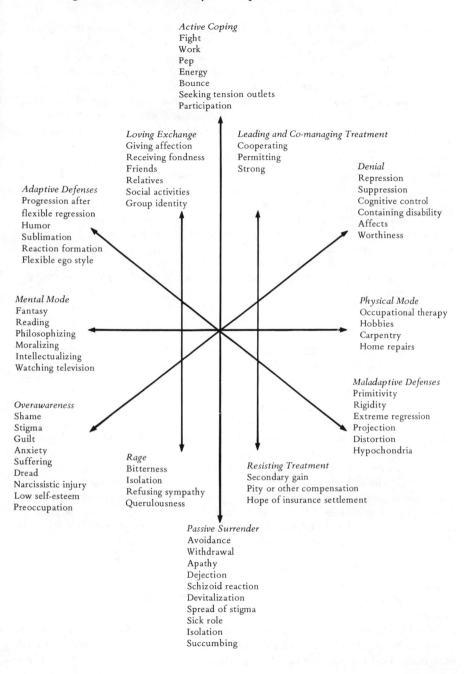

Active Coping
Fight
Work
Pep
Energy
Bounce
Seeking tension outlets
Participation

Loving Exchange
Giving affection
Receiving fondness
Friends
Relatives
Social activities
Group identity

Leading and Co-managing Treatment
Cooperating
Permitting
Strong

Denial
Repression
Suppression
Cognitive control
Containing disability
Affects
Worthiness

Adaptive Defenses
Progression after
flexible regression
Humor
Sublimation
Reaction formation
Flexible ego style

Mental Mode
Fantasy
Reading
Philosophizing
Moralizing
Intellectualizing
Watching television

Physical Mode
Occupational therapy
Hobbies
Carpentry
Home repairs

Maladaptive Defenses
Primitivity
Rigidity
Extreme regression
Projection
Distortion
Hypochondria

Overawareness
Shame
Stigma
Guilt
Anxiety
Suffering
Dread
Narcissistic injury
Low self-esteem
Preoccupation

Rage
Bitterness
Isolation
Refusing sympathy
Querulousness

Resisting Treatment
Secondary gain
Pity or other compensation
Hope of insurance settlement

Passive Surrender
Avoidance
Withdrawal
Apathy
Dejection
Schizoid reaction
Devitalization
Spread of stigma
Sick role
Isolation
Succumbing

Her mother, aged 44, is a tough, gruff divorcee. She is openly annoyed with the problems of her daughter and is much more interested in her sons and 7-year-old twins. She feels that the patient was a problem in school and had trouble learning long before the accident. She has encouraged Charlene toward the goal of being a matron in an old persons' home somewhere in the country. Charlene attends a special class for the handicapped in a regular school, but is often absent; she spends most of her time alone at home watching television and seeking solace from her dolls. In her relationships with the nurses after surgery she is quite obedient and childlike.

At the time of our follow-up interview, Charlene took a compliant role in the waiting room with her mother and seemed to be familiar with the staff and manageable in attitude. She related initially in a controlled way, appearing downcast and apprehensive, but began to talk after a while. She tended to answer questions by denying that she knew anything in order to avoid being pushed or pressed. The predominant tone seemed to be one of resentment, stress, fear, and apprehension. She was clearly aware of the purposes of the follow-up burn clinic. She is in the sixth grade and currently attending school, but had to be pressed to tell she was in a special class for crippled children. She talked about her birthday next week and used as few words as possible to answer all questions. She said that she plays with her brothers; they also fight with her and she has the most trouble with the 10- and 14-year-old, but overall her mother protects her. The 7-year-old twins are less difficult. She has only one girlfriend—"I don't like any other girls." She has a 12-year-old boyfriend, but "I never see him because he doesn't go to the same school." At first she said that she did not like her teachers; then it evolved that she had only one teacher and preferred going to school than being at home and would rather be at home than in the hospital.

She said she was sad in the hospital, but could not explain why because she said she did not know what would happen to her in the hospital. At first she began to talk about other people being treated badly or suffering, but she seemed afraid to pursue this subject. She liked the nurses and had some favorites. She said she was quite frightened of what would happen to her in the hospital—"They gave me operations." She did not know what was planned for her.

She rarely goes to church, and denied that anybody made her uncomfortable in public: "Nothing bothers me . . . nobody makes fun of me." She spoke of playing cards, rocking in bed at night, and wetting the bed. Although she watches television, she could name only one television show, "The Courtship of Eddie's Father," and said she hoped when she grew up she could marry and have children. Her ambition is to be a nurse and work with old people. She said that this is what her mother wants her to do, but that she also wants to do this; however, her attitude was very blank about the future. She said that she gets down-in-the-dumps but when I pressed her on this she absolutely denied it; she has no fears except about operations and being punched by her brothers. She drew a picture, but it was appropriate of a much younger child and overall indicated ego restriction and mental handicap, with marked efforts to evade and deny problems.

It is not difficult to see how Charlene's style may be imposed on our schema. She followed a pattern of general passivity, with intermittent active resistance to treatment; her modes were largely nonintellectual, though she fantasized a lot about her situation to the play ladies on the ward and the nurses who came to know her over the years. Her mother and father were not very affectionate, and the suggestion of having her work in the country in an old peoples' home was a clear manifestation of the way the family rejected her. Her statements of denial were in contrast to her general shyness, passivity, and almost freezing in the presence of strangers, and her assumption of a childlike role with almost all who approached her. She showed some adaptiveness in continuing overall with her treatment, relating to the hospital staff, and being able to form relationships with all the people who showed interest in her. However, her rigidity of style, regression, and lack of help from her environment all aimed her life toward low-level adjustment.

MATURATION IN A SHUT-IN

Case History: Mary L.

Mary is a 14-year-old black girl who has always been passive and who had received a good deal of social casework help before her injury. Her pattern has been one of continuous social shrinkage.

Mary was burned at age 18 months. Her pajamas caught fire when she was playing with a space heater. She was initially treated for a long period of time at various hospitals. She underwent multiple grafting procedures up to the age of three. Subsequently, she has undergone three plastic surgical procedures on her left ear and hip. Her skin is extensively scarred down her left side, including face, ear, neck, anterior chest, and upper arm and hip. An extremely taut band of scar tissue runs from far down on her left lateral chest up to her left wrist, in one broad continuous band.

Mary's mother, sisters, and social worker generally felt that Mary contained her feelings, even at home, and was likely not to tell anyone, including our hospital staff, about her feelings regarding her appearance or wishes for surgery. They reported that she did well at summer camp and seemed since to have acquired a few friends. Her mother expressed the feeling that Mary was somewhat less depressed than last year and functioned well in school, where she is in the sixth grade. Mary clearly dislikes coming back to the hospital and tries to avoid her appointments.

Mary apparently likes children and does well with them. She has a job after school, working with younger children. She has enjoyed this very much and has proved herself to be reliable. Her mother wonders if the scar tissue across her abdomen will prevent her having a successful pregnancy. Mary is very modest about her body and attempts to simulate her missing breast by placing padding in her bra. The stages of a breast reconstruction were explained to the mother but she was advised that it would be best to wait until Mary has achieved her full development. Further concern was expressed about her ear: "Will the thing [keloid] be left there? Will further work be done on it?" Mary's mother was somewhat bewildered by what she considered to be vague answers from the doctors who saw Mary, and wished to have some outline of a prospective plan. It appears that despite her disfigurement, Mary is making efforts to look like a woman and assume a feminine role.

Mary played with a doll and remained extremely withdrawn during her visit, responding to questions in a barely audible whisper. She feigned disinterest in my presence, but when I asked her if she wanted to ask me anything, she asked my name. Mary is a shy individual, but a person constantly and carefully observing and sizing up situations and people. Although she did not respond visibly, she was very much aware of everything and everyone around her. On occasion she responded to others through actions. She seemed starved for friendship, but too frightened to act appropriately to get it.

It had been noted by her mother and by the group workers that Mary never talked about herself, her burns, or her hospital experiences. She withdrew each time attention was focused on her by other people. Mary has at times exhibited stubbornness, which could be a manifestation of a great deal of anger that she has never been able to express. Establishing a trust relationship with Mary through which she could ventilate her feelings has been a long, slow process, according to her social worker. The goal has not yet been reached.

Although Mary had come a long way in the past two years with respect to developing relationships with peers and getting along in school, she was not yet able to vocalize any of her feelings about her appearance. She was very much concerned about it, however, as indicated by her interest in makeup, different hairstyles, and clothes. A rather unfortunate incident occurred in school when a girl to whom Mary had told that she had only one breast told the rest of Mary's class. The class responded by teasing Mary and she ran home, refusing to return to school for several days.

Her mother, who is a concerned person, is willing and able to reinforce a helping person's efforts when she herself is reached out to. She is a gentle, accepting person who is best reached through a pragmatic approach.

Mary's withdrawal, self-consciousness, and enormous shyness dominated her presentation, but she clearly was able to function intellectually and had a good capacity for relating with some people. Even her indiscretion in telling of her missing breast was an effort to relate to a peer. She derived support from her mother as well as social agencies, and made slow but clear use of this. She began to co-manage her treatment, gradually, as she developed patterns of relating and communicating to those around her.

UNEXPECTED COPING SKILLS
The patients seen at the Shriners Burns Institute do not include psychotic individuals who set themselves on fire, but the following is the case of an adolescent whose previous emotional upsets and family difficulties made everyone feel he would fare much worse than he did, an example of heroic response to adversity. Some surgical reports [38] and psychiatric investigations of suicidal patients have cited examples of persons who make suicide attempts and subsequently proceed to better adaptation.

Case History: Rick O.
Rick was first seen at the Shriners Burns Institute when he was 15 years old. He was initially treated at another hospital, where he was estimated to have burns over 75

percent of his body, sustained when he set fire to himself with gasoline. According to his parents, Rick tried to commit suicide at the age of 15 because of a recent incident in school. He had written antireligious slogans in his religion course book. The priest there became angry at Rick, put him on suspension, and told him that he would never allow him to become a priest. Rick had expressed a desire for the priesthood.

Rick, who is the third of six children, has a history of emotional problems dating back to the time when he was about 4 years old and set an aunt's sofa on fire. From the time he entered school (all parochial schools), he has had trouble with his teachers and has talked and fooled around in class. Mrs. O. said everyone knew her at his schools because she was called down there so often. His schoolwork had been poor for three years. He had been a truant, and he had been depressed and negative in the family for a long time. He also is accident prone, especially over the two years before the accident. About a year before, while Rick was on his paper route, he had exhibited himself to little girls. At this time the parents took him to a psychiatrist whom he saw a few times. The parents withdrew him from this treatment because they neither liked the doctor nor felt that he was helpful to Rick. ["All he did was fiddle with his pipe."]

Rick and his 19-year-old brother do not get along. The older brother is constantly denigrating him. He had always done better in school than Rick and let him know it. Rick and his older sister are close, but his main confidante is his 6-year-old sister. Apparently he has talked incessantly to this sister ever since she was able to speak and understand. The parents have not seen this as a sign of real emotional disturbance and loneliness, but rather felt that this was very helpful to their daughter, who is now older for her age and smarter because of Rick.

He has just recently started going out with a girl, but this is nothing serious, according to his mother. His main interests are reading, swimming, and playing the drums in the school band. This year he tried out for the swimming team and did not make it, but intends to try next year. In spite of his troubles at school he was described as friendly and emotionally open, prior to his burn.

Mr. and Mrs. O. did not like the hospital Rick was in before because the staff seemed too busy for him. At one point, shortly after Rick's first skin graft, he began hallucinating, thinking there was a man in his room trying to kill him. Rick asked the nurses to call his father, which they did. Mr. O. was pleased, because Rick is not in the habit of asking for help. He came right down and quieted him by reasoning with him, i.e., he connected the imaginary man with a television program Rick had just watched. The parents mentioned this in case our staff had the same problem with him.

Mr. O. is an attractive middle-aged man who works as an insurance agent. Mrs. O. is an attractive housewife. She does most of the talking and from time to time interrupts her husband; he allows her to "have the floor," but he answers questions directed to him. Mr. and Mrs. O. appear very intelligent but relate in such a way that one feels that they are onlookers where their children are concerned. They do not seem alarmed or noticeably upset and give the impression that they feel that all is in God's hands and whatever will be, will be. It is as though they play no part in what happens in their family. One can understand how difficult it has been for Rick these many years to reach them or rile them with his very *indirect* cries for help.

Rick seems to have made a series of "pleas" to his parents for help, in terms of his increasingly worse behavior, until he finally set himself on fire. The story is inconsistent, but it appears that up to the last moment, while he was holding the flaming paper, he had mixed feelings about what he was going to do, when the torch ignited the combustible fuel on his clothes. He denied writing sacrilegious remarks in his religion text, claiming that the boy who shared the book with him wrote them. However, he has written things at the Burns Institute and blackened out the name of God on cards, and has denied this also. Rick said that the disciplinarian's remark, "You will never get into the priesthood now," as well as the thoughts of facing his parents led up to his deciding to commit suicide. He told me his first thought was to use a razor to cut his throat.

In the hospital he complained a lot about procedures and asked for extra pain medication, but showed no evidence of psychotic disease or markedly aberrant mental functioning. He complained about his discomfort and cried out in pain.

Rick was seen for psychological testing two months after admission. At that time he had recovered from the acute phase of his injury and seemed to welcome the testing situation as a nonthreatening diversion. He was cooperative throughout, with minimal indication of anxiety, and in general presented himself as rather blandly pleasant and polite.

This image of emotional equilibrium and adequate comprehension of a reality situation was in striking contrast to much of his projective material. He demonstrated (particularly in reaction to unstructured stimuli such as the Rorschach test) considerable affective lability and at times a pathological inability to maintain an appropriate emotional distance. His responses ranged from the most primitive and bizarre oral-incorporative images to superficially well-organized stories with an almost fairy-tale quality of sweetness and light or grandiose happy endings. The underlying pervasive depression was clear, as was the disturbance in body image integrity and fears of mutilation and destructive attack. It was likely that Rick's recent injury had exacerbated his normal adolescent concerns about the defectiveness of his body and his adequacy in general, but it was also probable that these issues had always been of disruptive intensity. He was involved in identity conflict, much of which was taking place at a level of development well below his chronological age. Although the presence of homosexual fears and impulses was evident, and there may have been a convergence of many other areas of conflict around this issue, the disturbance in ego functioning and stability of identity seemed to be of a more generalized and long-standing nature than that associated with an adolescent turmoil in which problems of masculine identification are prominent. (One can speculate that Rick's ambition to become a priest represented salvation in several senses, and when this one concrete means of acquiring a safe and structural identity for himself was threatened, he became overwhelmed by feelings of helplessness, fear, and anger.)

At best, Rick appeared to utilize hysterical defense mechanisms, but it was clear that his tendency to deny, his extremely limited insight regarding both his emotions and his behavior, and the superficiality and lability of his object relationships were of sufficient magnitude as to suggest more severe disturbance. One consultant called him schizophrenic, but while all gave a negative prognosis, most diagnosed depression. However, his responses to the protective and structural aspects of his hospitalization, and to a therapeutic relationship with a caseworker, were encouraging, and it was strongly recommended that he be placed in a residential treatment center that would provide the environmental support and controls he needed, as well as the opportunity for individual psychotherapy.

The social worker who dealt with the family after Rick's discharge noted that both Rick and his family had a strong unconscious desire to "do him in." They would many times unconsciously try to sabotage plans made for him. They vacillated as to whether or not to continue psychiatric treatment, but stayed with it. Mrs. O's sister had shot and killed her own teenage son and then herself five years earlier for supposedly some of the same behavior problems Rick had in school. All in all, the entire family was full of surprises. They appeared quite normal, but unconsciously or beneath the surface this was not so.

Rick himself was full of surprises. One would think all was going well, and then he would do something in a subtle way to shock people. (The incident of setting himself on fire was a shock in that no one had predicted he would do it.) He had showed no signs of depression or anxiety. While he was in the hospital a photograph was found that showed pubic hair. Rick had just been given a new Polaroid camera. One cannot say definitely that this photograph was taken by him or that it was truly obscene, but Rick had done things like this in the past. It has always been difficult in working with Rick to know when he is lying and when he is telling the truth. Once he said that he did not get to a certain movie with a hospital aide as planned, but she later said they did go. The most recent shock incident occurred when Rick came back to the Shriner's outpatient clinic. He was there for hours, telling everyone that all was well and that he was happy when his head and absent ear were exposed, which could hardly be true.

One year after his release from the hospital Rick was seen for psychiatric re-evaluation at the Burns Institute in conjunction with the planning for his future training and therapy. I have known this boy since his original admission here, and he now appears considerably advanced in his maturation. There is no question that the underlying depression and sense of family discord persist. However, he seems to present no suicide threat at this time and appears to have made progress in training to proceed with his life and to live as much on his own as possible. He seems to be content living in the Young Men's Christian Association (Y.M.C.A.) and being centrally located in the city so that he has a sense of independence. He works and goes to high school, and his parents cooly *permit* all of this without much support. It seemed inadvisable to probe very deeply into his underlying difficulties as he will not be working with us in any direct way.

Mr. and Mrs. O. feel that psychiatric in-patient care is advisable for Rick. We can understand their feeling, but we agree with the caretaking social agency that he is making an excellent adjustment in being cooperative and managing his difficult situation competently. It seems clear that for his progress it is important for him to continue to manage on his own as much as possible and to institutionalize him at this point would be a crushing blow to his self-esteem. It might be temporary relief for the parents, but would be likely to produce a more more long-term hazard to this dejected young man.

The striking thing about Rick is that in spite of being suicidal he has, with help, been able to function on a higher level than before his tragic injury. He now covers his missing ear with the currently stylish long hair and goes about with a forceful facade of self-possession. He epitomizes one type of patient who seems to show inner strengths not predicted from his previous performance or family background.

Case History: Paul N.

Paul, 18 years old, was burned at the age of 8 in a house fire caused by faulty electrical wiring; a brother died in the fire. Paul was originally treated on the children's service at the Massachusetts General Hospital, and then was one of the first patients transferred to the Shriners Burns Institute across the street when it opened, so that his recollections of being alone in the hospital are fairly accurate.

One of the striking things about this patient with burns involving 50 percent of his body, including his legs, shoulders, face, neck, chin, and ears, as well as some scalp (Figure 10), and requiring twenty-three surgical procedures over a period of nine years, was his grit and energy. At several points in his hospitalization when he was around 11 years old he would wait at the entrance to the elevator in order to frighten people with his scarred face. He was often rebellious in what was considered a nonangry, mischievous, boyish manner. Over the years, he would consort with other adolescents to break hospital rules, smoke in the bathrooms, or venture into restricted areas. All through this he was considered a well-liked patient.

Paul is tall and rather thin. At the time of my interview he was dressed in sport clothes. His hair is fairly long, covering the sides of his face, and there is a substantial amount of scar tissue all over his face. His sleeves were rolled up and there was also a great deal of scar tissue on his arms; both hands are rather disfigured. He is scheduled to go back into the hospital this year to have some more work done on his right hand. Both of his hands bore very noticeable paint stains and Mrs. N. explained that this is due to the work Paul does and the fact that it is very difficult

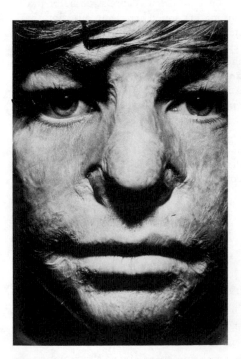

Figure 10. Paul N., with long-standing scars, has attained adequate adjustment through denial, activity, and family support.

to get the paint off his hands. Having lost many of his teeth because of his dietary problems after he was burned, he is now undergoing extensive dental work.

Paul tends to be nonspontaneous, for the most part responding to direct questions, in many cases with a simple yes or no answer. Throughout the interview, his parents were quite vocal. In fact, in most cases when Paul did not give very substantial or extensive answers to my questions, his parents would generally make some comment. (The social worker who continues to work with the family reported that Paul never talks about the way he feels about himself or the way he looks.)

He recalled with some reluctance the incident in which he had been burned. On the subject of the older brother who had been killed in the fire he looked somewhat depressed, as did his parents. However, they said little other than the fact that this had been a very upsetting experience for all of them (Paul has five surviving brothers and sisters). It was fairly evident that Paul has a lot of unresolved feelings about it, but was either unwilling or uncomfortable in talking about it.

After the accident he was in a local hospital for six months and was then taken to Massachusetts General Hospital and subsequently the Burns Institute, where he was hospitalized for a year, coming home only for Christmas. When asked how he spent his time in the hospital, he said that he slept a great deal, that initially he was the only patient on the ward. His parents described him as being the darling of the hospital, who got along very well with everyone and was extremely cooperative. They said he never complained and was quite willing to withstand all the suffering that he had to go through. During his hospitalization he was visited extensively by his parents and many friends of the family. His parents talked enthusiastically about how kind and helpful everyone had been. They had lived in their community only a very short time, yet many people became involved and would often go with them on weekends to visit Paul in the hospital.

During the recuperative period, which lasted for about a year at home, many children would come in to play with him. He also had tutors during this time so that when he returned to school he entered the fourth grade, being held back only one year. Paul described his recuperation period as being fun because he received a lot of attention and everyone was always coming to visit him. He denied any problems upon returning to school and claimed that the only thing he has been unable to do in school is climb the ropes in the gymnasium.

He denied having any problems with peers because of his experience and said that he has many friends. However, when asked about a girlfriend he responded very quickly that he did not have one. Discussion of going out with girls made him become very uncomfortable and he stated that he is really not that interested in them. However, there was a pained expression on his mother's face and neither parent responded when he made this comment.

He engages in school activities and takes gym, but the school is somewhat protective toward him when it comes to games like baseball, which they do not feel he should participate in for fear of injury. He does play those games outside of school, however, and enjoys them. His major hobbies are working on his car, spending time with friends, fishing, and making model airplanes.

He is currently a junior in high school, enrolled in a college course. The future in terms of a job as well as his academic work seems to be a sensitive one and, in fact, an argument between Paul and his mother ensued when this was questioned. He said that he has no idea what he wants to do after he finishes school and has never given any thought to any particular area he would like to become involved in. He is currently getting Cs and Ds and mother said that she thinks he could do better. At this point he became defensive and said that he had received only one D on his report card, and that this was a mistake and in actuality he was supposed to get a C– that was given to another girl.

Mrs. N. said that he had done very well in school until he was about 16 years old and began to look for part-time jobs with no success. Many of his friends were able to get jobs, but for some reason he was unable to. At that time he was given a car in the hope that this would make things better, but there was no improvement in his grades. When questioned about his feelings as to why he could not get a part-time job he looked somewhat uncomfortable and began to rationalize, saying that there just were not that many jobs around. His mother did come to his defense in this issue, saying that there seemed to be a shortage of jobs. He did refer, though, to a couple of positions he had applied for where he was told that they would call him but never did. When the factor of appearance was brought up in terms of its affecting his getting a job, he became defensive and said that he did not think this had anything to do with it. (His father has been able to secure some painting jobs for him, which he does on vacations and weekends.)

His parents said they thought he would like to become a commercial artist, because he is a good artist who really likes to draw. When asked about this, Paul admitted that sometimes he does enjoy drawing and had recently won an art prize in school, but had no thoughts about pursuing it as a career. His father wishes that Paul had decided to go to vocational school rather than taking a college course, but his mother said she could not imagine what he would do in vocational school because of the difficulty he has in using his hands. She seems more realistic than the father about Paul's ability to make use of his hands. Paul also tends to use denial here, saying that he is not prevented from doing anything. However, in looking at his hands, it seems fairly obvious that he must be rather limited. It is difficult to say whether one parent is more realistic than the other, and both seem to use a certain amount of denial. (For example, when Paul said that he has some difficulty with writing, his mother interposed that sometimes his handwriting is really beautiful, although when he first went back to school it tended to be somewhat shaky.) Mr. N. tended to rationalize a bit about Paul's future, saying that it is not unusual for a boy of Paul's age not to have an idea of what he wants to do, though he does have higher hopes for his son than being a painter. However, here again, Mrs. N. tends to be more realistic and concerned. She commented that Paul is 18 years old and she is very worried and concerned about his lack of any specific goal. Paul and his mother ultimately agreed that when people are uncertain as to whether they would be successful in anything, they are often ambivalent about indicating what they would like to do or making any kind of a commitment.

Mrs. N. is definitely protective. Paul has been asserting his independence, and she is somewhat uncomfortable with it; these parents would like to be able to direct their child. When Paul was asked if he ever got to make some of his own decisions, he laughed and said that once in a while he does. Mrs. N. expressed great concern, with very visible anxiety, when she talked about his desire to go into Boston on his own for his checkups at Massachusetts General Hospital—a distance of some 40 miles. She said that recently on a couple of occasions he did go on his own but she worried a lot. They appear to be a very closely knit family in which the parents do exert a strong influence on the children. However, Mrs. N. did say that because of her husband's extensive working schedule he spends less time now with the children than he ever did. He responded that he realized this but did not think there was anything he could do about it; the money was needed to maintain the family. She works also.

Because of the thinness of the tissue on his hands, Paul is constantly cutting himself. To protect them, he said that he usually wears gloves. However, his mother gave him a knowing look, and it certainly appeared from the stains on his hands that he does not wear gloves that much. It would seem that Mrs. N. has as a major concern the condition of his hands, as she made remarks pertaining to the fact that she has tried to clean them with many different kinds of cleaners but lately has been rather unsuccessful. Perhaps Paul engages in various counterphobic activities, tries to overcompensate by using his hands extensively in situations in which he has a great deal of difficulty.

In reviewing things that helped the family and Paul get through these trying times, they felt that it had been the support, reassurance, and good care that he had received very consistently at the hospital. He still receives Christmas cards and an occasional letter from various nurses, which makes him feel good. Paul said that he would continue going back as long as they wanted him to. He stated that he was very satisfied with the results of his surgery, and both parents expressed their amazement at the kinds of things that had been done for him.

When asked about his experiences with people in general, in relationship to his appearance, he commented that the only burned people he has ever encountered were in the hospital. He denied having any uncomfortable feelings about meeting new people and claimed that no one ever makes any comments. He then enthusiastically talked about the fact that last year his class had gone on an outing to Boston and that he and some classmates had been walking around downtown Boston for an hour and this had not bothered him at all.

As with most adolescents, the thing that came across most strongly was his tendency to deny and repress feelings. He tended to be inhibited and nonspontaneous, but his affect was friendly. Reality testing was adequate and there was no indication of thought disorder. However, he is experiencing definite underlying emotional conflicts that are likely to emerge to a greater degree as he grows older. This will most likely occur if he does not find some area in which he can achieve success and gain some degree of recognition. The area of heterosexual relationships is one of concern to him and one that he currently avoids. Although he denied having any concerns or feelings about having relationships with girls, it was evident that feelings about his appearance have a great deal to do with this. It was also obvious that he is ambivalent about presenting himself to other people in terms of trying to get a job. (In fact the social worker said his parents had noted that in the past year he had become much more self-conscious about his appearance.)

In many ways Paul seemed to be a very personable young man who, on the surface, is coping fairly well with his condition. Feelings of underlying inadequacy and poor self-concept were fairly evident, even though he consistently denied having any such feelings. In many ways he appeared to be compensating competently. Certainly he is struggling very much to develop a sense of independence. His mother's discomfort at this can be resolved only with time and his gradually developing a greater sense of independence. At various points Paul's inner strength and positive attitude were referred to by his parents; this attribution by the parents seems to be both supportive and realistic, and this is something that has undoubtedly helped him cope with his difficult circumstances. If this is true, it will likely help him extensively in the future in dealing with the frustrations he is bound to encounter.

The following are responses Paul gave to an oral questionnaire form that is used to assess adolescent responses to catastrophic illness. He shows a classic adolescent style of response that is quite emotionally retentive but consistent with his overall style. Denial, physical activity, and hospital and family support have all been striking modes in his adjustment. The questions were asked by the author.

Q. *What are your hobbies?*
A. Model building for one. I like to tinker with anything. I like fishing, camping. I do a little art in my spare time. Painting.

Q. *What do you do during the summer?*
A. Mostly camping out. I do a lot of walking in the woods. Not very much fishing. I remain at home most of the time. I'd like to get a job . . . anything I can get.

Q. *What course are you following in school and what do you plan to do with it?*
A. I'm taking the college courses right now, which I chose on my own. I have no idea what I'll do after high school.

Q. *What are your favorite school subjects?*
A. Math. It's just fun to do. So is history.

Q. *What is your least favorite subject?*
A. English. It's boring. Half the stuff doesn't make sense.

Q. *What kind of grades do you get?*
A. Anything from Bs to Fs. They sort of drop off and come up. Usually at the beginning of the year I get a B average. Then they start getting lower.

Q. *What do your parents think of your grades?*
A. I don't really know. They're concerned—when I bring home the low marks and slack off. My mother thinks they could be better. My father thinks I'm doing all right.

Q. *How is your social life?*
A. I think it's all right. There's not very many fights. There's fights but not any ruckus. I have quite a few friends. I made quite a few friends. Except I don't see many of them. I live in the country. They live in the city. Except for a few close friends near where I live.

Q. *Do you take part in school sports?*
A. I'm not really interested in school sports. There isn't anything I can't do. The only thing I can't do is climb the ropes in gym. I don't know if I could ever do them, because I was 8 years old when I had the accident.

Q. *What do you hope to get out of high school?*
A. An education, I guess. Probably the math will help me in filling out forms, income tax. It will depend on what kind of job I take after high school. Math will come in handy. English will come in handy. If I went to college, everything will come in handy then.

Q. *How has your disfigurement affected your life?*
A. I don't see any problems. None. I don't think it affects it at all. I don't think it would. I tinker with stuff. I fool around with cars, electrical stuff. I have nothing to give up. I get along with everybody all right. Not hard to make friends. I don't like talking very much. Conversation. I don't think I have any problems. I don't know. I'm not handicapped.

Q. *Do other people think handicapped people can work?*
A. I think they would. Depending on the job. A person who has lost a leg might have difficulty in walking outdoors.

Q. *Do people think it is harder to make friends with a scarred person?*
A. Why shouldn't they get together with other people? There's nothing wrong with it. No, I don't think so. I have no troubles.

Q. *Do your buddies have trouble with this?*
A. I don't think so.

Q. *Have you thought about marriage?*
A. I haven't thought that far ahead. It's healed up quite a bit. In eight more years it might be complete.

Q. *How about marrying a person with burn scars?*
A. I don't know.

Q. *One who has lost an arm or leg?*
A. I don't feel anything.

Q. *About marrying a person without a leg?*
A. I don't see what's wrong with it.

The material from the several hundred children and adolescents who were seen made it clear that there were so many intervening variables that prediction about the outcome of individual cases was difficult. We could not readily determine whether particular traits in childhood would correlate with particular outcomes because the usual traits examined in personality studies of normative development tended to be swamped by the overwhelming trauma of the burn injury, the succession of family and medical traumata that followed, and the societal reactions that confronted the children.

Although many children did not spontaneously talk about being stared at, all the disfigured children who were familiar with the people questioning them spoke about the problem of being stared at and felt this as a personal burden. This is consistent with the general reaction of people in terms of social conventions about staring; people ordinarily are irked and less willing to respond to a request when they are stared at. The disfigured person generally must constrict his awareness to keep himself comfortable, and he may also generally inhibit some of his social functioning in order to avoid unpleasant or self-torturing situations. As Kriegel indicates, " . . . a struggle for identity, is always with him. He can [always] be challenged in his illusions of sufficiency . . ." [11, p. 428].

This is a common experience when children go out of the hospital, either alone or in groups, and have to face the shocked looks of the public, an experience repeated in schools, shops, and theaters, as well as other public and semipublic situations. The undying attempt to elicit a human response from others, to affirm one's own humanity, requires much difficult effort and is fraught with anxiety for these children, as they try to evolve an identity that is valid, objective, and bearable.

REFERENCES

1. Parsons, T. Definitions of Health and Illness in the Light of American Values and Social Structure. In E. G. Jaco (Ed.), *Patients, Physicians and Illness.* Free Press, Glencoe, Ill., 1958.
2. Freidson, E. *Profession of Medicine: A Study of the Sociology of Applied Knowledge.* Dodd, Mead, New York, 1971. P. 277.
3. Goffman, E. *The Presentation of Self in Everyday Life.* Social Science Research Monograph 2. University of Edinburgh Press, Edinburgh, 1956.
4. Pless, B. I. Adjustment of Chronically Ill and Disabled Children: Selective and Critical Review of the Literature. Report from Department of Preventive Medicine and Community Health, University of Rochester School of Medicine, 1973. Unpublished.
5. Barker, T. X. *Hypnosis: A Scientific Approach.* Van Nostrand Reinhold, New York, 1969.
6. Jones, M. C. Psychological correlates of somatic development. *Child Dev.* 36:899–911, 1965.
7. Richardson, S. A. Some social psychological consequences of handicapping. *Pediatrics* 32:291–296, 1963.
8. Freeman, R. D. Emotional reactions of handicapped children. *Rehabil. Lit.* 28:274–282, 1967.
9. Kleck, R. Self-disclosure patterns of the nonobviously disabled. *Psychol. Rep.* 23:1239–1248, 1968.
10. Davis, F. Deviance disavowal: The management of strained interaction by visibly handicapped. *Soc. Prob.* 9:120–132, Winter 1961. Reprinted in H. S. Becker (Ed.), *The Other Side: Perspectives on Deviance.* Free Press, New York, 1964. Pp. 119–139.
11. Kriegel, L. Uncle Tom and Tiny Tim. Some reflections on the cripple as negro. *Am. Scholar* 38:412–430, Summer 1969.
12. Mayer, J. *Overweight, Causes, Cost, and Control.* Prentice-Hall, Englewood Cliffs, N.J., 1968.
13. Fisher, S. Experiencing your body: You are what you feel. *Saturday Review,* July 8, 1972. P. 27.
14. Coleman, J. S. *The Adolescent Society.* Free Press, New York, 1961.

15. Jansen, G., and Esser, O.   Quoted from preliminary notes on *"Das Koerperbehindeite Kind." Time,* December 12, 1971.
16. Tizard, J., and Grad, J. C.   *The Mentally Handicapped and Their Families.* Oxford University Press, London, 1961.
17. Rosenshine, A.   Unpublished manuscript. Library of the University of California at Los Angeles.
18. Woodward, J. M.   Emotional disturbances of burned children. *Br. Med. J.* 1:1009–1013, 1959.
19. Abel, T. M.   Personality characteristics of the facially disfigured. *Trans. N.Y. Acad. Sci.* 14:325–329, 1952.
20. Tauber, E. S.   Cited in B. Landis, *Ego Boundaries.* International Universities Press, New York, 1970.
21. Schilder, P.   *The Image and Appearance of the Human Body.* International Universities Press, New York, 1950.
22. Schmitt, R.   Ph.D. thesis, University of Houston, 1971.
23. Remensnyder, J., and Constable, J.   Personal communication, 1975.
24. Gifford, S.   Cosmetic Surgery and Personality Change: A Review and Some Clinical Observations. In R. Goldwyn (Ed.), *The Unfavorable Result in Plastic Surgery: Avoidance and Treatment.* Little, Brown, Boston, 1972. Pp. 11–33.
25. Morris, J.   *Conundrum.* Harcourt Brace Jovanovich, New York, 1974.
26. Freud, S.   *Interpretation of Dreams.* Basic Books, New York, 1954.
27. Freud, A.   Normality and Pathology in Childhood: Assessments of Development. In R. S. Eissler et al. (Eds.), *The Writings of Anna Freud,* Vol. 6. International Universities Press, New York, 1966.
28. Greenacre, P.   Fetishism and Body Image. In R. S. Eissler et al. (Eds.), *Psychoanalytic Study of the Child.* International Universities Press, New York, 8:91, 1953.
29. Bibring, E.   The Mechanism of Depression. In P. Greenacre (Ed.), *Affective Disorders.* International Universities Press, New York, 1950.
30. Erikson, E. H.   *Childhood and Society.* Norton, New York, 1950.
31. Yuker, H. E., Block, J. R., and Young, J. H.   *The Human Resources Foundation.* Albertson, New York, 1966.
32. Wright, B. A.   *Physical Disability: A Psychological Approach.* Harper & Row, New York, 1960.
33. Thomas, A., Chess, S., and Birch, H.   *Temperament and Behavior Disorders in Children.* New York University Press, New York, 1968.
34. Waelder, R.   *Basic Theory of Psychoanalysis.* International Universities Press, New York, 1960.
35. Rogers, C.   *Client Centered Therapy.* Houghton Mifflin, Boston, 1951.
36. Kardiner, A., and Ovesey, L.   *The Mark of Oppression: Explorations in the Personality of the American Negro.* World, New York, 1951.
37. Vaillant, G. E.   Theoretical hierarchy of adaptive ego mechanisms. A 30-year follow-up of 30 men selected for psychological health. *Arch. Gen. Psychiatry* 24: 107–118, 1971.
38. Berger, J. C.   Suicide attempts related to congenital facial deformities. *J. Plast. Reconstr. Surg.* 51:323–325, 1973.

4

Disfigurement and Adult Life Course

The case histories described in this chapter and Chapters 5 and 6 are all those of persons who have been patients at the Massachusetts General Hospital. The patients were either known to the burn group or the plastic surgery group, or were located through a survey of hospital records dating back to the time of the Cocoanut Grove fire in Boston on November 28, 1942. This date marks the beginning of large-scale and continuing interest in the treatment of burn injuries at the hospital. From the surgical and psychiatric experiences of that tragic event have followed major research and treatment efforts for military and civilian casualties.

SELECTION OF PERSONS FOR FOLLOW-UP

The number of patients treated for burns at Massachusetts General Hospital runs into the thousands. A number of determinants entered into the choice of cases for follow-up study. First, the cases selected were limited to those who had sustained facial burns with some residual disfigurement. Second, a surprising number of patients simply could not be located; they had no known telephone or forwarding address. The many physicians, both general surgeons and plastic surgeons, who cooperated and offered their records could not locate former patients either. General surgeons who worked with burns occasionally were able to name a patient whom they had followed for many years, but most of them had focused their efforts on the first months after the burn. Then the patients went on to rehabilitation services, to orthopedic surgeons for their joint sequelae, and to plastic surgeons for much of their reconstructive work. Also, some surgeons acknowledged that they did not care to pursue these cases. However, the most widespread opinion was that these patients withdrew from all treatment, suffering the "social death" described by MacGregor et al.[1]. It was a rare patient who was seen over many years for his residual problems. Cosmetic surgeons described various cases they had seen, but related a common story: patients would work with them for years and then break off treatment, sometimes discontinuing all medical contacts.

The Massachusetts Rehabilitation Commission reported very poor results in getting facially disfigured individuals back to work, and remarked that their experience had been that only people for whom they had provided service would be willing to be interviewed for follow-ups. This seemed largely true for the hospital group, many of whom were very much attached to their surgeons, but the numbers we actually located were miniscule compared with the original numbers of burn patients and the estimates of large numbers of facially burned and disfigured persons. Dermatologists rarely saw burn patients, and said their patients were suffering mostly from dermatoses that would not be considered on the same scale of disfigurement.

As the number of follow-up cases dwindled, and the suspicion grew that social death was indeed a continuing problem, we looked in the suicide and psychiatric clinic figures, but could find little to help us as the statistics do not list disfigurement. The experience of these clinics was that they did not see people with such "reality problems."

We checked the records, the cases of the surgeons, city directories, and telephone books, and wrote to local burn surgeons and cosmetic surgeons, while continuing to follow some of the active cases seen in Massachusetts General Hospital and the Shriners Burns Institute. (With children and their families it was easier to secure data as this was largely current or recent material; some of these personal and family experiences will be described in Chapter 9.)

The problem of selecting representative individuals remained. If most of the patients were out of reach, we could not assume that our sample was characteristic of the whole group, but we did come to feel that it was probably typical of the patients who were making an adequate adjustment. These more successful adaptations have become the inevitable focus of our adult follow-ups. Some less successful examples are included as well, along with discussion of the variables involved. Men and women have been selected who exemplify problems of early adult-hood, middle life, and later life, with their views of what they experienced as the fundamental data.

In choosing the particular case examples, it was felt that cross sections of different phases of life and different types of people were needed, but that they should be essentially physically intact individuals who were not psychologically abnormal. We sought individuals who had experienced a traumatic injury that had altered their body image, an injury with such a profound effect on facial appearance that this became a major organizer of personality functioning. The diagram outlined in Chapter 3 (see Table 1) has served as a means of arranging the themes, but does not presume to encompass the detailed environmental or personality variables that determine outcomes. It is hoped that the cases presented here will lead to further investigation of these problems among the groups of people we were forced to leave out, the numbers of individuals we did not reach. In describing these cases, which exemplify some of the ways people react to sustaining this type of injury in different developmental phases, it is hoped that some clear beginnings at establishing types of response can be laid out.

DISFIGUREMENT IN YOUNG ADULTHOOD
After his accident the young man described in the following case history found his life totally altered and was nearly crushed by it.

Case History: Robert C.
Robert, a 21-year-old soldier going home on leave, hitched a ride in a car. The driver collided with an oil truck, and the patient, who was thrown out of the car, went back to pull out the driver, who was dead. Robert sustained terrible injuries, described laconically in the record as third-degree burns of the arms, neck, and face, with loss of facial skin, both ears, nose, four lids, and eight fingers; he was still undergoing surgery years after the accident.

An only child, he lives with his mother and father, and is supported by his insurance settlement. Although he has lost eight fingers, he can, with considerable difficulty, dress, eat, and operate at home. His clear statement is that the worst thing he has to manage is his facial disfigurement.

During the initial period of several weeks in the hospital he was largely obtunded by the nature of his physical injuries. Subsequently he began to have intermittent periods of apprehension and terror intermixed with feelings of hopelessness and a sense that he would not be able to bear his situation. The staff was very much worried about how much he could see of his disfigurement, and they tried to keep him from looking at any reflecting surfaces. However, he did begin to get some image of himself but thought that most of this would be repaired. In the beginning he had no idea how frightening he looked to the nurses. The staff showed a reaction that later was characteristic of strangers who saw him—a feeling of dread and horror that took time to overcome. Each person who looked at Robert had to make an effort to think of him as a human being (Figure 11). Some children have come up to him when he was sitting in a car and asked "what he was" and how he came to look that way.

Robert has undergone much of the regression that is inevitable in his life of injury—increased dependence on other people, having to be fed, waiting for others to take action, needing help in bathing and going to the bathroom. His anxieties, or feelings of dreadful things about to befall him, can be ascribed to the realistic fear he has about future pain, surgery, dressing changes, and other necessary medical procedures. However, his anxiety bursts out sporadically. At night, while he was in the hospital, he would suddenly become agitated and frightened and feel he could not manage his situation. He felt helpless rage at the fate that had reduced him to his present situation. All these sensations were augmented by the clear awareness he had of being a normal boy a few years before.

His irritability brings to mind the quote from a novel by Mary Shelly, "I am malicious because I am miserable . . . if any being felt emotions of benevolence towards me I should return them, and an hundredfold" [2, pp. 146, 147]. The speaker, of course, is Frankenstein's monster.

It is fair to say that it was possible to discharge Robert four months after injury only because of the devotion of his family and his personal stamina, since he had no function in either hand and his appearance was such that he could not appear in public and had to be extremely careful as to who saw his face even in the half-light when at home. In contrast to some burn patients, he is more comfortable at home than in the hospital. Six months after the injury it was possible to consider the first stages of reconstruction.

After a year his surgeon wrote: "Although from a functional point of view, a reasonable reconstruction of the face will eventually be obtained, this will never be

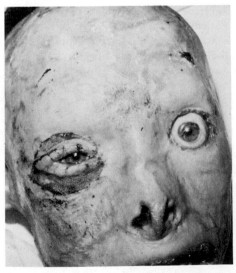

Figure 11. Robert C. in an early phase, when some patients begin to talk about their appearance.

cosmetically satisfactory. He will never be able to go out in public without it being immediately apparent that he has a very severely scarred face which has sustained a great deal of surgery and which, at the best, will be sufficient to just 'pass'. We will be satisfied, obviously, if we give him sort of a human face. There can be no reasonable attempt to reconstruct his face as it was before the accident.

"Concerning his employability, I think it is difficult to be didactic, but considering what I know of the patient, considering his original plans to be a printer and considering his educational background, I believe that he is totally disabled for life for any employment."

When seen three years after the injury, Robert was wearing sport clothes and a wig, and was accompanied by his mother. As he spoke to me alone he began to talk about the hopelessness of his life and how people always turn to look at him. He said he could bear small children because they said what was on their mind, but adults were "more sneaky" and pretended not to see him, then turned around and nudged each other. Each time something like this happens he is apprehensive about going out for a while. He felt that he would never have a date and that no girl would look at him. While he was visiting a friend's house, a teenage girl walked into the room and saw him. She said what a horrible-looking mask he was wearing and tried to remove it. Everyone was shocked. He never returned to that house. A nurse at the Veterans Administration Hospital had been of the greatest help to him in forcing him out into group activities two years after the injury, making him go to sit in the music room at the hospital and attend other activities. He had been seen by a psychiatrist there but this was apparently in connection with his recurrent nightmares of the accident.

He is awaiting news of further surgery and when a prosthesis can be made for his arm. He watches television, he cannot feed himself except sometimes to hold a sandwich, he cannot put a shirt on but sometimes can put on pants, and he wears loafers (no laces). Generally his parents feed him and wipe him in the bathroom. He had some hope of setting up a business with another disabled burn victim, and talked about his membership in the Disabled American Veterans organization. He has had little contact with other disfigured people.

He feels bored and restless a good deal of the time. I talked about the need for him to be active, and to try training his feet to type even though ultimately he will be typing with his hands and to do the Royal Canadian Air Force exercises as much as possible to burn off excess energy and also to get himself into the fittest condition. I think there is no good solution to his anxieties, but the supporting interest of a female social worker or nurse clinician who shows interest in him and keeps pursuing him not to give up would be the best road to follow.

He is not totally without hope. His mother is a remarkably sanguine lady. She seems to handle him well, and she spoke quite candidly of how trapped she felt being unable to go out and having a child as helpless as an infant at a time in her life when she thought she would have more freedom. Nevertheless, she seems to have accepted her tragedy with some resignation. Her husband seems more defeated, but overall they do all that can be expected.

Robert shows a mixture of posttraumatic symptoms, depressive symptoms, and the shame, anxiety, and impotent rage produced by the situation. Diagnostically it would be hard to put all these signs under one heading, but certainly correct to describe them as a depressive neurosis and gross stress response. This young man will need constant rehabilitation help, social assistance, and psychiatric and psychological treatment to mitigate his suffering.

In attempting to chart his adaptive defenses I have used several parameters, following Table 1 in Chapter 3.

1. *Active coping versus passive surrender.* Robert has clearly surrendered to his fate; he avoids the public, looks apathetic most of the time, and has withdrawn into isolation and the role of a sick person. There seems to be little available energy, or seeking for any activity.

2. *Loving exchanges.* He is turned in upon himself, and while he is seen by his family, they are constricted, silently unhappy, and apprehensive about his ultimate future. He shows sadness and some overflow of anger, but most of his rage is turned against himself and is manifested in depression. While a few loyal friends come to visit, he goes out for rides infrequently. Therefore, he has limited opportunities for expressing affection and, because of facial scarring and immobility, cannot display humor; but even so his voice is quiet, tremulous, and unhappy. He feels lost.

3. *Mental versus physical personal mode of expression.* His limitations physically have interfered with any carpentry or sports, and he appears more characteristically involved in watching television and reading magazines.

4. *Denial versus overawareness.* In the first few years of his incapacitation he expressed many of the usual hopes for miraculous transformation through the use of plastic surgery, wigs, and prostheses, intermixed with sudden panic reactions about how he looked and special concern about ptosis, which he had had slightly in one eye in the past. (Ptosis was a major early problem because his eyelids had been replaced by grafts. He had a picture of himself in uniform near the bed to show his original image to visitors and staff.) There was not enough denial to permit him either relief or hope.

5. *Leading versus resisting therapy.* From initial helpless compliance, he moved through several short phases of anxious and angry complaints about the staff and procedures, and later made some suggestions about postponing surgery. However, he never truly co-managed treatment, but rather was carried along.

6. *Adaptive versus maladaptive mental mechanisms.* He showed a consistent ability to test reality without totally abandoning cooperation in treatment, but no ability to sublimate much of his anger in crafts or hobbies, and little humor, flexibility, or progression after his major posttraumatic regression. On the other hand, his rigidity, ego restriction, and retrogressive level of functioning were not in any way marked by primitive, bizarre thoughts, extreme and unwarranted aggressiveness, hypochondria, or distortion of medical advice on the objective situation.

7. *Environmental resources.* The family had modest means, but they were absolutely devoted to him in spite of their sadness and their concern about his ultimate future after their own incapacitation and demise. He had loyal friends, and continuing medical staff to follow him. The arrangement was largely a division of services between the Veterans Administration Hospital in the area and the private hospital where he had had reconstructive surgery. Continuity of care was assured because he had received an enormous sum of money from the insurance settlement, which permitted private hospitalization for some of the highly specialized procedures in cosmetic surgery that could not be accomplished at the Veterans Administration Hospital and because the same surgeon was on the staff of both institutions.

Robert did not appear to be particularly religious, and though he prayed intermittently and desperately when alone and in the hospital, this was not a major feature of his adaptation. His priest did visit him, and Robert appreciated this.

Rehabilitation facilities at the Veterans Administration and Massachusetts General hospitals were available to him, but the organizing factor in his rehabilitation remained his original surgeon.

The helplessness of Robert is unquestionably due in large measure to his lost fingers. However, it was not easy to find persons who had sustained only facial burns. The industrial situations in which some were injured, and the exposure of face and hands in such situations, made for combined injuries, and any large burn that involved the face was also likely to have involved other areas, with all the scarring, contractures, and associated orthopedic problems. The so-called lung burns, which are actually toxic or chemical pneumonias rather than direct thermal injury, were common killers in patients who had severe facial burns.

It is worth noting that Robert was considered an example of social death by most of his caretakers, all of whom had given hopeless prognoses for him when the assignment of damages came up for his insurance claim. In the eight years following the accident he had undergone numerous cosmetic reconstructive procedures by a skilled plastic surgeon and looked quite different from the period three years after the injury, though in no way could he be considered anything but grossly disfigured. At that time, however, he had opened a small business selling electronic tapes, and was able to function in limited contact with the public. All of his surgical work had been carried out by the same surgeon, to whom he had been very much attached, and who has seen him at Massachusetts General Hospital, in his private office, and at the Veterans Hospital. His overall personality is fundamentally unaltered, but he is heavily focused on his work as the keystone of his adaptation.

The following case history is an example of severe burn injury that did not destroy the continuing life of the individual, although it created enormous problems.

Case History: Paul D.
Paul was burned at age 19 while working as a cook at a Boy Scout camp. He was seen at home five years after the accident. He grew up in a small town near Boston, was a high school graduate, the fifth of eleven children.

Paul appeared older than his chronological 24 years because he wore a mustache and beard to cover his scars. His lips, one cheek, and part of his chin where no hair grew looked livid and scarred, and his hands showed reddened cicatrices. He was working at a paper factory, operating a loading machine. He feels that things slip out of his hands and he is unable to work as a machinist, a trade he had been learning in a work-study program at the time he was injured.

He recalls the accident and vaguely remembers running to get out of the building. He was in the hospital with Mr. R., who was burned in the same accident, and was a patient of the same surgeon from the first. He spent three months in the hospital and then had to be home for several months. At first he did not mention having had problems or worries of any kind, but then began to talk about the first time he looked in the mirror and saw what a "mess" he was, and how discouraged he was. He told one sister not to visit for fear of upsetting her. In the beginning he had nightmares that reenacted the accident. Both the patient and his mother said they do not remember how many operations he has had. He said that pain, which was so much trouble during the dressing changes, became less of a problem and he is not bothered by pain now. He denied being changed in social poise, but said he was somewhat more nervous and fearful of driving in the city.

When he went back to high school, he was given special permission to grow a beard to cover his facial injury. He does not attend church very regularly, but this is not different from before. He has never been athletic, but likes to watch sports. He smokes a pipe, rarely drinks, and takes no medication. He finds camping, bowling, and tropical fish good hobbies. After being discharged from the hospital he gained nearly 30 pounds, being inactive, but has lost most of this now that he has returned to more active work. He thinks that he will try to become a draftsman; he cannot be a machinist and does not wish to continue working in the paper factory.

He has a girlfriend, who does not seem bothered by his scars. Occasionally people will look at his hands and be somewhat embarrassed to ask what happened. He talked about how badly he feels for disfigured children and about the ones he saw in the physical therapy department in the hospital. He spontaneously recalled a badly burned child who led him to wonder if the child would not be better off to have died. He denied having any special phobias or current depression. He had been rather anxious at the beginning of the interview, but calmed down when he realized my follow-up purpose.

Mrs. D. is a matter-of-fact woman who was somewhat concerned about the purpose of my interview. She spoke positively about the medical care her son received, saying that at first she did not believe the doctor's opinions about the scars and what would happen to them, but now feels Paul has progressed exactly as predicted. An operation is planned to amputate the fifth finger of the right hand, which has been immobile and frequently injured. She described her initial horror at his appearance, but also said it would have been worse for a girl. She recalled the redness and rawness of his chin before he grew the beard and said she accepts this as a cosmetic aid even though he looks "hippyish". She is proud of the fact that every day he was in the hospital she visited him, with all ten children coming along in two cars. "At first people would stare at him in public and I would say, 'We have to get Paul out of here,' and Paul would say, 'They have got to get used to me and not bother.' " She said that she and her husband have a daughter with speech trouble due to neurological damage from meningitis and she feels they have treated Paul's disfigurement the same way they handled their daughter's disorder. Paul's father has been a patient, taciturn, and utterly reliable part of this, but less the executive in all his caretaking. He is not a devalued father but a durable, laconic workingman.

The most striking thing about Paul's overall adaptation is his extended family system and its effectiveness in supporting him. Intact large families appear to function very well in providing the vital, if conventional, sources of help, and also permit a variety of shifts in the emotional support system as circumstances require.

His physical emphasis in his life was clear, even though he watched television, and chatted, socialized, and did some philosophizing with his family. He did not show much of the increased tolerance or breadth of thinking that Wright [3] described in the handicapped, but he did seem sanguine about his situation and tough-minded in his approach. He showed a reasonable mixture of denial and over-awareness. In his reaction to therapy he did not lead, but went along with the suggestions of his surgeon, whom he relied on greatly. There was a letter from his doctor on the mantle, and his mother told of the family writing and keeping in touch with one of the nurses who had been particularly supportive and helpful.

Paul showed an ability to regress flexibly and did show decision-making ability in choosing and shifting to a new career. He grew a beard to cover some of his scars, and he was able to joke about some of his past experiences, and also was able to repress and suppress some of the horrors of his experience, as well as to share with his older fellow victim, Mr. R., some of their experiences, though their lives turned in very different directions after the initial care.

In comparing the adult follow-up groups with the on-going group of patients seen at the Burns Institute, several observations kept recurring about the social context of burns. In the children's group, we were struck over and over by the fact that the majority of children were injured under conditions that were full of emotional tension, psychopathology, poverty, and social instability; divorce was the major family finding, and the children were frequently retarded—about 20 percent in one sample of cases—and many had learning disabilities. For several of these children a hard life might have been predicted even if they had never been burned. For the adult patients seen in follow-up, the reverse was the rule, with intact and supportive, stable families, and all the conventional assets save one—the face. Of course, it is hard to know if these persons are representative of all adult burn patients because of the previously discussed impediments to our selection of persons for study. We believe they represent the more successful types of adaptation.

Though Massachusetts General Hospital has an active pastoral counseling service and Protestant, Jewish, and Catholic chaplains are all available, there was only one patient in the entire follow-up series of 1000 for whom religious help appeared decisive. He was a 19-year-old college student who belonged to the Greek Orthodox church and was visited regularly by his priest, who told him that the Lord would see him through. The patient stated emphatically that he needed no other emotional help because he had his faith to guide him. He had a close family, but they were not as religious as he, and he made his way to normal recovery, with only minimal facial disfigurement, never appearing to expose the underlying depression that almost all patients experienced. The role of the pastoral counselors in our experience will be touched on further in Chapter 8.

Dr. Richard Goldberg, Research Director of the Massachusetts Rehabilitation Commission, reported that "strong personalities overcame a catastrophic illness, and weak ones did not"[4].

HOSPITAL TURMOIL AND LATER SUCCESS

Though the young woman in the following case was regarded as a psychiatric problem during her hospitalization, she displayed a remarkable emotional resilience.

Case History: Katherine M.
At age 25 Katherine was burned in an automobile accident. She was extensively burned over her face, right ear, eyelids, cheeks, neck, and hands, particularly the right hand and wrist, and some hair was burned off her scalp. Psychiatric consultation was requested after she had been in the hospital one week because she was agitated, uncooperative, depressed, and reportedly totally unreliable as to her moods or her statements about them. When first seen by the psychiatrist she was sobbing uncontrollably and said that her life had been "going downhill" ever since the age of 18, when she and her fiance had been accidentally overcome by automobile exhaust fumes and he had died. She did not complete high school. When she was 21 years old, her pelvis was fractured in an accident. It was while she was on vacation from her secretarial job that she was burned.

Her sister and mother came to the hospital and worked to support the patient. They described her as a normal, cheerful, reliable person who had been less happy since the death of her fiance. The nurses felt that the patient was very difficult, and that her sister was more helpful than her mother because her mother was so determinedly overprotective about Katherine's sobbing, screaming, and complaining, which the staff found uncontrollable and intolerable. Katherine was followed psychiatrically for three months during this hospitalization; in the succeeding four years she was seen intermittently by a psychiatrist as well as the surgeon who had attended her.

In the hospital, she had sleep problems, and was troubled by pain, despair, and anxiety; she required considerable medication for all of these for the first month. After several weeks she began to sleep better, to be comforted by her mother, and to accept support from the psychiatrist and the nurse clinician on the ward, and her panic decreased. She continued to be demanding and to be considered infantile by the nurses. Her mother told the staff that Katherine "will never be the same mentally. She might as well be dead." Katherine began to hit at the nurses during the painful dressing changes. However, she responded quickly and cooperated for short periods when hypnosis was used to help with the dressing changes, and this seemed also to improve her ease of management. She poured out her thoughts about being the youngest of four children, about feeling she was used by the others, and about always having to try to be very independent and how tired she was of these efforts to run her own life; she was aware that these had crumpled totally under this experience.

With gradual improvement and the attentions of her mother and sister, she began to sit up and to ambulate during the next six weeks. She began to type after two months, partly to exercise her hands, and partly to give her some focus for her interests. After ten weeks she was up and socializing with other patients and smoking in the lounge. Nearly three months after hospitalization she called for psychiatric help because she was depressed about "the way people look at me—my face is so twisted." However, she was willing to keep trying to make short visits out of the hospital. Two weeks later she was depressed again, but less so. "I worry most about my appearance. If only the doctor could show me pictures of what plastic surgery could do." She even began to show a previously absent ability to joke about her plight. Her course after discharge seemed to be consistently on the positive side, marked by outward buoyancy and optimism, with few relapses into brief, intense depressions.

When seen two years later, she was well-dressed and seemed quite unaffectedly composed about her facial disfigurement and the deformity of her hand. She acknowledged that people look at her. She found that she had lost memory not only about the accident but also about many issues from her past. She gave the impression of being more content and more aware of her direction in life than during her hospitalization. "I want to settle down and get married. I don't want to do office work and go back to that. I realize I still have hard problems, but I find I am now in a different religious attitude. I do not just think that if you do some-thing bad you will be punished by God! I fear about some things happening to me and I find I am very sensitive to anything critical my family says." Also, she has some hope of writing a book, which seems to be a way of further coming to grips with her fears of trauma and disability. She was reading a popular book by a plastic surgeon, Maxwell Maltz, *Psychocybernetics*, and had read another book of his, *Dr. Pygmalion*.

I saw her six years after her accident. She is a rather attractive, well-groomed woman who has obviously done a great deal to offset her appearance in terms of dress, makeup, and hair style. It is evident that she has been burned. Scar tissue is apparent on the right side of her face, but more so on her neck and also her right hand. She wore a blouse that covered most of her neck, and her hair covers most of the sides of her face and ear area, falling below the neck. She mentioned that she was wearing a wig, but this was not apparent.

She summed up her situation by saying that she had accepted it as the most important thing in her life. As far as adjustment is concerned, she said that in the past year she had started in a business management course in college. When she did not find it interesting, she dropped out of the program, but was able to get a position working as an instructor's assistant in the business program. This job involves filing and some other clerical work as well as looking for books for students and showing films. She said that her main interest is really getting her life organized and working toward the future. A job is not essential because she received a very good settlement from the insurance company, which she has invested, some of it in real estate.

Life had been very good at the time of the accident. She felt that being young helped her adjustment and pointed out that this was not her first disappointment in life. She feels that one of the things that has really helped her through this particular crisis is that everyone, friends and family, has been very supportive. Her family is very close. She also feels that religion played an important role, as she prayed a little during her hospitalization and has been a very devout churchgoer since that time. Before her accident, she said, she was not particularly religious. She often stressed that she enjoys life and views herself as a fighter and feels that this has helped her a great deal.

She now lives on her own in a small apartment and stressed that she is no longer a young girl who needs to have someone living with her, and that she prefers this kind of independence. She superficially touched on the fact that she has been dating a man for a while, but is not sure that anything will really come of it. There seemed to be a note of disappointment in her voice when she talked about this and I sensed that she really did not want to discuss it too much. However, I did pursue it and she told me that she had gone out with a number of men, none of whom had ever made an issue out of her scars. She was then quick to point out that there are enough people around who are very kind, so it is not necessary for one to really bother with those who are not. She also pointed out that she has a number of friends in her home town with whom she is close.

We talked about the issue of appearance and she said that she knows there has been marked improvement, because from time to time her family has taken out pictures of the way she looked soon after the accident and talked about the fact that she has undergone a vast improvement. She feels that although she is still self-conscious in some ways she has resolved this to a great extent. She mentioned that she goes to the beach and does wear a bathing suit that is up to her neck and also covers her arms. In the past she used to put on leg makeup to cover the graft donor areas but no longer does that. She is mainly self-conscious about her hand. She pointed out that this is something she will always think about from time to time, as it is very apparent, and that she cannot run away from the problem. She said that while in the hospital she never believed that she would be very repulsive looking and always felt that things would be improved. She had a tremendous amount of faith in her surgeon. She feels that he gave her a lot of love, attention, and kindness. She stressed the issue of love, saying how much one needs it, and this caused her to talk about the nurses she had to deal with and her belief that they were somewhat callous and unfeeling. Her rationalization for this was that they are used to dealing with scarred patients and have become somewhat hardened.

It is interesting to note that she said that she ought to see the plastic surgeon while she was here, but it was evident that she was quite ambivalent about it. When I confronted her with it she became a little defensive and said that he would probably like to see her because he likes to see his patients doing well and this makes him feel good. Nevertheless, in the final analysis it was evident that the thought of stirring up a lot of feelings and having been burned was something that she would like to avoid, in relationship to her experiences at Massachusetts General.

She realized that looks are not everything rather suddenly. It was at the time that she was flying to Florida to spend a month with an uncle there. On the plane she sat with two other girls. She said that initially she was quite anxious about this and knew that people were looking at her or at least glancing at her. Her way of dealing with the anxiety she experienced at that time was to begin talking to the two girls and she said that in no time at all they were engaged in a very pleasant conversation and there was no real discussion of her appearance. She said that this caused her to be more assertive in social situations. That is, rather than waiting for people to question her about her appearance and suffering anxiety about how they perceive her, she will inform them very quickly as to what happened to her and she feels that this generally wards off extensive questioning. She said that she had always enjoyed talking with people and is usually a very outgoing person; however, sometimes she can be very quiet if she has nothing to say.

She feels that in terms of personality she is pretty much the same now as she was before her burns, except that now perhaps she is a more sensitive person. When I asked her what she meant by this she said sensitive to and understanding of other people's problems.

From time to time she does get depressed, but she deals with this by giving herself a little pep talk. She indicated that when she was in the hospital she realized that she would not die. This caused me to ask her about her feelings in relation to death. She said that when she first arrived at Massachusetts General Hospital she did have suicidal thoughts and if she had had the opportunity she might have killed herself. Although she did think about suicide at that time, she felt that death was a very final thing and as long as one were alive there would be hope. She sees herself as a very impatient person. She feels that if she had had to wait a long time between operations this would have pushed her to the breaking point. But things did progress very quickly and very well so it was not as distressing an experience for her as she felt it might have been.

She indicated that the future is something that she really does not have any real plans for and that she will just take it as it comes. She made the remark that she would like to marry and have a family of her own and when she was saying that she looked a little unhappy. I asked her if she thought that she would be doing something like that and her only comment was that she hoped she would be.

From all indications it would seem that in some ways she is more or less drifting aimlessly, without any real goals. I wonder how she would be if she did not have the very loving and supportive family that she states she has, and also the financial security. She mentioned to me that she had no high school diploma and came from a rather poor family that had struggled a great deal and that she views herself as someone who has had to be on her own very much since she was 15 years old. So, in many ways it would seem that she is basically a very strong person who had some good coping mechanisms before she sustained her injuries. There is certainly some amount of denial and there obviously are underlying feelings of depression and anxiety about her condition, but she has developed a fairly effective style of coping with these feelings. When I asked her about her interest in real estate, she said that there was an interest but she really did not know where it would go and mentioned that she only owns one small building now but perhaps would like to acquire others. She laughed and said that she would like to become a millionaire, and I feel that although she was joking, striving for something like this at least on the fantasy level helps to compensate in some way for the feelings of inadequacy that she has in relationship to her disfigurement. All in all, it would certainly appear that she is a well-integrated individual who has adapted quite successfully to her condition.

This young woman shows a striking difference between her regression during the posttraumatic period and her later, active style of coping.

She did not use much blanket denial, but rather rushed into doing lots of things that frightened her, which involved active mastery. She actively worked with her therapy for part of the time, but then seemed to evade seeing her plastic surgeon (at a point where she could cover up part of her defects, so her attitude was not unrealistic). Her reliance on traveling to fend off depression, and keeping active at the same time, did lead to her moving ahead with her problems. She had evolved a particular social style, first reported by Sir Harold Himsworth, Visiting Director Emeritus of the British Medical Research Council [5], who met her when he came to visit the hospital. He described how she sat so that her damaged hand was covered and how she immediately began to interact by talking earnestly and making eye contact steadfastly. Her lids were not quite normal in appearance, but she had very mobile brows and forehead and she used this part of her face to put people at ease and to establish that she was a competent person. She also was quick to involve people in social conversation, immediately pointing out to the visiting British doctor that she was Canadian, not American, and rapidly establishing a pleasant, chatty atmosphere.

It is in this area of social skillfulness, a quality that is really a composite of personality features, that runs as a major theme in coping with burns. In Katherine's case it certainly means covering over depression, and appearing optimistic. This also seems true of a number of our patients and harks back to the problems of stigma management discussed in Chapter 3 on altered body image. It seems to involve the active control over the first contact with a stranger by the facially disfigured person; and it requires a definite amount of emotional energy always to do this. There is a counterphobic component and firm control over conscious depressive affect. It borders on bravado.

Another example of a switch from marked regression and disruption of care to good coping is Craig I.

Case History: Craig I.
At age 18, Craig was burned while working in a garage. He sustained extensive third-degree burns on his nose, cheeks, ears, shoulders, hands, and neck, which left him markedly disfigured.

He had been dissolute and failing at a nearby college and had always been indulged by his parents. After the accident, long after he was out of danger, he was a major management problem on the ward. He screamed, cursed, refused treatment, pushed the nurses away, and would not cooperate. At one point several months after his injury, the rehabilitation staff sent him home rather than struggle with his rage and rebelliousness.

He was readmitted for minor plastic surgery three years after the original accident. The chart noted that he had abruptly refused to give blood to the laboratory technician, but when a psychologist and I came to interview him, he quickly sat up and began to talk without interruption for the next 45 minutes. He said he was now much better; before, he had been unable to use either arm, and now he had a good left hand, which he showed in spite of scarring (his right hand is still markedly deformed). He has long hair, major scarring all over his face, and no visible ears. However, his tone throughout was that of the successful young executive; his manner that of an assured, driving salesman. He now has his own business, an auto repair shop, with a partner who had been badly crippled and was now fully rehabilitated. Craig is in charge of sales. (His surgeon later stated this was done largely by telephone.) He had tried to borrow money from the bank and was turned down, but his parents had been very helpful, paying all his medical expenses and giving him some money to get started in business.

When I reminded him of how difficult he had been to the staff and how changed he seemed, he agreed he had been difficult, passing it off as related to his immobilized arms. He talked about all the family efforts to acquire special equipment such as a Hubbard tank and how good his family and relatives, as well as his friends, had been in giving him special attention. He invited the interviewers to visit his office in Maine. Only in passing did he mention that his scars had looked much worse right after getting out of the hospital.

He presented a picture of having no major problems. His pressure of speech and forceful way of chatting served to contain his own affect and also to control the interaction with his interviewers, who did not try to crash through his defense.

REFERENCES

1. MacGregor, F. C., et al. *Facial Deformities and Plastic Surgery: A Psychosocial Study*. Thomas, Springfield, Ill., 1953.
2. Shelley, M. *Frankenstein*. Dell, New York, 1964.
3. Wright, B. A. *Physical Disability: A Psychological Approach*. Harper & Row, New York, 1960.
4. Goldberg, R. Personal communication, 1975.
5. Himsworth, H. Personal communication, 1974.

5

Disfigurement and Middle Life

Allport [1], Bühler [2], and many others have discussed the *directedness* of life, what people live for, be they goals or special objectives of higher purposes. In dealing with the cases we reviewed of burn victims in the age range of 30 to 50, this attitude evolved as important in evaluating how they functioned. Allport mentioned the loss of directedness in people who commit suicide, and, of course, Durkheim's [3] *anomie* refers to this. In considering the shattered lives that many of our subjects have suffered, we have not come across this phenomenon in any clear way. For the most part, we have examples of cases in which life directedness is fought for in spite of the multiple handicaps imposed by the burns, the disfigurement, the associated stigma, and the physical as well as financial and social handicaps. For those who manage to cope, the organizing direction of life seems to be maintained. We have anecdotal reports of a number of men who struggled with their disfigurement for eight or nine years and then violently killed themselves, e.g., three cases of auto accidents believed to be suicides, but these are not proved. The suicide statistics were not aligned in a way that would allow us usefully to extract the information we wanted, and families did not come forward to tell us about these tragic outcomes.

More commonly, we heard about people living solitary lives, typifying the accounts given by MacGregor et al. [4, 5] of social death.

These individuals sat at home, without hope, hiding from the world. There is a spectrum of activities among these shut-ins. Some did work. One was a night custodian in a suburban school, who kept to himself by day and did his work in isolation at night. He had no family, and was gossiped about in the town and used as a symbolic bogeyman for children.

Some kept in touch with old friends and sustained some sense of worth and direction through their focus on past activities. Weisman [6] has spoken about consultation with handicapped elderly people, and the need to help them reminisce effectively so that they can look upon past activities and previous levels of functioning in order to maintain some sense of worth. This has much to do with the "good-old-days" reflections of so many older people, serving as it does to keep a sense of purpose in life. For persons disfigured in the prime of life, there is a sense of being thrust into old age. Unlike the muted tragedy of our society in which people gradually lose vitality and status as they get older, till they become a burden to their families and to society, many burn victims are cast aside as useless by the world with tragic abruptness. In the elderly this often is associated with diminished psychic energy, a drift into reverie, and the quality of apathy or devitalized sadness, rather than the anguished dejection more common in the clinical depressions of younger people. For most people in middle life, their lives are focused on work or family, and the cases to follow hinge largely on this adaptation.

The next patient was a moody, anxious woman in her thirties who was able to continue to relate to important people around her but was always complaining while coping.

Case History: Meredith J.
Meredith is a fairly attractive 36-year-old divorcee. She had noticeable red scar tissue on both sides of her face up to the hairline in the ear area and around the outer edge of her right eye. A great deal of red scar tissue was also noticeable on her neck; it seemed that she tried to conceal as much of this as possible since she was wearing a long-sleeved blouse buttoned up to her neck and it was a rather warm day.

There was a definite tenseness in Meredith's voice and she appeared anxious throughout the interview. She mentioned attending a group that apparently is a day-care type of program run by a local mental health clinic. The last time she went they baked a cake, and she could have stayed home and done that, she said. She sees the group as a means of having social contact, and I noted that she had been sitting in her car talking with another woman for several minutes before our appointment. In spite of her apparent anxiety and tenseness, her affect was friendly and she was not defensive at all about talking about her injuries.

She had accidentally ignited a book of matches which set her nightgown on fire. She did not pass out immediately and remembers screaming to her 10-year-old son, who was in the room at the time, to get help. She also remembers being sent to Massachusetts General Hospital. During the first four weeks of her hospitalization she was delirious most of the time and under heavy medication. After her skin graft, she was able to walk about the hospital on her own. Initially she was rather shaky but she did enjoy going around and helping and talking with other patients. It was her feeling that this was something that helped her a lot, that is, seeing people who had been burned more badly than herself and who were unable to do things, such as eat, on their own. She also spent a great deal of time watching television. She acknowledged that she was depressed from time to time and experienced a great deal of pain. She said that she prayed a lot when she was suffering; however, she views herself as being almost an atheist.

When she went home she said that the state welfare department had offered to provide her with a homemaker, but she did not want anybody coming in to help her and preferred to do things on her own. This is consistent with the information on the chart that indicated that she was a person who did not like outsiders to become involved in her life. She said that her legs had ached a lot and so she took medication while she was at home and did not realize how much medication had built up in her system. The result was that she had an overdose shortly after returning home and needed to be hospitalized for a short time. This was an issue that she really did not want to discuss, but she does continue to take diazepam (Valium). She criticized the hospital, feeling that her medication should not have been increased during the time that she was experiencing a lot of pain and, in fact, said that she would ask for medication only when she felt she needed it. She referred very positively to one surgeon, saying that she never worried about how things would turn out because she had a great deal of confidence in him and would have done anything that he told her.

Graft areas are apparent on her face and neck. She became tense when this was mentioned and denied that she was upset by the scars, saying she is much too busy to spend time brooding about her appearance. She went on to say that if she were 18 years old she would mind the scars but it is really too late for her now. She did admit that sometimes when she looks at herself in the mirror she is upset, but this passes quickly. She has a boyfriend who she feels cares a lot about her; she said that he still expects her to be disturbed by her disfigurement, but she claimed that this has not happened. There is some denial of reality in this situation and an avoidance and inconsistency in dealing with the way she really feels about her appearance. She stressed the fact that she is too busy living to be concerned about things like this; it is her feeling that she has even benefited in some ways from the injury, that it has taught her to enjoy life.

She felt that the experience had been rather traumatic for her son. When she was burned he was very frightened and thought she was dead. It was not until she called him on the telephone a few days later that he really understood what had happened. He had been one of her major concerns while she was in the hospital. For a while he stayed with a neighbor and then a great-aunt; however, because he was a very active boy, after a time he was placed in a children's home. This was something she was initially reluctant to allow; nevertheless, the social worker convinced her that this was a good thing to do for both herself and her son. In terms of her reaction to fire, she said that she is not traumatized by it, but is more careful than she used to be. She then commented that whenever she lights a match and her son is in the room, he tenses up.

There were many young volunteers in the hospital who were very good to her, but at times she found them somewhat irritating. For example, one time a volunteer wanted to get her up to come to a cookout being held at the hospital and she did not want to go to it. This seemed to tie in with her concerns about being near fire or some reluctance to socialize because of her appearance, but she was defensive and not very clear about why she had not felt like going. Initially, she said, the only person who visited her while she was in the hospital was her boyfriend and he visited her daily. She went on to say that she did not want her son to see her, because she was all bandaged up and this would have been very upsetting to him. She then spontaneously mentioned that she has a brother, but since their mother died they have not been on friendly terms, having had a monetary struggle over the will. There were some inconsistencies around the issue of visitors; she claimed she had friends, but then stressed that the only one she saw was her boyfriend.

During the time she was hospitalized, she said that she worried about her son Michael a great deal. They had never been separated even overnight and they are very close to one another. She minded very much not being able to see him. Her hospitalization seemed very long and she often wondered if she would ever get home. There was a definite note of depression as she discussed the separation. She added that she called her son every night and this helped a little. She referred to him as a sensible boy who had a very good attitude. She went on to say that as a result of this separation he has become more independent. However, she may resent the fact that he is not as dependent on her as perhaps he was before she went into the hospital.

She had been concerned about finances, but welfare has taken care of all of her hospitalization costs and she receives disability payments now. She did complain a bit, saying that she never seems to get the same size check and it is very hard to adjust to living under these circumstances. She also has some funds through money that was left to her, but she was reluctant to discuss this. She said that she was being evicted. (While she was in the hospital she received a notice from her landlord saying that because she had created a nuisance, the fire, he was evicting her. However, her lawyer became involved and the whole matter was dropped.) She rationalized a bit about the issue of moving, saying that she wanted to move to a better neighborhood where her son could go out and play more and be near more children. Her plan is to move to a wooded suburb and, in fact, she has put a deposit on an apartment in such a town.

Meredith is an isolated woman of average intelligence. Her environmental resources are limited, centering mainly around financial support that she receives through welfare and a close relationship with a boyfriend and an aunt of hers. She is obviously very attached to her son and depends very much on him for emotional support. She does seem to have a lot of underlying anxiety and it is evident that she uses denial and repression a great deal. Depression seems to be a definite factor here; however, she had been in a state of depression even before her accident. She is a guarded woman who does not allow others to learn too much about her, and this apparent isolation is used to defend against hurtful environmental forces or pressures. There may be a lot of underlying anger with regard to her life in general and her injuries in part, but she tends to use reaction formation here, referring to her life as being much better since she had this experience.

In a number of cases where life was strongly built on a career or a job that could be realistically pursued after the injury, the job also provided an opportunity to focus attention, to relieve and divert unpleasant feelings. These people did better. Professions provide this type of adjustment. Goldiamond [7] reported the ultimate example of this type of adjustment when he made himself the subject of studies in behavior modification after becoming paraplegic in an accident, a kind of self-objectification that serves both personal and public purposes in a most admirable way. One facially burned lawyer arranged to do most of his legal work by telephone. An architect with burn scars on his face and largely damaged ears grew his hair long to cover as much of his scarring as possible, and then withdrew to his drafting room to work mostly in solitude. These adaptations, of course, involve all the benefits of social class and education. For persons with a particular craft, such as an artist, this pattern may also be followed. The following case is that of a talented Japanese pianist with frightening disfigurement from childhood burns. In spite of her disavowals of concern over appearance among Japanese people, Japan with its long and exquisite awareness of appearances and enormous aesthetic literature, as well as a vigorous cosmetic surgery industry, appears very similar to Europe and America in regard to stigmatizing the disfigured.

Case History: Tanizara K.
Tanizara, a 34-year-old single Japanese woman, was burned in childhood and grew up with her scars. It is only recently that she has undergone plastic surgery, having had fifteen plastic surgical procedures during the past five years. She had been in Baltimore on a two-year music scholarship and was planning to return to Japan to visit her family. However, while she was visiting a friend in Boston her friend had suggested that she might look into the possibility of having some work done on her face. Tanizara stated that she had never really been concerned about her face at all and in no way had ever considered trying to improve it. At this point she does not know whether she will be having any further surgical procedures, but is leaving it up to the surgeon. She emphasized the tremendous amount of confidence that she has in him, referring to him as having somewhat of the temperament of an artist. She has always felt that he is really concerned about her. She has faced each surgical procedure with a great deal of optimism.

In the beginning she had continued her musical studies, but being in and out of the hospital interfered with her being able to study for examinations as well as keep up with her practicing and performing. She sees herself as a good student who has always enjoyed school, and thus it bothered her not to be able to devote her attentions to academic work. Therefore, she has given it up for the most part. However, she continues her musical training on a private basis and looks forward to being a concert pianist.

She recalls very little if any effect that her burns had on her life as a child. She is the daughter of a teacher who was the director of a school in Japan. Both parents are still living as are all of her brothers and sisters. She stated that although they are apart from one another she does not feel isolated from her family, which she views as a close one. Her father was always very protective of her, and while her mother did not make an issue out of her burns, she has always been very supportive and given her a tremendous amount of reassurance. Tanizara placed great emphasis on religious training. She said that her mother always emphasized spiritual beliefs and these were instilled in her as a child. Since becoming an adult, she has been very occupied in so many other areas that religion is not of any great importance to her. In spite of this, she feels that her religious training as a child has been helpful to her as an adult. Periodically she and her family exchange visits.

Tanizara claimed that she has never really given much thought to her disfigurement. She said that she has never been thrown in with large numbers of people. Because of her family's social position, she was never subjected to any situation that made her uncomfortable. During her early years, at the time of the Second World War, community relations were somewhat disrupted anyway and there was no real chance to concentrate on her condition. Involvement in activities such as her music or studies at school gave her a lot of confidence.

She acknowledged some feelings of depression, but indicated that they occurred mainly when she began to have skin grafting on her face. The depression was due primarily to the fact that her life was somewhat disrupted and she was not able to pursue the kinds of things she really wanted to. However, she feels that she has adapted to this by becoming interested in other areas, such as learning how to make her own clothes. For the past year she has also been working part-time as a technician in a university physics laboratory. She said that she enjoys her work and that it gives her an opportunity to meet people.

Socialization has been limited or at least structured in her life. Basically, her social contacts are with a close circle of friends, most of whom are involved in her area of interest, that is, music. It is obvious that she wishes to expand her social horizons and talks about wanting to see people more than she has in the past. She views her career as the most important factor in her life now and she would like to establish herself as a concert pianist. Eventually she hopes to marry and have children. I found her to be a very warm and outgoing individual. She sees herself as more alive than she used to be. I asked if this had anything to do with the fact that she sees a difference in herself because of the surgical procedures. She was really not sure of this, but views herself as someone who has adjusted well to her particular problem, and has never felt any great concern about her face. This might be viewed as denial or repression of her real feelings. However, one might also take into consideration her cultural background as a determinant in this area. I talked with her about her relationships with men and it appeared that she was slightly uncomfortable. Nevertheless, she indicated that she has had dates on numerous occasions. Here again, I emphasize that her social activities have centered on her music; social contacts for her have been selective ever since she was a child. A message that comes across very consistently is that of acceptance of what has happened to her. She has never had any real contact with persons who have been burned other than seeing them in the hospital. As far as working or being involved with a person who has been burned, she said that she has no real thoughts on it at all, that it would not really bother her. She exudes a tremendous amount of optimism and one gets the impression that this is a life-style that would exist regardless of the deformity.

We discussed the issue of financial problems and she indicated that during the past five years she has received support from the Massachusetts Rehabilitation Commission, which has taken care of all of her medical costs. When it was needed she has also received financial support from her family, and through part-time work has been able to earn enough to live comfortably. She emphasized that since her financial needs are not particularly great, there had never been any substantial pressures on her as far as earning money was concerned.

An interesting facet of Tanizara's personality is her firm negation of concern with the fact that she was burned. A number of times she mentioned that she had never thought about improving her face or had never been concerned about it, but always felt that one must make a life for oneself and be a productive and creative human being. She has always been achievement-oriented and has certainly established herself successfully in some areas of her life, such as her studies and her involvement in music. One has an immense feeling that she has coped very well with her deformity, which has been a handicap for her in most areas. There is clear repression of feelings or denial in direct relationship with social issues. One could wonder how fulfilled she feels as a woman and also how well she would be functioning if she did not have a profession in which she feels successful. There is a special tunnel vision in which little but career is seen.

For the physically disabled working-class person, the focus of his life can be destroyed, or turned into an "antidirection" where he must strive to show how disabled he is in order to maintain his workmen's compensation insurance. This is the adaptive style of the man described in the following case history.

Case History: Frank M.

Frank is 36 years old and the divorced father of four children who live with their mother. He was burned at age 34. At the present time he lives with his mother in his apartment. He is a tall, well-built man who was neatly dressed in sport clothes at the time of my interview. The locus of his burns was some reddened tissue on his forehead, and when he took off his sunglasses it was apparent that his eyelids had been reconstructed. All of his fingers with the exception of his two thumbs are missing down to the first joint. He is quite spontaneous and initially seemed apprehensive and even suspicious of our interview, looking around the room a great deal.

He and four other men had been injured in a gas explosion due to a gas leak at a construction job. The gas was ignited when he lit a cigarette, but the other men harbor no ill feelings toward him. He commented that he had to walk most of the way to the hospital. Two iron workers who had been around at the time of the explosion put him and a couple of the other men in a car to drive them to the hospital; however, they stopped and let them out because they could not stand the smell of the burned flesh.

He spent five months in the hospital. He talked very positively about the kind of care he had received there, especially about the surgeon assigned to him. He considered himself lucky because this surgeon used to visit him every day, if only for five minutes. This helped him develop confidence that he would get better. His fellow workers who had been burned did not have the same kind of care and became more depressed than he. He felt that the nurses were not used to taking care of a burn patient and seemed to get very upset. When his fingers were amputated he was told that he would have to feed himself because it was good therapy; however, he could not stand to look at his hands, so he did not eat very much. He remarked that while in the hospital he lost 40 pounds. (Now he is slightly overweight.) They had wanted to amputate his thumbs as well, but he refused to allow it. When interviewed after discharge, he talked a great deal about his hands and the fact that he was very jumpy when the dressings were changed. He rationalized, saying that this was due to the sensitivity in the nerves. Very often a couple of people had to hold him down when his dressings were changed because he would become very upset. He complained that he did not like other doctors who were in the process of learning surgery coming around and looking at his burns. He had wanted medication for his pain, but very often his doctor would tell him that he did not need it. He denied that this made him angry, but it was apparent that he was bothered by the doctor's refusal to give him medication. He was pleased about being put on a beer diet at one point and proudly talked about consuming very large quantities of beer while he was in the hospital. While there he watched television and walked around for the most part. He described himself as pacing up and down in the hospital like a caged wild animal.

He emphatically stated he was never concerned about how things would work out; that is, never worried about whether or not he would live. He had had sixteen surgical procedures, and indicated that he had just accepted this as a part of the way things were, that it did not really bother him. However, he did acknowledge that he needed a great deal of encouragement and made reference to eleven people dying of burns during the time that he was in the hospital. He went on to say that many of these people had been not physically well off to start with, while he was a very strong and healthy person so that this had undoubtedly helped him a great deal.

His mother had visited him often when he was in the hospital, as had many friends. He had hoped that his wife would bring the children to see him; however, she never did.

When he was discharged, his appearance seemed to upset the children. They would ask a lot of questions. For example, his 6-year-old daughter asked him when his fingers were going to grow, and this used to bother him. However, he said that they are now well adjusted to it. Commenting on other people's reactions to him, he said that he feels that people often stare at him. He turns around and stares back. Or they ask a lot of questions and feel sorry for him, which he resents. An issue that he seemed to pursue was the fact that children often made comments about the way he looks, and although he said this does not really bother him, it obviously does.

At the time of the accident he had been working for a year and a half as a construction inspector for a trucking company. He was classified as a temporary employee. The company calls him a great deal about coming back, but when he asks them what type of job they plan to give him they are very nonspecific. He is quite suspicious of this and feels that because he was a temporary employee they will take him back and then lay him off, and that if he goes back to work his pending lawsuit will not hold up in court.

He said that he has had more or less to reorganize his life to try to keep busy, but that it gets very depressing being idle. He proudly talked about the fact that he ran a baseball team for 16- to 18-year-olds this past summer and that they took first place in the league. He tries very much to stay out of the barrooms, and that is a problem because there is always someone in the barroom to talk to and he has a tendency to drink heavily. (It is also his belief that "you don't find your jobs in the union hall but in the barroom.") He attends many sporting events. He had been seeing a girlfriend before the accident, and he said that she is very understanding and that he has a good relationship with her. If he were not going out with her, he would find it very difficult to learn to relate to another woman. He sees his children every weekend. His former wife has remarried since the accident and he feels that she resents his contact with the children because he takes them out and has a good time, while she has to take care of all of the problems and daily chores. He finds that very often she resists letting them go with him, and, in fact, this past summer he rented a summer cottage where he was going to take them for three weeks but she claimed that they were sick. They are going to court over this. During the first four weeks that he was in the hospital, when he was not being paid by the trucking company, his wife complained a great deal about not receiving her alimony payments. He has many negative feelings toward her.

His life is construction and he was a union carpenter. He had gone to college for two years with the plan of becoming a teacher; however, during the second summer in college he worked for a construction company and made a lot of money and so decided to quit college and stay with construction. As far as returning to this type of work, his comment was that they would never let him on a job because of insurance. He thinks he could do the work, but then admitted that the only thing he really could do is supervisory work. He went on to say that if he could not go back to construction work, he could always officiate at sports events and this would give him enough money to get by. In fact, a suburban school system has offered him a job as an assistant coach for the baseball team and referee at their various sports events. However, if he took this job it would affect the workmen's compensation that he presently receives. He expects to win his lawsuit, but much of the money will have to go to pay his hospital bills and lawyer's fees. He is concerned about his future and even talked of buying the apartment house in which he lives because perhaps it would give him a small income. He said that he never received any help from the union and is no longer a member. Here again, he stated in a somewhat depressed manner that he feels they would not take him back because he could no longer do the work. He said that he has heard about the Massachusetts Rehabilitation Commission but no one ever told him where it is. He did have a long interview with the welfare department, as a result of which he has been receiving a check for $233 each month. They sent him a check in the beginning for $2500, which he used to buy a new car. At the present time he is making more money than he ever did but is skeptical about how long this will go on.

Frank seems to show a very definite tendency toward what might be viewed as overcompensation, or at least conveying the message that he is a very independent person; for example, he said proudly that he used to use a cigarette lighter to light his cigarettes but now uses matches. He also pointed out that he drives a car and ties his own shoelaces. This led him to talk about the things he does, such as play golf, pool, and shuffleboard and do simple repairs around his home. He stressed that one cannot lock oneself in a closet—one has to go on living and make the best of things. He would like to start a small construction company with his insurance settlement, but he does not know if this is realistic. He acknowledged that he had had a number of minor accidents in construction work. His rationalization for this was that if one were in construction he had to face the fact that he would get hurt at some time or another.

In talking about changes in his personality, he feels that he used to be a rough-and-ready man whose hands were his weapons, and he tended to be loud and outspoken. However, now he has been humbled and many of the people who used to be very frightened of him are now much more aggressive in relating to him. He feels that he is more mature now and that perhaps the accident was a good thing, clearly a major rationalization and denial of his feelings. There seemed to be some underlying fantasies here about the fact that perhaps he was destined to have an accident in which his hands were hurt because he had used his hands to hurt other people. He sees himself now as being somewhat more sensitive and a bit more compassionate than he used to be. After talking extensively about these changes, he said that he still feels he is a pretty tough fellow who can take care of himself if he has to. His attitude toward life is that one should live a day at a time. He feels that he is a realist. He has much underlying bitterness, especially toward the job because of the difficulties he has had and also, in some ways, toward the other men who were burned with him but who did not suffer the extensive injuries he did. He did say that if the money stops coming in, then he will really start worrying. It was at this point that he talked again about the fact that he gets depressed from time to time.

Frank appears to be a man of average intelligence whose major modes of adapting are in the physical area. He certainly denies a great deal and avoids confronting some of his feelings even though he does see himself as being very much of a realist. His relationship with his girlfriend provides some opportunity for loving exchanges, but there is great discomfort in his relationship with his children and his former wife. He seems to demonstrate underlying rage in the form of bitterness and a tendency to be very distressed about accepting sympathy. He seems to be a rather energetic person who in many ways does utilize active coping mechanisms. There is evidence, at present, of environmental resources, especially in the area of money. He seems to live with the fantasy of coming into a great deal of money that will change his life in a positive way, yet he has some realization that things might not work out that way at all. At the same time, he feels that if things don't work out, they don't—there is nothing he can do about it. He has been telling his fellow workers who were in the accident with him that they should live on a day-to-day basis and not count on anything. Although he denies it, he is counting on a great deal, especially in the area of insurance money, which he can use to make certain of a positive future for himself. At this point, he really has no direction. There is vast underlying rage and bitterness that will emerge should he suffer any great disappointment in the future. His tendency to try to present himself as a very strong person who is holding up very well seems to be a brave pose. He may be much shakier than would appear from initial observation.

A middle-aged woman who had won her life battle to overcome disfigurement yet always dreamt of eradicating it, brought out this inner goal by coming for surgery when her family was grown.

Case History: Angela M.
At the age of 2, Angela opened the door of a pot-bellied stove at home. The flame blew out, burning her face, upper shoulders, and left arm. She presents now, at the age of 45, with old scars on the face and on the left arm. These apparently healed under simple medical care and nothing further was done. She grew up with the scars, having accepted them her entire adolescent and adult life. Since her children, except for the 14-year-old, are now essentially grown up and seem to be on their own, she is seeking cosmetic surgery for her facial scars.

She said, "I deserve something for myself." Her husband said, "It doesn't matter to me one way or another—what she wants, I want. Beauty isn't skin deep. For me, she's always been the most beautiful girl in the world." She answered, "I have such an ugly face." She laughingly gave the actress Ann-Margret as a model for a way she would like to look.

Angela was the seventh of twelve children, and the whole family worked together to treat her as normal. Children stared at school, but never teased her though she always feared that people might laugh at her. Her mother once tried blessed water (from Lourdes) on her face and one sister advised surgery. Otherwise, no one has suggested it and she has never prayed for a miracle.

Angela knew her husband as an adolescent. They married when she was 21 and he was 18. For twenty years he was in the military service, stationed in Rhode Island, Alaska, and California. Sometimes he was away for months at a time so that she estimates that they were separated eight out of the twenty years. She attends church regularly. She completed tenth grade and is interested in citizen-band radio and the supernatural, but has always avoided dances, public jobs, and going anywhere for business meetings during the past six years that her husband has been in private business. She described herself as domineering and moody, going from high to low and back quickly. Her husband said she is almost fanatically religious.

The following summary comes largely from the plastic surgeon's admirable interview:

On being asked what she would like to have done, she states that she would like to have the scars removed, or changed, so that she would look better. She stated she would feel differently about herself; she feels she would be much more acceptable to the people around her. She stated that she has lost one job because of her facial appearance. Whenever she is out in new company, she is aware that people stare and ask about her face. She would like to go back to school and earn a

diploma; however, she is fearful that her appearance will cause comment among
her classmates. Her husband volunteered that she has been a woman who has been
admired and loved, but that she always has avoided company and organizations.
He describes her as going out very little and participating in no women's club
activities or church activities. He is active in the Veterans of Foreign Wars, but she
has never come to a dinner meeting with him because she is basically fearful of the
public effect of her appearance. She listened quietly as he made these matter-of-fact
statements, and she agreed [with] them. One senses that this woman, while having
satisfactorily established good relations with her husband, and raised a family, has
essentially removed herself from any other social intercourse.

Mrs. M. is quite short and slightly stocky. She has a fundamentally attractive bony
skeleton to her face, over which is traced old scar tissue, particularly on the right,
and what appears to be very prematurely aged skin, throwing the entire face into
multiple wrinkles, irregularities of skin, and basically warped lines. Specifically, the
burn scar extends from the right ear, which is somewhat thinned out as the result
of the scar, down across the entire right cheek. This scar is basically flat, white, and
somewhat irregular, and has varying degrees of hyperpigmentation at the edge,
none of which calls very much attention to it. Beneath the right corner of the
mouth, there are two or three very sharp ridges of scar, disposed primarily trans-
versely; these approximate 2 to 3 cm at their longest. In both upper labionasal
folds, there are old leonine scars which have long since undergone hypertrophy
and softening, leaving her with very wrinkled, vertically disposed scars in these
areas. There is a good deal of wrinkled, pale scarring on the left cheek near the
corner of the mouth that is very similar. The remainder of her face shows premature
aging changes with exceedingly deep labionasal folds, a very full, excessively
wrinkled lower lid tissue, and cheeks that are by no means smooth even in the
unburned areas. They are quite deeply furrowed and show large pores. Her forehead is quite wrinkled, and the glabella area exhibits some multiple frowns. Crow's-
feet are not prominent.

I discussed surgical correction and in this discussion I took most of the lead,
since questions directed at Mrs. M. evoked intellectualisms in return; in fact,
she broke out in embarrassed giggles at times. I do not rate these giggles as abnormal
but rather as giggles of delight at discussing what she clearly hopes will be magical
surgery to correct the facial disfigurement that has caused her lifelong embarrassment.

I counseled her that she should think carefully about these possibilities and talk
them over with her husband before making any decisions about facial surgery.
Likewise, I observed that she is a woman whose emotions are clearly influenced
by her facial appearance and that I felt that before any surgery was carried out she
should receive psychiatric evaluation to help her examine her own motivations and
expectations. Interestingly enough, she seemed very eager to do this and even suggested she should do it whatever she decides about surgery.

Angela epitomizes a normal life managed with great energy and
humor in spite of the circumscription of her social life. She has done
as well as her many siblings. In striking contrast to Angela, who looks
more like 55 than 45, is her very youthful-looking husband who appears about 38 years old. Her hearty laughter and her ability to laugh

at herself and her troubles appear to be long-standing traits. She says that at no time did it occur to her to ask for heaven to help her, but now she looks to cosmetic surgery to offer her a better life. During her marriage there were separations that lasted years, while her husband was at sea or stationed in inconvenient places on both coasts, attesting further to her ability to manage things independently. Jackson [8] found that burn disfigured women are mortified when their children do not want to kiss them after they return home scarred. However, Angela's children have not commented much about her appearance though they have been known to be occasionally embarrassed by it.

Deviance and respectability are tied to each other in everyday life and each individual tries to construct an image of himself that is normal, acceptable, and plausible to himself and to the people who are important to him. People who are disfigured struggle for acceptable roles, and this is part of the unification of their lives. (This can also be so constricting as to leave them "closet cases.") A clear example follows of the coping of a man whose face was completely shattered. With the help of his family and friends, he managed to maintain most of his previous sense of worth and respectability in spite of losing his nose, ears, hair, and almost all the normal skin of his face, so that he presents a mask of scars to the world.

Case History: Carl M.

Carl is a 49-year-old married man who is currently a clerical worker at an electric company. Fifteen years ago he was burned over 50 percent of his body in an explosion while working as a maintenance man with heavy electrical equipment. He has subsequently undergone dozens of surgical procedures. He lost all the fingers of his right hand; both ears; most of his hair, nose, mouth, and chin; and for three years had an indwelling tracheostomy tube. I first saw him when he came for a psychiatric consultation in the hospital.

He was quite willing to talk about his injury and how things had gone in his life since he was burned. He views himself as much more fortunate than many other people who have had his experience because there were no financial limitations on treatment or on his ability to continue supporting his family after he was burned. He described himself as someone who has always been optimistic, and he attributes part of his success, being able to bear up under everything that has happened, to always believing that each surgical procedure would produce a positive outcome. He would also keep his mind on other things, that is, things that would give him some type of gratification. For example, when he had plastic surgery on his mouth he thought constantly of the fact that when it healed the first thing he wanted to do was to eat two sirloin steaks. Another factor that he feels helped him greatly was that shortly after every operation he was up and on his feet. He was able to walk around the hospital, and this gave him the opportunity to see many other surgical patients, whom he perceived as being much worse off than himself. Also, his normal deep voice remained, even when he had a tracheostomy, so people could always identify him regardless of the bandages or edema.

He said that he had never had deep depression because he always felt that things would turn out all right and he managed to keep himself busy all the time. He also stated that there were so many surgical procedures (about fifty, according to his hospital record) that he really did not have a lot of time to think about what was going on between them. We discussed his talking with a group of doctors about his experience. "They asked me if I prayed before going up to an operation and that kind of junk." He treated religion in a matter-of-fact way, and one had the feeling that he was not terribly involved in it, nor did he view it as having a positive effect on his ability to survive what had happened to him.

Things had gone very well with his family. They have been very much behind him. He was especially talkative about his two children, whom he is sending through college. His son wishes to become a dentist; his daughter is studying to be a nurse. He indicated that his relationship with them is quite good and that he is proud of them. They both accepted him well after his disfigurement, but his son feels embarrassed by him in public.

He pointed out that he thinks this whole experience has been much harder on his wife than it has been on him because she has had to manage so much and a lot has depended on her. She felt this was especially true during the first few months following the accident, when he was really "not with it." She fought to hold back her tears after his injury. The surgeon encouraged her and advised her about what to tell her husband at different times. Carl talked about the shock the first time he saw himself and indicated that fairly early on, once he knew that he was going to survive, he decided then and there that he was going to have to face this because he had a family to support and that without him they would have a great deal of difficulty.

"At first you're a celebrity and hero in the hospital, everybody admires your courage, but then it ends and you say "What the hell, either you go out the front door or you move into the corner and stay there.' I think my wife and kids kept me going. As a single guy I couldn't go through it, and, to tell you the truth, if I didn't have the company paying all the bills, I don't think the doctors would have given me such good care. I don't think I would be alive. My doctor always knew when to let me go or when to push me. We got along well. I had no mouth and they fixed one up after surgery. I used to pray every time I went up to the operating room, but now I have been so many times I hardly think about it."

His family has tremendous reverence for Carl's primary surgeon but very little liking for the plastic surgeon who rebuilt his nose. They have newspaper clippings of the doctor's appearances, announcements of promotions, and Christmas cards he has sent. And Carl's hospital folder has several congratulatory letters and cards to the doctor, showing the mutual communication of interest and friendly regard. The family even had a fond nickname for the surgeon, who reciprocated with cordial respect for the patient and his family. They have been in contact for 15 years, and the doctor has performed most of Carl's many procedures.

He made numerous references to the fact that he has been given a tremendous amount of attention and that it makes one feel very important to receive such attention. It has certainly had a marked ego-building effect on him. He expressed great interest in trying to help others who have been burned and spoke about wanting to write a book, partly from a desire to continue being a center of attraction.

He works full-time and drives his own car with a special knob so he can manage the wheel. He dislikes the paperwork he is now doing and would have preferred physical work, but accepts it, saying repeatedly, "What the hell can you do?"

Concerning the reaction to his appearance of the people who work in the office, he said he is now more or less just part of the woodwork. When he first returned to work, some of the women indicated that he did make them feel rather uncomfortable. However, he said he did not let this really bother him. Since his accident he has had to develop a very different personality. He described himself as basically a rather quiet person, somewhat of an introvert. Now he is much more outgoing; however, this is forced. He feels that if he does not extend himself, perhaps no one would really relate to him. He expects that no matter where he goes people will notice him and react in different ways. In discussing the reaction of people to him, he displayed affect only when talking about how children respond to him. Although he tried to treat it in a matter-of-fact way, saying that children are like that, this bothered him. He did stress that his own children had never reacted negatively to him since the injury.

He makes an effort to put strangers at ease. Many people, who try to not notice him, give him a quick greeting and flee. Because he has a skin graft on his cheek from his thigh, he said that when people are uncomfortable on meeting him, he will point to his cheek and say, "Do you want to kiss my ass?" When pressed, he said he did not know what went on in his wife's mind but that she has never shown repugnance about his appearance. "People shy away, people look at me in public and sometimes walk into a lamp pole trying not to notice me. They wonder if this guy is a real person. I don't know what they think. I always try to be forward because they don't know if I can talk. If they hear me talk, then they know I'm OK. I try to draw people out." His wife said that when people seem to be staring at him she tries to engage him in conversation; she was surprised once when he said he knew she did this.

He tends to joke a lot about his appearance, or at least he said he does. For example, he said that he is lucky because he does not have to shave any more. He talked extensively about how he had had two wigs but gave up wearing them because they were a nuisance (and his wife thought they looked silly on him). He did mention that he uses facial makeup to improve his complexion, but aside from this, he does nothing to enhance his appearance. He said that he has always liked expensive, elegant clothes and liked to keep himself neat.

He described his wife as someone who never belonged to clubs or gossiped with the neighbors during the day, but was always at home, and he would always come directly home after work. He feels his social life has remained the same since the burns. That is, he and his wife have a close circle of old friends, most of whom reside on the same street. Almost every Saturday night they go out somewhere, dancing or to a banquet or some other type of affair. Offhandedly he said that when his wife is all dressed up he is sometimes told that it really does not matter how good she looks because people are always going to look at him anyway.

Mrs. M. stated that her husband was a strikingly handsome man and that she used to take pride in being seen with him in public. She thinks this makes it all the more surprising that he has accepted his disfigurement. Contrary to his statements, Mrs. M. said her husband did not want to go out of the house for the first three years; he did not answer the door and had nightmares—all of which has now changed. His physical energy, sexual performance, moods, working around the house, and heavy smoking and moderate drinking are all the same as before the accident. He was somewhat bothered by guilt over whether he had caused the accident, but has been reassured by the company that this was not so. Prior to the accident Carl used to wash the kitchen floor, paint and repair the house, and do all the shopping and driving, taking his wife everywhere. "I was quite dependent and had to grow up a lot after the accident," she said. He still does a great deal around the house, sometimes cursing when he cannot manipulate something with his missing fingers. She was told by the doctors that she would not be able to tell what he was feeling because his rebuilt face is immobile. However, she feels she has learned to judge his moods from his face and body positions.

In the course of psychiatric practice one is exposed to expressions of bitterness. Many patients talk of life passing them by, of time wasted, of lives blighted, and of bad luck. The hospitalized patient with a malignancy or a heart attack will often wail, in some form, "Lord, Lord, why hast Thou forsaken me?" This seems strangely lacking in most of the patients we have seen. Either they are too crushed by *what* has happened to be acrimonious about *why* it has happened; or the many burdens of surgery, deformity, and medical care keep them from expressing it. The children, parents, and spouses of adult burn victims talk about the cruelty of people who make remarks about burn disfigurement, but the main focus is on bearing the tragic events. Nevertheless, some patients do become sour and vehement, even when they make successful adaptations.

One example is the case of Shirley F., who in 1942 survived the tragic Cocoanut Grove nightclub fire. When she was seen for follow-up, she was 50 years old. She had gone to the nightclub with a date after a football game, and he had died in the fire. She was hospitalized for four months, underwent a dozen operations, and remained permanently scarred. She lost all four fingers of the right hand and part of her scalp was burned off, leaving considerable raised scar tissue on her forehead and neck. She had married and raised two children, and had been able to work outside the home for several years. However, her anger toward some of the doctors, and toward men in general, seemed to run through her report of what had happened. When she was caught in the fire, she told the policeman that "dogs walked over her," referring to men who had trampled her. Later, she told of being propositioned by men. When she rebuffed them they asked her, "Why are you so fussy?" She described dates who fled from the sight of her. Nonetheless, she had great regard for her plastic surgeon, and several other hospital workers. She kept in touch with her nurses long after treatment. She always struggled with being stared at for her burns, but she told of being unattractive and fat prior to her injury. She checked up on her interviewer, calling several people at the hospital to make sure he was what he claimed to be, and then complained to him about some of her unpleasant associations with his hospital.

Perhaps it is partly due to the interview focus on lesions, the rehabilitation emphasis, and the surgical style that has helped patients filter out the expression of bitterness. Perhaps the most bitter ones are shut off, and then drop out of the medical care system, so that they are not interviewed at all, or only when they are profoundly depressed and relatively quiet. However little pride and sense of accomplishment she expressed about it, Shirley does show an interesting balance in attitudes between her negative picture of herself and her ability withal to relate and to go ahead with her life. She also kept the pictures of herself and her date on the fateful evening out in her living room, clinging to the images of the past and what might have been, slanting her life toward nurturing lost fantasies rather than the realities. She described her husband as someone who had not originally interested her but who, from their earliest relations, was a model of kindly considerateness in his dealings with her. Yet, she found him "too short."

Many contrasts might be drawn between Shirley F. and Carl M. A striking one is the use of humor in dealing with their burdens. We regard this as an adaptive defense in dealing with burn disfigurement. A number of patients have shown flashes of wit, and some of the children have told children's jokes, while the adolescents have engaged in the traditional raillery, with each other or with the doctors. The humor —irony, sarcasm, one-line gags, slapstick—is quite varied in style and often too difficult and evanescent to capture as a distinctive style, yet the phenomenon remains a critical one. What is conventionally called "personality" in talking of a well-liked person is often an indication that he is either good-humored or humorous, or both. A punster expects only hearty groans as a response, but the very situation is one of complicity, between the person punning and his audience, and this is already a step from *thing* to *friend* in our disfigured group. Carl showed a hearty style, and underlying it was a network of loving exchanges between him and his family, and the friendly support from his doctor, his friends, and at least the acceptance of his co-workers. He showed a flexible balance toward awareness of his disfigurement, and seemed to "*contain*" the effects of disability so that they did not obtrude in all aspects of his life. In contrast, Shirley seemed to intrude her hurt and devalued feelings into all relationships along with their corrosive bitterness; without denying the nasty sexual overtures she received, the sense was that all her relations were tinged with acrimony, including those with her husband; nevertheless, she was up and around, and had made a life for herself.

Energy and seeking tension outlets are axes in our burn coping sche-ma; while there are some patterns of applying them that are more appealing, it is unquestionable that many people get along by discharg-ing their energy in unpleasant ways. This again contrasts with the altruistic style described earlier. The person who turns this energy largely against himself is hobbled by it; the one who spews it out may be unpleasant, but can sometimes salvage himself if social relations are not destroyed. Ideally a more pleasant sublimation of energy and hostility in humor is best for the patient and those around him. The vignette of Shirley has been given in less detail than the other case histories and does not include other aspects of her functioning that did show some evidence of affection and fond ties to other people; how-ever, the waspish characterization is valid.

REFERENCES

1. Allport, G. *Pattern and Growth in Personality*. Holt, Rinehart & Winston, New York, 1961.
2. Bühler, C. *Die Menschliche als psychologischer Problem*. Ogrefe, Bonn, Ger-many, 1959.
3. Durkheim, E. *Suicide*. Free Press, New York, 1951.
4. MacGregor, F. C., et al. *Facial Deformities and Plastic Surgery: A Psychosocial Study*. Thomas, Springfield, Ill., 1953.
5. MacGregor, F. C. *Identity and Transformation*. Quadrangle, New York, 1974.
6. Weisman, A. Personal communication, 1975.
7. Goldiamond, I. A diary of self-modification. *Psychol. Today* 7:95–102. Novem-ber 1973.
8. Jackson, D. Personal communication, 1972.

6
Disfigurement and Aging

Our society treats all the signs of old age, with their implications of infirmity and the proximity of death, as disfigurement. An "ugly old woman" or similar expression conveys this attitude. The extended family is no longer a helpful structure for most people; as energy and vitality wane, dependence increases, and for handicapped people these factors become critical even sooner.

APATHY

The following case illustrates the passive surrender that can occur when a person undergoes disfigurement in old age. This response is probably more typical of these persons than are the active coping and successful adaptations described in the succeeding cases.

Case History: Francis D.

Francis, age 72, was burned 24 years ago. Scars clearly disfigure the right side of his face. He has not worked since the burn injury, existing from one welfare check to another, becoming progressively more dependent, and gradually restricting his activities to sitting at home watching television and having his younger but quite maternal sister care for him. He is a shy bachelor with very little social life who has built his life around his facial defects by steady constriction of his life in line with his previous passive personality style. He has been managed medically by a succession of doctors and fears that there has been no special one whom he could seek out if the need arose. He has always been fearful of going back to the surgical clinic because of his becoming confused and anxious about all the red tape involved

111

in further care. He looks older than his age, and his manner is one of apathy rather than acute depression; no depressive ideation is expressed, but he is an inarticulate and indrawn person.

Cameron [1] pointed out that the social matrix has provided the strongest security for the aging person, particularly as the weakening individual is forced to depend progressively on others. Our experience with older patients who had the added problems of disfigurement was consistent with this view.

In North American life the social system tends to push the elderly to one side more quickly and more abruptly than in some other cultures, but the pressures are the same in other societies that focus on productivity. Chronically ill patients generally tend to move downward in the socioeconomic scale, and as they change their status they become obscured in the problems of the poor and its effects on the aging process. Poverty makes them ever more anxious and concerned about personal safety. This augments the trend toward withdrawal and diminished social contact and availability. In addition, there is threat of the disfigured person's continuing apprehension about social embarrassment from his appearance. These notions, however, are only partially substantiated by our experience because of the difficulty in finding a sample of older people who would respond. In this age group, the interval between medical care and follow-up was greater, more people had moved, and more had died. But our general problem of locating elderly patients seemed dominant. Some of the surgeons hypothesized that the facially disfigured patients of 30 years ago, when burn medicine was less sophisticated, were more likely to have died of pulmonary injury or of shock, since most patients who had sustained facial burns had also sustained other severe burn injuries.

In Erikson's view [2] older people are in a phase of life where the basic conflicts lie between a sense of ego integrity and a feeling of despair. He feels that people have to accept the wholeness of their life cycle, and achieve a sense of renunciation and wisdom, which enables them to face the end of their life courageously.

Our older patients were well beyond the group described by Goldwyn [3] as requesting plastic surgery, namely, professionally active and energetic persons, usually women between the ages 40 and 58, who want to "reaffirm to themselves that they are still youthful, optimistic, and effective in thought and action." There were exceptions to this, one of whom is described in the following case of a woman who is trying actively to cope:

Case History: Paulette E.

Paulette was a 68-year-old domestic worker who was referred for psychiatric evaluation by a plastic surgeon she had sought out for a face-lift. She was widowed and receiving Social Security benefits but wanted to go back to work. She had two grown children who were not much help to her financially. Her repeated statement was that she did not want to look beautiful, but that she wanted to look eight or ten years younger so that she would be employable. She felt that she was able to work and was full of vitality, but that she was discriminated against because she seemed old.

The plastic surgeon felt that she looked appropriate for her age, and that surgery would do little to alter the lined appearance of her face. He told her this several different ways, but it did not seem to register with her; she submitted to the psychiatric evaluation, but was furious when she found the same line of reaction from the consultant and said that the surgeon should have told her in the first place that the operation would not be much help. She said she would get along without the operation. She still intended to work and to fight off the social disengagement.

One could cite many individual examples of hardy folk who have handled adversity and facial disfigurement because they had a strong will and marked abilities. President Charles William Eliot of Harvard University, who was active long after his retirement from the university, bore a lifelong disfigurement of a port-wine stain on the side of his face. The poet Henry Wadsworth Longfellow grew the beard that gave him such a striking patriarchal appearance to cover a burn scar (Fig. 12). Allegedly his facial burns occurred while he was pressing his young wife's face against his chest to shield it; she had ignited her hoop skirt making wax candles, and died of her injuries.

If we return to the burn adaptation chart (Table 1) it is evident that the process of aging itself shifts all the variables.

1. The tendency is toward passive surrender, away from active coping.
2. Affectionate exchanges tend to be limited to a smaller group, and anger comes out more. But Erikson has stressed the challenges for the older person to achieve wisdom and accomplish personal integrity rather than succumbing to despair. This applies to normal or disfigured people.
3. The coping mode is not so likely to shift from a physical to an intellectual one. Rather, both physical and mental activities tend to be constricted.
4. Both denial and overawareness become muted. The group we saw was no longer involved in active treatment and handled denial and overawareness by decathecting or distancing problems.

Figure 12. Henry Wadsworth Longfellow grew his beard to cover facial burns sustained in a fire in which his wife died.

5. The elderly are rather settled in their defenses, not seeking new adaptive modes and protecting even the limited status quo.
6. It is the area of environmental support where the sharpest contrasts can be seen. The need for external sources of help increases greatly with old age.

In citing an example of long-term adjustment of a socially well-off woman who has been aided by her social status and a large supporting environment, financial and status variables clearly enter:

Interview with Elizabeth S.
Elizabeth is 68 years old, the wife of a professor. They live in a large suburban home and also have a summer place at the seaside. Elizabeth is very well groomed

and exudes dignity and good breeding. The obvious facial disfigurement showed in the pale scar tissue around the lower part of her face as well as her neck, but most predominantly along the lower right quadrant of her face. Her burns extended to her chest, arms, and back. She seemed determined and anxious, but related in a spontaneous manner.

She remembers quite vividly how she was burned even though it happened when she was only 5 years old. She and a friend were dancing around the Christmas tree and she brushed against a flaming candle, which ignited her dress. She said that in those days one did not go to the hospital for such things and that a local doctor, and many nurses, treated her at home and this is where she stayed.

An only child, her fond parents gave her a tremendous amount of attention. Some of her early recollections are that her parents tried very much to encourage her to have a normal life and that they pushed her a great deal to be assertive and to get out with people. She prefaced this remark by saying that she felt that they pushed her more than she wanted. Upon entering school, she was teased a lot by other children. This was rather upsetting to her and she had a desire to quit and stay at home, although here again her parents would not allow withdrawal. She recollected that in 1918 she first went for plastic surgery.

She acknowledged the fact that she was very depressed and used to have a strong desire to withdraw from relating to people but received a great deal of support and encouragement from friends. At the time of our follow-up interview, she said she was particularly self-conscious about her appearance and hates to go to big parties and meet new people. She said that most of this has developed since it was discovered three years ago that she had skin cancer on her face. She had had three operations for this, which left some white blotches on her face.

She stressed that her parents' pushing her had caused her a lot of conflict and she had had some psychotherapy in adolescence. This was around the time of her coming out as a debutante, when she was apprehensive about going to the parties and balls. She said that her doctor was helpful and supportive to her during this time and that he would tell her parents which affairs she should attend, thus enabling her to avoid situations where she would be confronting many new people. (She used to enjoy masquerade parties, where she could wear a mask and not feel conspicuous.) The doctor who treated her for pyelitis also gave her a lot of emotional support.

Her education consisted of private day and boarding schools. She much preferred attending the day schools because it enabled her to come home to her own four walls, making her feel more secure. She did not attend college, a fairly typical pattern for girls of her social status. When she graduated from finishing school, she became involved in volunteer work in hospitals. She worked for five or six years prior to her marriage at the age of 24. Over the years she feels that she has done many things that surprise her, that is, things that call for a lot of contact with people, which now is something that makes her very uncomfortable.

Her experiences in the hospitals lately have caused her to develop some very negative feelings about hospitals and she does not want to have any part of them if she possibly can avoid them. She mentioned that after her fourth or fifth surgical procedure for the burns, she began to feel very frustrated and her nerves were on edge. She was always scared and worried about how she would react to the operations and also how things would turn out. It was at this time that she decided that she would not go back for any more reconstructive surgery. She acknowledged that she wishes there were some way of getting rid of the scar tissue and commented that it is just on her face that it bothers her, not on her body, which can be covered up.

When she was an adolescent and young adult she developed an attitude that people would have to accept her for what she was and this type of positive thinking helped her a lot. However, she had worried about whether or not she would ever marry. She went on to say that her husband and four children have been tremendously supportive and made her feel secure. She is a rather dependent woman who needs a lot of support and reassurance. Her family has given her something to live for and without them, she said, she would really have nothing. She also said that marrying into a big family was a great help to her. Her husband's six brothers and sisters have been supportive and involved with her. They and her children and ten grandchildren live in the area. Thus, her life revolves around the family. She also reads a great deal. At the present time, she works one day a week in a hospital bookstore. I commented on her doing this in relationship to her feelings about being in hospitals and she said that she has no contact whatsoever with the patients in her job.

She talked quite a bit about the fact that she sees herself as having changed in terms of personality over the years and said she is more in a shell now than ever before, because of her appearance. However, on two or three occasions she did say that maybe some of her feelings have to do with her age. She thought that as one gets older one becomes more sensitive and has a tendency perhaps to withdraw. She made numerous references to her desires to become involved in areas that did not call for much contact with people. However, it was obvious that the pressures she experienced from her family to become involved with people were the ones that she really responded to.

She talked a lot about her feelings toward other people with disfigurement. She is intolerant of people who feel conspicuous because they have to use a cane or a crutch and said that they do not know what it is like to feel really conspicuous. Once at a social gathering she met a woman whom she was able to identify as someone who had also had plastic surgery for burns. Aside from this and the hospital, she has never seen other burned people, but she did indicate that she has seen a lot of disfigurement in terms of facial blemishes or birthmarks and has a great deal of empathy for people with this problem. When asked whether she had ever been made uncomfortable by people's reactions to her, she mentioned that this has come mainly from children and referred to an incident after World War II when she was in Italy with her family. A number of small children gathered around her and were interested in her appearance. She laughed and said that this was probably a good time to be traveling because one might assume that she was a war casualty. At one point she referred to a friend of the family's child who was in the hospital for burns. She went to the hospital to cheer up the child and talked about her own experience and it made her feel good to be able to give someone else this kind of support. She said that she would be very interested in talking with people who had been burned. However, she again expressed the issue of being uncomfortable in hospitals and emphasized that although she very much would like to make a contribution in terms of working with burn patients, she would not want to do it during their early recuperative period. The parents of many of her nieces and nephews have often asked her to talk to the children about the dangers of fire. She does not mind doing this, but she is not sure that it really has any preventive effect.

Elizabeth is candid about her feelings. She shows evidence of passive surrender in terms of dejection and some withdrawal, and apparently these issues are more noticeable now because there is evidence of active coping during her earlier years. The environmental resources are quite obvious in terms of loving exchanges from her family. Because of her social position and family support it seems that she has not been subject to the harshness of reality experienced by disfigured patients under greater pressures, such as having to earn a living. She has married, traveled, and raised a family, but I think this coping is mainly due to the fact that environmental resources have been quite extensive. She is certainly quite open in terms of talking about her sensitivity about her appearance. At one point she said that a plastic surgeon had strongly recommended that she use makeup, but she claims that if it gets wet it runs, and one ends up looking worse than before. Thus, it would appear that rather than trying to cover up the disfigurement, she is manifesting a tendency to withdraw from social interaction where she would have to be concerned about how she was being viewed by others. It seems that there is a certain degree of overawareness of her disfigurement as is evidenced by the issues of anxiety and a sense of stigma. She seems to have fairly good ego strength, at least that has been manifested in the past, but I would tend to question how effectively she could function if it were not for the supportive matrix of her family. Notable is the resurgent concern about her appearance in recent years; in addition to the burn scars, the aging of her skin and the fear of cancer are stirring up threats to her sense of intactness.

The following is the case of Josephine I., who was burned when she was in her sixties. This interview took place three years later, when she was back at work but experiencing some financial problems, and functioning still within the general framework of her social environment.

Interview with Josephine I.
Josephine is a 65-year-old widow who was burned in a factory fire. She is plain looking and was attired in slippers and a housedress. Her injury was apparent in scar tissue on her hands and arms as well as face and neck; she had also burned her back and broken a clavicle in the fire. She explained that her eyes had not been burned because she had covered them with her hand. It was evident that her nose and ears had not been rebuilt in any way; however, some plastic surgery had been done on her mouth, which she said was smaller than before the fire. She had great confidence in all her doctors and had only positive reports on her care. She had been in for six operations since her initial hospitalization after the fire, but stopped having further surgery because of the pain she experienced on her leg where skin was taken for the grafts. She added that it really did not make much sense for her to continue having plastic surgery, because she was not a young girl, she was not looking for another man. Josephine has had two husbands, both of whom died,

the second one four months before the interview. Later during our talk, she joking-ly hinted that maybe she will find another man. However, in spite of this guise of humor it became rather evident that she is serious and, in fact, her parting com-ment was to repeat that she would like to meet any available older men.

During her hospitalization, she never really thought about death at all but took each day as it came and never gave much thought to her situation. She discussed this issue rigidly, and denial was evident; also apparent was a tendency to repress her real feelings. She mentioned that she was given whiskey every night, only at that time she did not care for it very much. Since then she has developed a taste for it. The issue of drinking came up a number of times, giving the impression that since her injuries she drank somewhat, but not excessively. While she was hospital-ized, her family and friends were very upset and came to visit her a great deal; however, she talked most about her second husband to whom she was married for 30 years.

She referred to him as a rather odd man who, although graduated from high school, never impressed her as being very bright. She viewed the situation by saying, "He worked and I worked and he had his way of life and I had mine." One of the big issues was money. He would often squander it foolishly and, in fact, during the time she was in the hospital he gambled away a substantial amount of the money from her bank account. At first she said that her husband's attitude toward her was not much different after her injury than it had been before. However, in talking further, she did indicate that there had been some very definite changes. She said that he felt sorry about what had happened to her, but selfishly seemed more con-cerned about himself and his own needs. Sexually, their relationship had always been very superficial, and was virtually nonexistent at the time of the fire.

Josephine views herself as a strong-willed woman who does have a temper. She stated that once she has become fed up with an individual, she severs her relation-ship with him. There were many battles between her and her husband, all centered on the issue of money, and, in fact, at one point she actually told him to move out of the apartment. He took up residence in her daughter's apartment on the floor above. She explained that her husband had had a heart attack this past year, and that six months ago he had been able to return to work. However, one evening while driving home he had had another heart attack and become involved in an accident with his car. It was shortly after his death that she learned he had signed over all his insurance policies to his brothers, who, out of pity for her, took care of his funeral expenses. Her bitterness and resentment toward this man were clear. Nevertheless, in many ways she tried to make light of it and actually denied having any negative feelings towards him.

She viewed the fire as something that changed her life, especially with respect to her husband. She had always viewed him as odd but never really understood him until she was hospitalized. Basically, she saw things as going downhill from there on in, but her resentment is somewhat reality-based as it relates to finances.

She currently works five days a week for about four hours a day. It is no great strain for her to go to work, she said, as the bookkeeper for the company lives nearby and gives her a ride. None of her hospital bills have yet been paid because her lawsuit has not been settled; her attitude is somewhat pessimistic as she feels that eventually everything will work out unsatisfactorily. She makes enough money to take care of things, and, in fact, does have savings and is able to save a little more money now. The house belongs to her daughter and they share expenses, which are not very great. She added that she makes her own clothing. She is not living quite as comfortably as she might like to, but she is not under any great financial stress either. She seems to be a rather clever and resourceful woman who is well able to take care of herself.

Initially she denied that her appearance bothered her. She then indicated that it did distress her, especially in the beginning, although her own sisters told her that she looked pretty much the same as she always did. When asked if she had ever looked at any old pictures of herself, she was quick to indicate that she really did not know if she had any except for a wedding picture. When we were discussing appearance, she tended to rub her hands over the area of her face that had been burned. At one point, she began to rub the area of scar tissue that had been covered by the sleeve of her dress, saying, "I don't have to be more beautiful and nobody would want me anyway." She was looking for reinforcement and the way she talked about the relationship with her sisters gave the feeling that she looks for this a great deal. She said that in the beginning she was very concerned about her appearance and that children would notice her. However, no one has ever made derogatory remarks about her appearance. In fact, she said that the children never said anything, but sometimes they made faces. She denies that anything like this bothers her now. She also said that she had not encountered another person with very obvious burns since her accident. She is not really sure how she would react. As far as negative or painful feelings, she said that sometimes she feels nervous and depressed, but relates this to being overtired. Upon questioning she did admit that she does wonder why life turned out for her the way it did.

She seems ambivalent about religion. She does have a certain amount of faith and feels that everyone must, that religion is important but not really that important. She is Catholic, but declared that she is not devout. A subject that tended to come up spontaneously and often was reference to death, but when asked directly she claimed that the issue of death does not really bother her because she has seen a number of deaths in her own family.

Josephine is a gregarious and friendly woman, very much in touch with reality. As far as her defense structure, there was evidence of the usual denial along with repression, some reaction formation, and a tendency toward rationalization. Although in many ways she appeared to have accepted her situation, there is some evidence that she has not completely done this. She is obviously a woman who needs close relationships, such as that provided in a marriage. Her two marriages involved hostile, dependence-type relationships. In both cases she seems to have been the dominant and controlling force, with both men being somewhat inadequate, weak, incompetent, unreliable individuals. She had a very strong dependence, which was highly evident when she talked about needing help from her daughter and grandson upon her release from the hospital; yet, she stated that she took care of herself most of the time and that she really could not rely on anyone else. She said that she had to be self-sufficient because this is what her mother had taught her; she had been the oldest child in her family and so had a tremendous amount of responsibility in bringing up her siblings. She tried to present herself as being a rather happy-go-lucky type of person, emotionally very stable. There is a definite underlying depression here. Some tendency toward avoidance is manifested by the fact that she was extremely verbal and made a point of trying to discuss areas that were not directly related to the burns, and it was often necessary to bring her back to the main topic. This tendency to be distracted was perhaps intentional, but she was very quick and would immediately answer any question and was easily brought back to the specific issue being discussed. She was very responsive to being interviewed and quite honestly enjoyed the attention; she remarked several times at the end of the interview that she was available for more questions anytime.

It is obvious that Mrs. I. has coped with her situation quite well, utilizing excessive denial. While she is willing to express her feelings, admitting that she does get nervous or depressed, she denies that this is related to her injuries. Her tendency to be extremely assertive and gregarious seems to be an expression of an unconscious feeling of "Look at me—even though I look this way, I'm comfortable in relating to people." Here, again, she seems to be compensating for what can probably be viewed as a rather poor underlying self-image and feelings of inadequacy.

The cases presented are mostly examples of what would be called good accommodations. This again relates to the intrinsic measure we have in our follow-up process; we assume that people who are unavailable, have no known address, no telephone, and do not respond to our efforts are making a worse adaptation. This also presumes a value system in which active adaptation, rather than passive acceptance (a tolerant and ascetic life), is best. This goes against Plato and a host of other philosophers, but all the systems for judging adaptation for the multitudes, rather than for selected individuals, would likely be focused on the importance of the social nature of man and the maintenance of communal ties and interaction. Einstein was known to have remarked that the solitude that most people hate and fear was "delicious" to him. Much more common would be the elderly who demand attention and do not acknowledge awareness of physical unattractiveness, like a dried up 90-year-old man who has numerous senile keratoses on his face, lipomas, and some scars from removed epidermoid skin carcinoma. He pursues his grandchildren to kiss him whenever they meet, despite their tendency to be physically and emotionally repelled. The earlier-mentioned hurt feelings of disfigured mothers whose children don't kiss them is related.

We had some reports from surgeons about patients who withdrew from treatment and disappeared, but we were unsuccessful in tracking them down. Some depressed people had made suicide attempts, but we had no data about them when they grew older. Except for Francis D., all our examples were of people who were working and had succeeded in maintaining affectionate interchanges with the people around them, and resisting social disengagement with different degrees of success as they grew older.

MAJOR TRAUMA NEAR RETIREMENT AFTER LIFELONG ADEQUATE ADAPTATION

Interview with Rudolph P.

Rudolph, 65 years old, was burned three years ago when a gas leak on the floor below his office was ignited, causing an explosion. He sustained burns to his face, head, arms, hands, and torso, with resultant contractures in his hands and axillae.

Rudolph, a friendly, soft-spoken man, relates in a spontaneous manner. His hands are rather deformed, and there is evidence of scar tissue on his lower arms, forehead, right eyelid, nose, and the top of his head. The skin on top of his head is still tender and when he goes out in the sun he must wear a hat. He mentioned that he must wear rubber gloves whenever he handles any kind of detergent or harsh chemical. He stated that appearance was not really an issue of importance to him, especially since he feels that it did not turn out that bad. He joked about having lost his hair, commenting that he now parts it in the middle. He views his attitude as a very positive one, stating that one has to help himself, take the good with the bad. Discussing the extent of his burns, he voluntarily took off his shirt and began to explain the surgical procedures that had taken place. He was especially anxious to show me the areas where the grafts were taken and said that the greatest amount of pain was experienced not from the grafts themselves but from the donor areas.

In the months in hospital he never asked for any medication other than what was given to him, saying that medications made him lose touch with everything and only periodically be aware of things. He knew many people had come to visit him, including his wife four days a week, as well as various friends, neighbors, and co-workers, but he recalls almost nothing of these visits. He thinks that nature has its ways—when one is suffering a great deal the mind blots out the pain of physical suffering. He talked about hallucinating, talking to laundry bags in the hallway, and not really knowing what was happening to him. He went on to say that it was months before his mind came back to him. He was totally dependent on others for care, and his hands, arms, and head were completely bandaged during this period. He was unable to do anything involving the use of his hands, including caring for basic bodily functions. He seems to be a very independent man who was quite threatened by his inability to function autonomously. He also experienced some sensory deprivation in terms of his inability to use his hands for contact with the environment.

At the time of his release after his initial hospitalization he was highly ambivalent about coming home because his forehead was breaking out with pus pockets because of the graft and his head was covered with silver nitrate scales. He acknowledged that his appearance was frightening to him and certainly was upsetting to his wife. These problems had to be cared for, but he did not feel that it was really fair that his wife should do it. However, his doctor discouraged him from going to a nursing home or rehabilitation center, and encouraged him to return directly home and indicated that a visiting nurse would be made available. Rudolph said that this was the case, but nevertheless his wife still had to do most of the caring for him.

While he was in the hospital financial hardship was no great issue for them since he was receiving full pay and all hospital bills were being covered by insurance.

He did not return to work for 55 weeks. During this time he underwent four more surgical procedures for his hands and axillary contractures. He stated that he never worried about going back to the hospital because he had a great deal of confidence in his surgeon and felt that there was a purpose for each operation. For example, he could not lift up his arms very far unless they were operated on.

In talking about some of the physical problems that developed because of the burns, he said that mucus sometimes runs out of his nose and he cannot feel it. He makes a point of trying to be alert for it because it will happen just while he is eating or in other delicate situations and he finds this embarrassing. He also wears glasses now, and it is necessary for him to wear dark glasses out in the snow or bright sun. He feels very fortunate that he did not lose his sight. He is preoccupied with issues of care and being very cautious not to do any harm to himself. On two or three occasions during our interview he commented that he has to be careful.

He acknowledged that there were times when he became rather depressed, especially during his long recuperation. After he had been out of work for approximately 55 weeks, his surgeon urged that he try to go to work again. He said that he was very happy and felt like a new man when the company doctor who examined him told him that he could go back to work at the gas company the next day.

When he did go back, things were not quite the same as they had been in the past. During the year that he was out, he had been assured that his job would be waiting for him when he came back. However, when he returned, he was put on a rotation shift, which upset him. He pursued the issue for about a year after his return to work and was finally put back on the day shift on a regular basis. He retired at the mandatory age of 65. At the time of his retirement he was in the position of supervisor, and his feeling was that he was not really ambivalent about retiring because of the gradually increasing pressure experienced in the job. He said that he likes being home very much and that there are many things for him to do there.

In discussing the kinds of things that had helped him through this difficult period, he said that people were very good to him. He has saved all the get-well cards he received and from time to time will take them out and look at them. His major concern has been his inability to lift his arms; however, he feels that he is very fortunate that things turned out as well as they have. He sees himself as having to be more patient now because doing things with his hands takes longer. He indicated that another very positive experience for him was getting his driver's license back. During the time that he was recuperating his license expired and he knew his eyes were affected so he did not think he would be able to renew it. However, after being fitted for glasses he had no trouble passing the eye test. This made him feel very good because driving is something he likes to do.

When asked about his feelings in relationship to fire or danger, he said that he really never thought about it and pointed out that if he had, he would never have gone back to work for the gas company. He was burned at age 62 after working for the company for over forty years. Undoubtedly if he had not gone back at that time he might have lost a great deal in terms of retirement benefits.

Like many other former patients I have interviewed, he said that he had a chance to see many other patients in the hospital who were much worse off than he. He mentioned that on a couple of occasions when he went back to the hospital, the staff would have him talk with younger patients who had similar burns, to try to reassure them that things would work out all right.

He feels that he is a bit more short-tempered now but attributes it to age rather than his accident. He also commented that he does not smoke or drink any more. Before being burned he used to smoke two packages of cigarettes a day, but in the hospital he could not hold a cigarette because his hands were bandaged. He said that he lost the taste for smoking and has not smoked since. He described himself as having been a moderate drinker, but now the only time he has a drink is when he and his wife go out to dinner or visit friends.

Rudolph is a personable man of average intelligence who, from all outward indications, has adapted very well to his situation. There is evidence of some tendency toward repression, rationalization, denial, and reaction formation. He seems to have a fairly flexible ego style and a good sense of humor. Certainly environmental resources in the form of medical personnel, loyal friends, and adequate finances have played an important role in his adjustment to disfigurement. Loving exchanges in terms of receiving fondness from friends and relatives seem to offset greatly any rage that may exist. He is Catholic, and though not considering himself a religious man, he does have faith in God and feels that this played a role in his getting well. There seems to have been a balance between the mental and physical modes of adjustment, with not too much emphasis in either area. He derived little in the way of secondary gains from his injuries.

He denies having any negative feelings toward the person who inadvertently ignited the gas, but rather feels that the gas company was at fault since the leak had been present for a couple of days and could have been taken care of earlier. Autonomous living plays a very important role in his life and one of the most traumatic aspects for him was the need to be totally dependent during hospitalization. He makes a big issue out of being able to do things for himself in spite of the difficulty he has using his hands. His adaptation and adjustment are good. There is no evidence of significant emotional conflicts and certainly he appears to be coping quite well with his situation.

In tracing what has happened to physically disfigured people, I have followed a few themes and concepts of personality development. My fellow interviewers and I subscribe to Wright's idea that physical abnormality as a "physical fact is not linked in a direct or simple way to psychological behavior" [4, p. 371]. She feels that there is no clear proof that impaired physique produces a standard response in overall adjustment and we concur. What I have been stressing is that facial disfigurement has a special import in the social and psychological world, and takes on important status in each stage of the life cycle. And each phase of the life cycle may be examined from Waelder's perspective of a parallelogram of forces in which behavior is not the result of the "all-pervasive motive, but the outcome of many usually conflicting forces . . . a slight shift within the contending forces can result in radically different behavior, just as a change in the vote of a small fraction of the electorate can lead to the adoption of an entirely different policy" [5, p. 9]. It was this kind of thinking that led our group to try to use a concept of different axes of adjustment (Table 1) in these situations at different ages. It was clear that normality prior to the injury not only was too complex and elusive a concept to lean upon, but it also was misleading, because some of our patients had the same traits before and after their injuries. What we sought were the features that left people, in Cox's [6] term, *going concerns*, so that they could respond to other people, continue to derive some gratification from their own lives, and make some contribution to the lives of the people around them.

The older person more obviously responds to the threat of death and the termination of his life. But most of the patients in our series had to face the threat of death after the original traumatic injury and in each of their courses of treatment and surgery. While this was not the primary focus of our examination, our sample did not yield people who talked of dying or wanted to end it all. The attitude reflected may have been coupled with escape from medical care, social withdrawal, and an unmeasured number of actual suicides. What we did see was a need to come to grips with the changed balance of forces, accompanied by constriction of psychological awareness and experience, to adjust body image and self-concept, and to reestablish a sense of personal worth [1].

With disfigurement we are dealing with an accommodation that requires continuing effort. Many styles of coping relate to complex personality patterns for managing catastrophe and alterations in the body image. Some of the interplay with the family and the medical care system will be explored in subsequent chapters.

REFERENCES

1. Cameron, N. Neuroses of Later Maturity. In O. J. Kaplan (Ed.), *Mental Disorders in Later Life.* Stanford University Press, Stanford, Calif., 1956.
2. Erikson, E. H. *Insight and Responsibility: Lectures on the Ethical Implications of Psychoanalytical Insight.* Norton, New York, 1964.
3. Goldwyn, R. Personal communication, 1975.
4. Wright, B. A. *Physical Disability: A Psychological Approach.* Harper & Row, New York, 1960.
5. Waelder, R. *Basic Theory of Psychoanalysis.* International Universities Press, New York, 1960.
6. Cox, R. D. *Youth Into Maturity.* Mental Health Materials Center, New York, 1970.

7

Psychiatric Care of Burn Patients

The complexity and severity of problems confronting patients hospitalized for severe burns are so intense that their treatment is distinguished from the general management of the sick. The problems of psychological care and the management of both burned adults and burned children are combined here because they are basically similar. In fact, the more dramatic presentation of the issues in burned children make them striking models for the adults.

ROLE OF THE PSYCHIATRIST

Bellak [1] made clear that all illnesses seem to involve some expression of anxiety, regression, and depression. *Anxiety* refers to the apprehension of an experience that will be harmful to the patient, and is distinguished here from fear as a similar psychological response to an objective and justified threat. Burn patients are fearful of their actual suffering and their realistic expectations of very painful procedures; these reactions overlap with anxious concerns about dangers that are unknown or unrecognized, conscious or unconscious. In children this is apparent and more intense because of the greater instability of their emotional reactions, the intermixed separation anxieties, and the lesser comprehension of the events surrounding them. However, vis-à-vis the adults, these are distinctions of degree rather than a qualitatively different experience.

125

Regression is more obvious in children, in the sense of going quickly back to earlier forms of behavior, such as stuttering, enuresis, and soiling, but it is also clearly apparent in the adult burn patient who is helpless and requires others to care for his products of elimination and clean and feed him. The major emphasis here is on the importance of understanding the degree of regression in adult patients, which many hospital staff have trouble recognizing and accepting.

The *depression* seen in both adults and children is profound at some point in a severe burn. This is sometimes ignored in children; some psychiatric theorists assume it to be only a minor issue or difference in the child's psychological structure. However, our observations of hundreds of children on the wards lead my colleagues and me to conclude that children of 4 years and upward manifest quite clearly the outward signs of conventional depression, with dejected faces, psycho-motor retardation, and withdrawal from their environments, along with hopelessness, crying, irritability, and emotional depletion. For children and adults there is an overlapping between depression and *grief*, a realistic sadness or melancholy in reaction to and proportionate to what has been lost. Of course, these patients have lost so much—loss of home, separation, the deaths of others in the injury, family disruption, income loss, and so forth—that grief pervades the picture.

The role of the psychiatrist in this has been reviewed by Lipowski, who said that the liaison psychiatrist "often serves the unserved, by helping to ensure the identification and appropriate management of mental and emotional aspects of illness throughout the hospitalization" [2, p. 624]. This whole approach has derived conceptually from an old tradition in the humanities.

At the Shriners Burns Institute, patients are cared for by a team headed by a surgeon that regularly includes a psychiatrist, social worker, and psychologist. In the first days after admission, while attention is focused on survival issues, the psychiatrist can help in getting to know the family and the circumstances of the injury and in building clear pathways of communication with the family. For the succeeding few weeks, an atmosphere of great anxiety about life and death persists. During this time parents need help in coping with the child's tragedy and planning for the future. The child and his parents need to have their communications monitored so that they do not become confused by the vague rumors about what is going to be done to the patient. There follows a long period of hard, repetitive work, with skin grafting, infections, intermittent isolation, feeding problems, bathing, repeated debridement, painful dressings, and the enlistment of the child's co-operation more actively in the therapy plan. Casts, skeletal traction, ambulation, and physical therapy are all used, and the associated despair, psychophysiological depletion, intermittent hyperactivity, and disruptive behavior produce problems of management that intimately involve the psychiatrist.

After months in the hospital the child begins to expand his life space and to think of long-range plans and of returning home. Families need help in preparing for the return of their damaged child, and in planning for the protracted period of further graft revisions and surgery for contractures that follows.

Throughout the hospital course the nurses are in most frequent contact with the patients and need the most support from the psychiatrist through formal conferences, group meetings, and individual consultations. The psychiatrist serves as a facilitator of communication between staff members at all stages of treatment and works with the morale problems that inevitably crop up after months of stressful, minimally rewarding work. No other aspect of nursing requires the staff to inflict so much pain on children in the course of necessary care. According to Galdston [3], surgeons and nurses say, "There is nothing worse than caring for a burned child." This complaint is made with pride and despair in appreciation of how the need to provide the indispensable care taxes and penetrates the depths of one's own being. An outstanding feature of the process is the extent of intimate contact between the caring person and the child.

Although the issue of human contact is a profound one, most mental health efforts shortly after burn injuries are overshadowed by the issues of shock, cerebral defect, pulmonary burn complications, and electrolyte imbalance, and psychiatric intervention is usually called for in regard to toxic psychosis, brain dysfunction, coma or lethargy, insomnia, hallucinosis, and confusional states.

The image of the psychiatrist needs to be clarified. He is generally viewed as "permissive," with the expectation that he will ask the nurses to tolerate bad manners, sex play, and deteriorating behavior. The nurses may become angry about truculence, which they feel they are expected to permit, when, in fact, the psychiatrist is on the side of firm limit-setting to help the nurses and also to reassure the children about controls in order to augment their own impaired regulatory abilities.

The tempo, the disparate people involved, the focus on technique and mechanical problems, along with needs of professional people to defend themselves against being upset by the burned children, all conspire to reinforce repressive mechanisms. It falls to the psychiatrist, through his own demonstrated attitude and his strategically placed comments and teaching, to make subjective interpersonal issues remain a conscious part of the treatment program.

The role of the psychiatrist is always challenging and usually must be an active one in order to be effective in this situation. His psychodynamic statements should be clear and his theoretical formulations, concise. The focus of the work shifts from the patient to his family, to his doctors and nurses, and includes teachers and physical therapists who are involved in his care. For some of the children conventional psychotherapy is indicated, but for the majority the psychiatrist should utilize his knowledge to counsel parents, consult with caseworkers and nurses, and advise other physicians. Hypnosis, drugs, play therapy, environmental manipulation, and education all have their place in this work. Methods of approach are necessarily flexible, but a consistent effort must be made to translate the attitudes toward handling burned children and their families from irate or moralistic opinions into psychologically aware professional positions, and this requires giving knowledge and continued support to the staff, which enable them to apply the information during the arduous course of burn treatment.

IMMEDIATE CARE

In the immediate care situation the psychiatrist can be an agent of clear communication for the staff and the family. He can assess parental reactions to the disaster and help them to cope with it. At the same time, he can share his understanding of the family with the staff so that they can adapt the timing and style of what is being told to the family. This establishes the psychiatrist as part of the team for later work with the family and gives him basic knowledge about the particular situation from which to work.

Seligman, MacMillan, and Carroll [4] did not isolate specific emotional factors in the survival of severely burned children. In their investigations no one trend or overall grouping to distinguish survivors from nonsurvivors was evident. Trends became elusive and patterns did not emerge. Previous work suggesting withdrawal as a survival mechanism seemed contradicted by this study [5]. Further research likely would clarify that both withdrawal and protest-type behaviors have an adaptive role, depending on other interrelated factors, including the timing of the behavior, other losses and their timing, and parental responses.

Seligman, MacMillan, and Carroll describe three possible trends for survival, excluding the obvious issue of burn extent and depth: (1) a poorer prognosis in preadolescents who lose a parent of the same sex and are close emotionally to the surviving parent, (2) a better prognosis in those with protest behavior and psychosomatic responses, and (3) a better prognosis for children with hopeful parents. Grasping at hope, parents often focus on the fight for life a desperately burned child makes: "Tony is really hanging in there," or "He certainly is trying." Larger series are needed to explain the significance of this in survival; it may be only a cultural attitude that effort will prevail.

THE MIDDLE PERIOD

In the burn unit the middle period is one of false hopes and magical optimism alternating with apathy and dread. It is the period for skin grafting, low-grade infections, fevers, intermittent isolation, and the beginning of playroom and school activity. Certain doctors are endowed with charisma; staff and patients feel that if things are not going well they will be set right by a particular surgeon or pediatrician. Occasionally the psychiatrist evokes this feeling if he does something dramatic, such as hypnotizing a child to relieve the terror of dressing changes. As part of the burns unit team, the physical therapist begins to take second place in importance only to the surgeons during this middle period. The staff's expectations of the patient's and his family's behavior crystallize at this point, if they have not already. There is a diminution in nursing flexibility and slackening attentiveness to the nuances of the patient's adaptation to the ward. The child's situation has been categorized "good," "hopeless," or "difficult." At this time, any obnoxious behavioral manifestations, which before were tolerated in the interest of survival, begin to cause irritation and can lead to an angry staff request for psychiatric consultation. It is also a period when most burned children begin to manifest depression.

By this time the psychiatrist or social service, or both, have made a comprehensive assessment of the family unit and their interaction with the hospital environment. The consultant psychiatrist must also discern any covert staff disagreements, i.e., orthopedists arguing with plastic surgeons about how to release contractures, or nurses feeling that the surgeons are too abrupt in changing dressings. This period often coincides with increasing pain for the patient as scar contractures are being stretched and rigid joints mobilized by the physical therapists. The staff shows relief when they feel that the consultant is going to *do* something. Supporting the child can be the assignment of a psychologist, resident in psychiatry or pediatrics, social worker, or volunteer. We found that nurses could later take over more of this. Also during this time there may be a change of house officer and nurses owing to routine staff rotation. Brazelton, Holder, and Talbot [6] stressed that continuity of one person attending to the patient and his family is essential for best overall care, yet this is frequently absent. The child psychiatry resident, a few nurses, and the child psychiatry consultant may be the only ones to remain. Hence, the psychiatrist can serve significantly to resolve further discord about changes in the style of management of the case. The child psychiatrist should support the staff, foster a unified group approach, ensure that the family is kept informed, and synchronize the team of social worker, play lady, and psychotherapist. Weekly rounds led by the psychiatric consultant with as many people from all disciplines as possible can be an invaluable asset to maintaining the unified group approach. These also serve well as a forum for teaching about children's reactions to illness. They can be the occasion for anticipating problems, pointing out that immobilization of an active youngster can lead to rage and depression, and that exposure of a child to the death of another child on the ward will produce deep reactions, even if not expressed, and can be traumatic. This is the period when the consultant may not be directly asked for his opinion or he may be taken for granted if things go well. His notes in the chart may not be commented on. The surgical staff tends to delegate problems of mental functioning and social adjustment and not be burdened by them, but when they become alarmed at some medical or surgical reverse or some social obstacle to the medical program, they want to have the psychiatrist's opinion immediately. If the consultant does his job well, things run smoothly and crises are avoided, and the psychosocial work is relatively invisible.

Proper handling of some specific aspects of treatment and the patient's feelings during this middle period can be crucial and warrant special attention.

The Physical Therapy Tub

The beginning of physical therapy baths, which usually are given daily, burdens the child with several specific assaults. The child is obliged to reveal to himself and to others the extent to which the surface that encloses his body has been destroyed. He is required to watch as blackened bits and pieces of himself float away into the bath water. Warming the treatment room, playing music, storytelling, and providing bath toys for diversion have proved helpful in supporting the child, and the attendance of a male burn technician has been helpful in attenuating the intensity of the experience. The bath is warm and the child is tended by nurses who support him in what he remembers as an experience of particular closeness between his mother and himself. Having male aides also makes the nurse feel backed up, and in several hospitals in different countries the nurses spontaneously say it is more like a normal family.

The bathing of the burned child produces intense, rapid, and extreme changes in affect and behavior. The sudden shift from shrieks of anxiety and pain to bouts of joyful water play is perplexing. The change from accusations of attempted murder to cooing proclamations of love is disconcerting [3].

Isolation

Visits by volunteers, aides, and others to the child who is isolated in a life island, an antiseptic room, or a bacteria control unit can be very helpful if they are willing to read to the child for long periods of time without expecting any return in understanding or gratitude. It is the voice of a real live present person to which the child responds. The child in isolation can stay mute and immobile while a television set is on, but he may be prompted to react to a person. Television is fine if used properly, but it is a poor substitute for active participation and human contacts.

Management During Dressings

A continuing problem is the necessarily painful dressing changes that are such a regular part of burn care. The fear these engender spreads across the ward in the course of dressing time. Dressing teams in a number of hospitals in Europe and the United States have found it helpful to use experienced people who work as quickly as possible. There are several important issues: The staff needs to be strong enough and numerous enough to move the child swiftly. They need to accept the fact that they are causing pain, and they need a place to express their guilt and anger over this. They need to be consciously schooled in the avoidance of counterhostility toward the children, who rage and curse at them in their own terror, pain, and fury. This requires that experienced nurses make this a conscious focus for discussion and that the psychologist and psychiatrist be involved in these discussions.

The pediatricians and surgeons also need to be involved to work out the best combination of medications for pain and anxiety, so that the child receives enough help well in advance of the actual procedure to feel more relaxed and to have some analgesia. It is also important that the staff *expect* a drug effect, so that they can proceed with more confidence. This is not merely suggestion, but part of the expectancy set. The effectiveness of hypnosis for dressings depends greatly on the expectancies of the patients and the nurses [7]; the use of hypnosis is discussed later in this chapter.

The staff needs a plan for managing difficult children and must have a sense of professional control to make it work optimally. Control is never easy for patients with severe burns because treatment always causes pain. However, we have found that when properly managed patients show little leftover rancor toward the nurses and attendants. In the beginning we kept our physical therapist from participating in the adolescent discussion group because she was involved in causing so much pain, but we found that the children were quite realistic about her duties in spite of their shrieks and accusations during the actual debridement in the tubs, and accepted her as a co-leader of their group quite readily.

Mealtime

During mealtime, child patients need supervision, help, encouragement, and patience, with foods they like and company. Resistance to eating is almost universal because of malaise and the fact that eating provides one of the few areas in which children can resist or express anger.

Emotional Needs

In consideration of the significance of the healing process, the concept of holding described by Winnicott [8] has been useful. The burn makes holding a child impossible, for the skin has been destroyed and the pleasure of its sensation has been turned to pain. The staff must provide the child with support, physical contacts, rocking, stroking, and patting. Their skill and ingenuity in offering themselves is important—there is a strange desire some patients show to have their ears cleaned to make contact. Being held in hydrotherapy, fixing hair, and holding hands or feet, all can be useful.

As a rough estimate some clinicians consider that the period of a turning point in prognosis comes around the time when half the burned area has been covered with grafts. Occasionally, dramatic improvements in emotional status occur as soon as the patient learns that most of his burned area is again covered with skin.

Jorgensen and Brophy [9] emphasized that in this period, which they designated the *recovery phase*, they have found psychotropic drugs and analgesics to be helpful along with aversive conditioning to deal with depression, grief, and hostility. Formal individual psychotherapy also is ameliorative here.

In this environment it is natural for the nurse to take an active role in the personal side of the patient's care, and a lot of personal attention goes out to these patients, both adults and children. In fact, Vigliano, Hart, and Singer [10], Woodward [11], and Jackson [12] seem to feel that the physician is unsuited to this role, and that while doctors can be sympathetic, their role and time commitments dampen this approach as does the pattern patients and their families have of seeing the doctors as threatening authorities. Nurses often take the initiative in directing attention to special needs of patients, in charting and controlling the depth of the unavoidable depression, and in bringing the verbal productions of the patients to the mental health workers. Nurses can regularly report to the psychologist, psychiatrist, social worker, pastoral counselor, or pediatrician who is involved. Some of the therapeutic assistants available in these settings are discussed in the next chapter.

Hamburg, Hamburg, and deGoza [5] noted that after four to six weeks, the emergency, protective defenses of the acute crisis period diminish, and a transient increase in depression may occur. They emphasized that patient concerns at this stage of treatment are summarized by three questions: (1) How long will I have to suffer this way? (2) How can I maintain a sense of personal worth? (3) How can I enhance prospects for recovering bodily functions? The management issues they outlined are the following: (1) mobilize hope for eventual recovery, (2) restore supportive interpersonal relationships, (3) provide boredom-relieving diversions, and (4) facilitate recovery mechanisms by utilizing the patient's ability to help in his own treatment.

A major aspect of clinical reality is a coincident family crisis. Multiple family deaths occur frequently in fires and emotionally tax the surviving members. The expected mourning period may be delayed or take a different form from the usual. Atypical mourning reflects the need of a patient's ego to deal with a more immediate task, namely, his own survival and eventual recuperation.

Hope

One of the most impressive observations in several studies of severely ill patients has been the human capacity to retain hope in the face of adversity. Under the most difficult circumstances, notwithstanding almost overwhelming evidence to the contrary, most people can maintain (if only covertly) the spark of hope that somehow, someday the situation will take a turn for the better. These hopes primarily concern a patient's physical condition, but also involve his interpersonal relationships. On the whole, this is one of the major sustaining forces in the midst of personal crisis. It is, in large part, a derivative of the patient's previous experience and perhaps of innate forces as well. It is also, however, influenced to a considerable extent by the attitudes of those in the patient's current environment. This remarkable capacity may on occasion lead to trouble, since some patients may retain fantastic hope of changes that are impossible. The maintenance of these implausible hopes may impair the patient's cooperation in realistic measures. The patient then crumples into despairing uncooperativeness with its attendant problems.

Hypnosis

At both Shriners Burns Institute and Massachusetts General Hospital poor eating and pain produced calls for hypnotic intervention, though we also use hypnosis to encourage ambulation and increase cooperation in physical therapy procedures. Underlying these requests are pleas to give hope to staff and patients. We have had the opportunity to observe the use of hypnosis in several contexts: (1) at the Burns Institute, (2) in Massachusetts General Hospital's pediatric intensive care unit, and (3) in Massachusetts General's adult burn ward. In each setting we have noted a familiar series of events. Hypnosis is usually requested by surgeons to help manage uncooperative patients. Prior to this request an atmosphere of discouragement along with a sense of imminent doom in regard to management and outcome had developed on the part of the nurses and the medical and pediatric staff. The problems of the staff are essentially those of chronic latent anxiety and tension.

A major factor in the care of burn patients is the impasse in which nurses find themselves because they must repeatedly cause pain. This is exacerbated in the care of children, and nurses often feel incompetent when parents observe the reactions of their children, whether silently or critically. The undercurrents of anger are intense and provoke guilt in the staff. This is tempered with adult patients, whom nurses exhort to be courageous, but it is less successful with children, who seem to be more helpless and cannot be expected to be stoical. Adolescents may fall in either category or vary between adult and infantile, adding to the uncertainty and feelings of staff and patient discontrol.

The official and unofficial sharing of information and undercurrents of feeling about patients establishes an atmosphere on each ward. Staff members hunger for specific procedures for improving morale, controlling patients, and changing the direction of a patient's course. Most new staff members, particularly the nurses, subjected to screams for mercy during dressing changes, helplessness, irritability, and fear of death, have undergone a depressive and hopeless reaction within months after they come to work in the unit.

Years ago we demonstrated hypnosis to the nurses and medical staff, first describing our technique of induction to them and the children and proceeding to hypnotize several patients. In the beginning exhibitions of hypnosis were carried out using a volunteer nursing student, and this had a dramatic effect on the staff and led them to cooperate with the new method. Usually I would take two or three weeks at a time to ensure good subjects and to extract as many reinforced positive attitudes as possible. The original results were striking. Hypnosis was suggested as a technique that would help in special situations. Public attitudes toward hypnosis made all of the nurses and some of the doctors expect almost magical transformation in mood, cooperativeness, pain tolerance, and appetite. Discouraged nurses approached patients with a new enthusiasm and positive expectations.

This interacting reinforcement between nurse and patient enhanced the efforts of the hypnotist to suggest other improvements to patients. Individual patient and staff morale improved. In spite of repeated efforts at realistic discussion of its limits, hypnosis became a popular device and considerable interest in it developed, with requests for more courses, training of the other staff members, and conferences with the anesthesia service, surgeons, and pediatricians. Enthusiasm for psychology peaked. Staff nurses began to make private requests to be hypnotized to cure smoking, lose weight, manage frigidity, and erase personal anxieties. Despite all efforts to be logical, nonsecretive, and scientific, there was always an aura of magic and secrecy about what was being done hypnotically. Inquisitive nurses and doctors kept "accidentally" walking in during inductions.

After this had gone on for many months, failures with hypnosis occurred. The children did not respond as markedly as they had, the nurses did not expect as much, and few of them remained nonsmokers or diet-controlled. The professional focus shifted back toward new chemical anesthetics, analgesics, and tranquilizers (see Table 2), while nurses began to feel that they could personally manage many of the patients' problems and much of their agitation, which they considered to be behavioral in nature and hence amenable to skillful nursing care. Etzioni [13] pointed out that nurses have traditionally provided humane care in a maternal tender role, and the selective use of hypnosis, using suggestive magic under the aegis of scientific wisdom and specific technique, helped the nurses to do this. As the confidence of the nurses increased with depressed burn victims, they wanted to assume once more the personal supportive function for the patients instead of merely executing detached technical tasks. Surgeons simply observed that care was running smoothly and special hypnotic interventions were less necessary. The requests for hypnosis decreased.

Marcuse [14] reported that hypnosis is a kind of "expectancy in the form of role playing," which partially explains what occurred in our group setting. As long as the role was clear and positive, the social matrix for reinforcement proved helpful. As the environment became less polarized and less positive, hypnosis seemed less effective. There is no doubt that Ambrose [15] was correct in writing that people who work with children and use hypnosis find it easier to deal with them. It potentiates confidence in relating to children. This is particularly true for psychiatrists in the burn setting. Bandages, isolation units, masks, and charred, desensitized skin all interfere with bodily communication

Table 2. Suggested Shriners Burns Institute Drug Protocol (for Children)

1. Barbiturates: only as specific anticonvulsant medication

2. Sleeping medication: diazepam (Valium) or meprobamate, or both, in adequate doses will remove much of the need for specific additional medication for sleep. An adequate dose is measured by achieving the desired effect. If this is not reached, it is almost safe to assume that the dose can be increased, until specific side effects appear. Generally matters are simplified if a single rather than a combination drug is increased to tolerance. In most situations adequate behavioral control can be achieved with one or two drugs and we generally avoid combinations of agents (such as Demerol, Phenergan, and Thorazine). Medications should be given four times a day, with a double dose for sleep.

3. Valium: a very safe general tranquilizer and sedative. May be started at 2 mg/kg/24 hr (70 mg/m^2/24 hr).

4. Meprobamate: also a safe drug. May be started at 1 mg/kg/24 hr (35 mg/m^2/24 hr), with dosage increased as necessary to achieve desired effect [in children 6 years or older].

5. Chlorpromazine (Thorazine) is also a very safe drug and will at times tranquilize an agitated patient without putting him to sleep when Valium or meprobamate has failed to do so. The initial dose can be 2mg/kg/24 hr, with whatever increases may be necessary in individual cases. Use only with patients over 2 years of age.

6. The need for specific pain and sleeping medicine can be reduced at least 75 percent with effective use of Valium, meprobamate, and Thorazine. The principal value of this switch is that the tranquilizers do not lead to the escalation problem that frequently accompanies both the sleeping and the pain medications. Once an effective dosage of the tranquilizer is reached it will usually remain effective for the patient at that level.

SOURCE: Norman R. Bernstein, M.D., Nathaniel Hollister, M.D., and John Crawford, M.D.

and physical contact. These children have a great need to be touched and constantly request that their ears, nose, and genitals be cleaned. Hypnotic induction with them is particularly easy when there is physical contact because they are so eager for it. Their physical discomfort makes them desperate to escape into the trance state. Once members of the staff begin to see that they can communicate with children in physical ways, they do so and ask less for hypnosis, which is then seen as a competitor for intimacy. The degree of illness definitely makes a difference; all severely burned individuals have a major threat to their lives and undergo exquisite agony, repeated surgery, and many frightening procedures. The multiple traumatic experiences and the massive assaults following 50 to 60 percent burns require forceful coping mechanisms that transcend many of the focused anxieties of patients who seek dental surgery or minor elective procedures. Perhaps it is for this reason that we have never seen burned adults or children panic during induction nor seen staff or patients regard hypnosis as a hazard. Parents have never interfered, if only because the permission required is so much less threatening than that needed for amputations or skin grafting (often with the parents as donors) and hypnosis also lightens the burden of emotional support. "We'll agree to *anything* that will help," parents often declare.

The social context of hypnosis needs to be examined further and the role of novelty explored in order to maintain a high success level. Currently hypnosis is being used intermittently at the Burns Institute, when there are enough new people to be fascinated by it, and to provide a facilitating milieu.

Hypnosis continues to be useful in handling particular patients who are fearful or uncooperative, most frequently now in physical therapy. For example, 13-year-old Joey grieved for his sister who had died in the accident that had caused his burns and rebelled at physical therapy, tyrannizing the new physical therapist. Hypnosis helped him to ventilate his guilt and diminish his provocations.

Barber [16], Rosenthal and Jacobson [17], and other workers in different fields have written about the ways that the expectations of the group in which a particular technique is applied will frequently determine the success or failure of that technique. These group expectations can vary over time in ways that should be examined systematically so that the milieu factors can be comprehensively managed to enhance the use of hypnotic techniques. At the Burns Institute this has been an experiment in nature because we have had the opportunity in a new and separate setting to see how a technique was evolved and to examine the ways in which social factors have extracted different results. The more systematically we can manage these group factors, the more our theoretical and clinical operations can be precisely employed.

LATE PERIOD

During the late period visitors decrease; the child and family are impatient for improvement and news of discharge. The patient may be taken touring around the hospital and spend occasional weekends at home. Contractures from burn scars may require casts, physical therapy, or traction. Skeletal traction for contractures with its visible nails and wires often horrifies the staff, but can be quite gratifying to the patient once he gets used to the sight. It is one of the few medical procedures in which the patient can completely understand the purpose of the devices and can see results as his joints straighten in response. Children also seem able to accept the immobilization surprisingly well. Some children in traction rattle the whole bed, as if their bodily tension overflowed from the limbs to their mechanical extensions in the bed and frame. Children also seem to exhibit themselves, to show off both their disfigurements and their intact parts. The boys aged 11 to 15 seem notably to ignore their nudity before the nurses, to expose their genitalia, and to masturbate rather openly. Of course, there is little privacy in such wards. Nurses need support in dealing matter-of-factly with these issues [18].

Woodward [11] has shown a very significant decrease in psychiatric sequelae when burned children under the age of 5 are visited by their mothers daily, as compared with children visited three times a week or less.

The child's regression now appears stable and it requires a concerted effort by the staff, including even the cleaning women, to reestablish the level of responsiveness the child showed prior to his hospitalization. The child struggles to maintain his dependence and to keep all the indulgences and services accruing to his special critically-ill-patient status. The outside world may not seem so desirable; strangers often make shocked comments about his appearance or turn to gasp and stare. Sibling rivalry recurs as the rest of the family's children assert their demands anew. They no longer have to defer to a desperately ill sibling. The world has not stood still waiting for the arrival of the former patient. Often it fears him. The child has to make a basic change in his reactions.

Also during this late period, the staff suffers from the disappointing awareness that with burned children much disfigurement is permanent. An undercurrent of strain for staff members at this time is a wish to be given credit, some acknowledgment of all the effort that has gone into the child's therapy, though they rarely mention it directly or at this time. The staff members saying goodbye to the child and the family often never saw the original, dramatic aspects of the case, but rather the more monotonous, chronic part.

Stabilization of Coping Mechanisms

Hamburg, Hamburg, and deGoza [5] described the ways in which patients cope emotionally. They charted some mental mechanisms used to adapt and illustrated how they are verbalized. Some of these are listed here.

Mental Mechanism	*Observation*
Delusion-illusion-hallucination	Patient says he is not in hospital.
Denial	Patient claims problem is minor.
Repression	Patient does not remember trauma.

Mental Mechanism	Observation
Constriction	Patient focuses on only one part of the problem.
Suppression	Patient's emotions are smothered.

In the experience of Hamburg, Hamburg, and deGoza, the severe injury was the primary emotional stress, but its impact was usually heightened by one or more of the following situational factors: separation from family, friends, and other major sources of gratification; emotionally painful circumstances associated with the accident itself; difficulty in initial hospitalization; disrupting effect of the injury on plans for future life; and effects on family welfare. The adaptive problem was usually further complicated by special, highly personal, sometimes unconscious problems having to do with the patient's interpretation of his injury, growing largely out of his past experience and personality. Prominent among these problems were interference with previously important activities, threat to capacity to be loved by others, conflict over extreme dependence necessitated by injury, tension over handling of hostility, sexual difficulties, and competitiveness and feelings of inadequacy.

Pain
Individual pain thresholds vary considerably as do extent and depth of burn. Our observations indicate that there are no broad truisms applicable to the nature or severity of the pain that the average burn patient experiences. For example, many patients with much full-thickness burn still experienced considerable pain. All our patients were treated with silver nitrate dressings, which are commonly believed to relieve pain once the traumatized areas are covered. Reactions to these dressings were, however, variable. Some patients experienced soothing relief; others complained that the dressings caused an intolerable stinging and burning reminiscent of the pain experienced at the time of their initial injury. Suffering was universally greatest at the time of dressing changes or debridement. Some patients experienced their worst pain in donor sites after autografting, while a few felt very little pain there. Pain threshold and capacity to tolerate pain appeared to decrease over the course of hospitalization. Pain is worsened by anxiety, and anxious expectation of the pain of anticipated surgery is the salient factor in causing its progressive increase. Likewise, patients whose pain reminded them of their initial injury suffered more as a result of the anxiety associated with those memories.

Fears about Deformity and Mutilation

Fears about deformity and mutilation begin to develop after the acute phase of injury has passed. Having passed through the initial shock of injury and having become familiar with hospital surroundings and routines, the burn patient begins to think about the future.

Patients generally harbor fear of cosmetic deformity. This concern, for which there is sometimes little basis, tends to be more commonly discussed among women but is endemic. Many of the concerns about deformity are not verbalized. The nurses hear more of these in passing, as the patients test out responses. However, as described in Chapter 2 on body image, these attitudes are visual, rather intricate, and shifting, so that word descriptions give only a fraction of the fantasies involved.

DISCHARGE PLANNING

Social workers have an important role to play beyond helping with practical, financial, and transportation problems. Their specialized training in dealing with families equips them to serve effectively as counselors for people important in the patient's life. Relatives and close friends can be told that it is normal for burned patients to wonder if they are still regarded positively by those close to them. Patients may test their families with unusual requests or special appeals for attention. In planning for the future, relatives should be encouraged to adopt an attitude that prohibits exaggerated regressive withdrawal, and yet helps the patient accept realistic limitations of future abilities. The patient should be consulted about family decisions regarding geographical moves, children's schooling, and so forth, just as he would be if he were home. The social worker with knowledge of vocational pathways is able to discuss future plans directly with the patient, emphasizing the ability of the patient to be active and constructive, even if this requires considerable change from the patient's former, preburn plans. Regular weekly meetings with groups of mothers have proved a valuable vehicle for exchanging experiences and providing support at this time from other parents who have been through it.

Reentry into Community

The patient and his family are all focused on leaving the hospital. The announcement of discharge needs to be carefully thought out so that its timing supports emotional progress. With emphasis on discharge, the staff can often undo much of the developed trust if future plans are not clearly stated for further contact and return visits. Unless he is clearly told about further treatment plans, the patient sometimes assumes that the staff has given up and finished its job. Often during this phase children talk of becoming nurses or doctors. This transient identification should be used in helping them formulate ways to help themselves, to acquire new skills, and to work hard at further rehabilitation. The staff who have been with the patient and his family all along may have difficulty in separating themselves, and they need not do so. Informal contacts (postcards, letters) and brief visits are rewarding on both sides. The child's school should be contacted and advised about special needs or limitations of the patient. We found that showing photographs of the child helped the teacher steel herself for receiving the disfigured child. This shaped the class response, too.

Whenever discharge was being considered, efforts to improve appearance were frequently noted, especially in young girls. Though somewhat less obvious in the men than in the women, such efforts could be observed in almost every patient. There was a good deal of preoccupation with facial appearance. In one case, the first sign of a period of depression was given when the patient, an adolescent girl, stopped using lipstick.

Resurgence of Apprehension

Before patients go home, a variety of behavior patterns are observed that serve one or more of the following functions: keeping distress within manageable limits, mobilizing hope, maintaining a sense of personal worth, restoring relations with significant other people, enhancing prospects for recovery of respiratory and motor functions, and increasing the likelihood of working out a favorable situation after the limits of physical recovery have been reached.

Bergmann and Freud [19] have written that in spite of the need for "mental first aid" for children in the hospital, no such technique exists. They concluded that "since therapy is carried out within the hospital setting, it has to involve not only the parents of the patient, as in child guidance work, but equally the nursing and medical staffs. Since the approach ranges from the human to the scientific and covers every aspect of the child's life, such as physical health, illness, normal and abnormal mental health, an orientation in these various fields will be essential for the worker, as well as observational skill and a thorough grounding in the essentials of a developmental child psychology" [19, p. 151]. They listed a spectrum of approaches, including working through inevitable trial and error, assuming the mother's basic role of giving comfort, acting as an auxiliary ego, functioning as educator or play therapist, providing a corrective experience, offering standard child guidance treatment, and providing analytical interpretation on rare occasions. The psychiatrist in a burn ward functions in these ways and as a coordinator for the actions of others using these approaches.

Awareness of Long Period of Adjustment

The nurses are the ones most likely to acknowledge and seek help for their angry feelings toward the patients and their apprehension and emotional depletion during the return of these patients to their families, friends, and schools. The covert frictions between doctors, pediatricians, orthopedists, and plastic surgeons about when to have children return for further surgery recur here in making long-range plans.

For a long time after hospitalization, many of the detrimental emotional effects of the burn injury involve both the child and his parents. Woodward [11] found that one out of six mothers sought medical attention for her own emotional reactions after the burned child had returned home. Their self-image as a competent parent was shattered; they found themselves unable to refuse the child any request and were prone to a smothering, overprotective attitude. This "vulnerable child" syndrome is seen when parents really expect their child to die.

Experienced Consultants Vary on Approaches

Hackett and Weisman [20] described four main directives for therapeutic consultation: (1) rapid evaluation of the most pressing psychiatric problems, (2) explicit psychodynamic formulations of the predominant conflicts, (3) proposal of a practical program of management, and (4) active participation by the psychiatrist. These apply to work with burned children, with some modifications. It is more and more evident that the psychiatrist should involve himself at the time of admission, even if he cannot act, because he will be privy to all the interactions that are visible from the very first, both on the side of the family and on the side of the staff in their contacts with the child.

Availability for psychiatric treatment after leaving the hospital is low, as we found that our subjects want to turn their back on the hospital and the traumatic experience. We have met great resistance to arranging follow-up interviews for our studies, though this resistance relaxed a little after twelve months had elapsed. Former patients do not want further entanglement with professionals. All problems are blamed on the physical damage. Referral is more successful when the medical staff clearly agree about further psychiatric care. It should not be merely something thrown in to make the record show a "total care" attitude.

Thesi Bergmann and Anna Freud have commented that "so far as surgery is concerned . . . any interference with the child's body, whether major or minor, is likely to arouse his fantasies and fears with regard to being attacked, mutilated, and deprived of a valuable part of his own self. It makes surprisingly little difference whether the intervention is . . . serious . . . or significant. . . . On the other hand, the differences between major and minor, serious and negligible, which are insufficiently reacted to by the child patient himself, loom very largely in the minds of the medical and nursing staff, who are used to an objective and wholly realistic appraisal of events" [19, p. 136]. In contrast, at the Shriners Burns Institute we feel that the intense, catastrophic, repeated, protracted stresses applied to burned children, coupled with the long absence of parents, and the inevitable fatigue, physiological depletion, and changes in and transient moods of the staff *do*, in fact, make a difference in degree that makes the experience different and ultimately changes the quality of the inner experience.

Hackett and Weisman [20] stated that it is useful to designate systematically four components of conflict: (1) age regulatory functions, (2) predominant emotional patterns, (3) object relationships, and (4) the nuclear elements of wishes and fears within a temporal context. They believe formulations should be down to earth and related to observed behavior.

At the time of this writing the psychiatric endeavors in the Burns Institute cover a variety of formal and informal activities. Table 3 outlines these endeavors. Each Monday there is a conference for individual patient planning, sometimes called the social service rounds. Tuesday there is a staff group run by the psychologist to ventilate feelings about acutely ill children. Wednesday there is the nursing project on interviewing, which the psychiatrist, social worker, and psychologist attend, where videotapes and records are reviewed about the interactions between nurses and children. A mothers' group* and an outpatient follow-up clinic also meet on Wednesday. Periodically on Thursdays the psychiatrist makes walking rounds with the surgical house staff at 7 A.M., and once a month attends the administrative meetings in his role as a division head. The psychologist and the physical therapist run a weekly group for teenage patients. Nurse leaders and the director of nursing have meetings with the social workers regularly to review problems. In addition, informal contacts between all professionals now cover many patient problems, and special meetings are held. Furthermore, any child can have a psychiatric consultation with

---

*Occasionally a father, boyfriend of the mother, uncle, grandmother, even a neighbor, does come, but these are usually one-time occurrences.

Table 3. The Functions of Psychiatry at the Shriners Burns Institute

I. Evaluation of children
II. Clinical care of children
   A. Direct
      1. Psychotherapy
      2. Hypnosis
      3. Drugs
      4. Milieu management
   B. Indirect
      1. Parent counseling, parents' groups, patient groups
      2. Supervision and morale maintenance for nurses and physical therapists; training nurses in patient interviewing
      3. Consultation with surgeons, pediatricians, anesthesiologists
III. Collaborative training in psychological medicine
   A. Surgical residents
   B. Pediatric house officers
   C. In-service training
      1. Nurses
      2. Burn technicians
      3. Aides
      4. Practical nurses
      5. Schoolteachers
      6. Play ladies
      7. Chaplains
IV. Clinical investigations
   A. Follow-ups on adaptive mechanisms of patients and their families
   B. Studies of expectations of plastic surgical patients and their parents and families
   C. Studies of reactions to transplantation of skin (in conjunction with the pediatrics department)
   D. Drug studies
   E. Body image research

a child psychiatry fellow, and cases can be followed by him or a psychology trainee, the director of psychiatry, or a social worker.

This type of consulting work needs to evolve not only in terms of individual children and their families, but also in terms of ripening staff roles, so that teachers, nurses, and volunteers can be deployed flexibly to augment the mental health professionals in patient management.

REFERENCES

1. Bellak, L. (Ed.). *Psychology of Physical Illness.* Grune & Stratton, New York, 1952.
2. Lipowski, Z. J. Consultation—liaison psychiatry: An overview. *Am. J. Psychiatry* 131:623–630, 1974.
3. Galdston, R. The burning and healing of children. *Psychiatry* 35:57–66, 1972.
4. Seligman, R., MacMillan, B. G., and Carroll, S. The burned child: A neglected area of psychiatry. *Am. J. Psychiatry* 128:52–57, 1971.
5. Hamburg, D. A., Hamburg, B., and deGoza, S. Adaptive problems and mechanisms in severely burned patients. *Psychiatry* 16:1–20, 1953.
6. Brazelton, T. B., Holder, R., and Talbot, B. Emotional aspects of rheumatic fever in children. *J. Pediatr.* 43:339–358, 1952.
7. Bernstein, N. R. Management of burned children with the aid of hypnosis. *J. Child Psychol. Psychiatry* 4:93–98, 1963.
8. Winnicott, D. W. *Studies in the Theory of Emotional Development.* International Universities Press, New York, 1965.
9. Jorgensen, J. A., and Brophy, J. J. Psychiatric treatment of severely burned adults. *Psychosomatics* 14:331–335, 1973.
10. Vigliano, A., Hart, L. W., and Singer, F. Psychiatric sequelae of old burns in children and their parents. *Am. J. Orthopsychiatry* 34:753–761, 1964.
11. Woodward, J. M. The burnt child and his family: Impact on the family. Section of Paediatrics. *Proc. R. Soc. Med.* 61:1085–1088, Jan. 1968.
12. Jackson, D. Personal communication, 1973.
13. Etzioni, A. (Ed.). *The Semiprofessionals and Their Organizations.* Free Press, New York, 1969.
14. Marcuse, F. L. *Hypnosis.* Pelican, Baltimore, 1959.
15. Ambrose, G. *Hypnotherapy with Children.* Staples, London, England, 1956.
16. Barber, T. X. *Hyponosis: A Scientific Approach.* Van Nostrand Reinhold, New York, 1969.
17. Rosenthal, R., and Jacobson, L. *Pygmalion in the Classroom.* Holt, Rinehart & Winston, New York, 1968.
18. Rubin, M. Balm for burned children. *Am. J. Nurs.* 66:296–302, 1966.
19. Bergmann, T., and Freud, A. *Children in the Hospital.* International Universities Press, New York, 1965.
20. Hackett, T., and Weisman, A. Psychiatric management of operative syndromes. *Psychosom. Med.* 22(4):356–372, 1960.

8

Burn Care Personnel and Their Attitudes

Surgeons have a crucial role in burn care, but the nurses are the sustaining heroes of a treatment unit. This does not denigrate the importance of physical therapists, pediatricians, and the congeries of other medical specialists, technologists, and supporting personnel who are involved, but the most continued and intimate contact is between the patients and nursing personnel. This is true for both adults and children. The burn ward at the Massachusetts General Hospital has been in operation for many years. With the opening in 1968 of the Shriners Burns Institute, where the children are treated, we had the opportunity to see the recruitment of staff from the first and, through an experiment in nature, to observe the evolution of staff attitudes toward the work, the children, and their families. The following is an account of that experience.

NURSES
When the hospital opened, there was an affiliation agreement that precluded making special financial or work arrangements for burn nurses, even though some prophets had told us that without special "combat pay" or shorter days we could not acquire a staff. The agreement merely assumed the same standards of work and pay for both institutions. With some delight I might remark that we have not only developed a staff but have had a fine group of dedicated young women

(only three in seven years were men, and they did not remain long) along with one male practical nurse.

There have been over 125 nurses during this time. Our turnover has been considerably less than that of Massachusetts General Hospital next door for overall nursing services. There is some selection in the people who choose to nurse burn patients, but in all cases—for those nurses who stayed with the work and for those who sooner or later turned to other aspects of nursing—the job was a very hard and demanding one. During the first months of treatment, the most exacting role falls to the nurses.

The nurses were eager to learn and quite willing to discuss and disclose their reactions to the work. This contrasted with some of the pediatricians and surgeons, who discussed the stresses of burn care only after they had worked together for months and then mostly in brief asides and jokes.

At the end of the first year of operation at Shriners Burns Institute, we interviewed nurses and gave them questionnaires. In following the nurses over several years, I have been able to identify a number of patterns in their behavior. Since the first year, these issues—described below in detail—have been incorporated into the orientation and in-service training.

Idealized Expectation

When the original staff of nurses were first interviewed (see Appendix 1 at the end of the chapter), they expressed enthusiasm for all aspects of the work they expected to do and the roles they expected to play. They knew that the work would be physically arduous, but they felt that this was an insignificant problem. They expected that in achieving the high level of technical competence and professional specialization required in this field, they also would acquire a prestige as avant-garde nurses.

The pervasively positive and confident expectations manifested by the nurses were in marked contrast to opinions and reactions they heard from outsiders. Without exception, every nurse mentioned the dramatically negative reactions of friends, family, and fellow professionals to her decision to work with burned children. Thus, the nurse who committed herself to this work was doing so in the face of strong opposition and was testing the strength of her own convictions and value judgments.

The nurses did not expect to be seriously upset or threatened about their personal worth and integrity. They confidently looked forward to becoming accepted as lovable authority figures by the children and their parents.

Confrontation and Confusion

At first the nurses were unfamiliar with emergency care techniques. This caused feelings of anxiety and incompetence. The relentless but necessary dressing changes and debridement became a painful task. The reactions of the children were intense; they invariably screamed. Often expressions of fear and anger were directed toward the nurse: "You're killing me," "I hate you."

Although the nurses were accustomed to causing pain in the process of treatment, and anticipated occasional outbursts of anger, the situation with the burned children was a protracted emotional assault. They were depleted by the repetitiveness of the stress, and frustrated by their inability to alter successfully the child's reaction. Most of all, they seemed ashamed and guilty about their own anger at the children's hostility and uncooperativeness.

When individual patient behavior troubled the nurses, they tended to express this in technical, depersonalized terms. All sorts of disturbing actions were referred to as "regression" or "acting out." One boy's episodes of abusive and threatening language was called "paranoia." Questions of "mental retardation" or "autism" were raised about those infants or toddlers who did not respond positively to a nurse's cuddling or playfulness.

Many nurses, as well as other staff members, reported experiencing bad dreams during this phase. These varied from nightmares to bad dreams of threatening destruction to replays of some of the horrible things they had seen on the wards. The dreams related, of course, to the personal lives of the staff members, but would be correlated with deaths on the ward and particularly ghastly visual experiences, such as seeing a 90 percent burn patient with a tracheostomy looking like an anatomical specimen while they had to keep working on the patient's vital functions. These dreams would also recur in veteran nurses when personal experiences or ward events stirred them or stressed them particularly (e.g., the death of a child resembling a sister). There was nothing remarkable about the dynamics of these unconscious events, except that they seemed to affect almost everyone who worked on the burn wards. Teachers and recreation therapists would also report these experiences, pediatricians sometimes, and surgeons almost never.

Ambivalent Identification

Mastery of techniques and routines of burn care was not accompanied by the expected feelings of accomplishment and gratification. Coping with hostile impulses toward the children and feelings of rejection and guilt over producing pain became less avoidable problems and were clearly threatening to the nurses' identity. Some of them said directly, with considerable anguish, "All I do is hurt him. How can he possibly like me or trust me?" One way of dealing with this was to question how real the child's pain was. If faking or overdramatizing were suspected, it obviously would be easier to tolerate the distress caused by a procedure.

Another notion to which many nurses clung hopefully was the belief that "they really know we're helping them even if they don't act that way." There was, of course, some reality to this, but it was difficult to maintain in the case of those children who, even with treatment, would remain severely disfigured and thus never really be cured or "helped." The nurses could incorporate many conflicting feelings about themselves and the children into a framework of an eventual constructive, benevolent outcome despite pain, anger, and disappointment; but if the end result was a damaged product, all the effort and struggles could be undermined. One nurse vividly expressed her ambivalence in talking about a severely burned 2-year-old who, if he survived, could be expected to lead an existence of lifelong agony. Years of hospitalization and reconstructive surgery would still leave him with missing or distorted features and extremities.

As a person you wish they'd go fast and go quietly. I'm just glad I'm leaving, and I won't have to see him when he goes home. You can talk to me until you're blue in the face, but you can't convince me that he's going to be a happy, well-adjusted kid. But then, you really don't know. Maybe he'll be a genius, but as a person, you wish he'd go. As a nurse, you have to do everything you can to save him.

Some nurses projected negative feelings on "outsiders" (i.e., anyone outside the hospital with whom the child came into contact and who responded with rejection) and were overly protective and defensive about the children in their own interactions with others. In some instances, a nurse would show overidentification, acting out to some extent the resentment, humiliation, and despair that the child presumably experienced when he left the hospital. There was a determined, sometimes compulsive effort to recognize and praise any and all positive features in a disfigured child's appearance and behavior.

"Realistic" Resolution

After several months on the job, the nurses showed a notable lessening of the intensity of response to problem situations. Mutual reassurance could be accomplished by time-related distancing. "Remember the trouble we had with that child! Nothing could be that bad." "Look at the difference between the way she used to be and the way she is now— I never would have believed it." Setting of more limited goals and narrowing of involvement became apparent. Some of this was due to practical considerations. On the ward, the nursing duties were suffi- ciently demanding to preclude spending time with a child returning to school, making home visits, or engaging in time-consuming sessions with parents.

However, there was a subjective factor. Although seldom acknowl- edged openly, there seemed to be a recognition by the nurses that even if they had time for these activities, they would not be able to bring about a significant change in the obvious reality. No amount of ex- planation could transform the aversive reactions of strangers toward disfigurement into understanding acceptance. No relationship with a nurse, however close and trusting, could make up for the loss of a previously attractive or normal appearance. No contact with parents, however extensive, could eliminate the anxieties and conflicts they experienced during the child's hospitalization and readjustment. With time there was less diffuse hostility toward outsiders. Instead, a more focused blaming of specific individuals (particularly the mothers of the children) and organizations (local clinics or health services) developed. In general, they settled into a stage of relative outward calm in which unresolved issues had been laid aside and internal conflicts were man- aged by an externalized distinction between the "good guys" and the "bad guys" surrounding the children.

Commitment and Acceptance

After approximately a year, it was surprising to realize that 75 percent of the originally hired nurses were still on the staff, a remarkable figure in contrast to the rate of turnover in general hospitals. It is clear that this was a special group, resulting largely from a self-selection process at the time of hiring. They could be described as more professional, more ambitious, and having a greater tendency toward counterphobic reactions, a greater need to prove themselves, and a more pervasive interest in the psychosocial implications of nursing than the average nurse. Undoubtedly, these characteristics of personality contributed to their staying with the job as well as the manner in which they resolved its challenges and conflicts and arrived at an equilibrium.

At the end of the first year, it was evident that though many of the original sources of threat to individual identities and to smooth group functioning still existed, the nurses were able to confront these prob- lems with considerable flexibility, objectivity, and ability to appreciate gains as well as mourn losses. There was indeed a shared sense of dis- illusionment and cynical acknowledgment of the discrepancies between promise and fulfillment, but this was usually expressed in constructive mutual supportiveness rather than destructive sarcasm. Denial was used in an increasingly subtle and selective manner when the situation demanded the nurse's involvement and participation in ongoing treatment despite the unalterable or hopeless aspects of the child's future. Humor was possible without accompanying guilt.

An attitude of acceptance and understanding developed in relationships of all kinds. The nurse who had barely managed to contain her anger and frustration with a patient, and could not stand changing his dressings once more, or had blown up at an exasperating, overwrought mother, could expect a helpful and tolerant response rather than precipitation of a ward crisis. Many problems could be referred to the social worker or psychiatrist to handle without the nurse's feeling inadequate to the situation.

The candor of the nurses was impressive, as was their unremitting application to caring for the patients and making a good adjustment to them. Nevertheless, the best nurses had limits of endurance, and informal questioning at burn centers around the United States, Canada, England, and Australia seemed to indicate that these nurses endure for about 18 months before turning to other kinds of work, either in nursing or in other fields. The nurses who stay in the work seem to move into teaching and administration, which permits a lessened dosage of direct care responsibilities; however, they continue to demonstrate procedures on individual patients and to work with particular patients they like or families they favor. The situation is comparable to any hospital nursing job, but especially to intensive care units. Also, in the natural course of nursing careers a majority of nurses leave the field and marry, sometimes to return after having children. In other countries the role of the nurse does not appear to be undergoing such rapid professionalization, and the relationship of the nurses to the doctors and to their tasks does not seem comparable.

Most of our nursing staff for both adult and child patients was composed of young women in their early twenties. The core staff tended to be around 30, with a rare few in their forties. All seemed to be influenced by current issues in the community and the new values expressed by youth in our society. As Yankelovich [1] has indicated, there appears to have been some shift in our society, with a new central theme of finding self-fulfillment within a conventional career. The new values he reports extant in the college-educated and the working class involve an alienation from religious establishments, and this was certainly true in our staff. Lack of intense interest in making money is nothing new among nurses, as they have always been expected to work hard for relatively low salaries. However, in sharp contrast to the failed idealism and lack of interest in caring for others that seem so prevalent today, the dedication of the nurses is striking (see Appendix 1). The private lives of many of the nurses were similar to the life-styles of college graduates: their experience with sex, drink, foreign travel, skiing, sunning, and marijuana was not markedly different.

Almost everyone on the nursing staff at some time pondered, "Why am I doing this? I don't need all this grief." This was as common among the long-term staff as among transients. The characteristics of old-fashioned devotion to patient care seemed to be blended with a modern semicynical Weltanschaung, an interest in modern technology, and achievement through mastery of a career in medical technology. There are similarities to the situation described by Hay and Oken [2] for intensive care nurses generally, who bear similar chronic latent anxiety and tension. They related that professional error may be life-endangering. Given the complexity of machines and procedures, a degree of residual uncertainty remains even in the experienced intensive care nurse. Although there is much in which she can take pride, her self-esteem is often threatened. Her patients die, even her major successes are usually still seriously ill and often merely transferred to other wards. The intimacy afforded by the amount and frequency of direct personal contact promotes attachment to the patients. Deaths provide a situation of repeated object loss, the intensity of which parallels the degree to which the nurse has cathected her patient. The special nature of the work and its conditions creates strong group bonds among intensive care personnel. Group loyalty reinforces work pressure in stimulating guilt about being absent from work. The group cannot refuse to accept additional work even when the total work load is unrealistic. This would violate group norms and threaten the shared fantasy of omnipotence linked to the concept of being special and to the defensive denial of anxiety about mistakes. The whole situation lends itself to perpetuation of the status quo and, when pressure becomes intolerable, to the absence of any recourse for the individual but resignation (flight).

PEDIATRICIANS

For adult patients at Massachusetts General Hospital a variety of medical specialists would be called in, but the surgeons felt appropriately competent to manage the fluid balance and special procedure aspects of burn care. At the Burns Institute, there was both a greater availability of pediatric specialists and a feeling that the metabolical status of the burned children was more precarious and that the dosages, heart murmurs, and fluid balance and nutrition issues were different from those of the adults. In addition, many of the surgeons felt uncomfortable with children in terms of gauging their reactions to fever, pain, or an ominous prognosis. Upset parents and shrieking, inconsolable children appalled others. The pediatricians came to work at the Burns Institute for two basic reasons: either they were simply fulfilling rotation as interns and residents, or they were staff pediatricians who had a specialty that was related to burn work, i.e., endocrine dysfunction, tissue regrowth, infection, or renal function. About 30 percent of them were women.

All were dedicated workers, but they all had a different relationship with the nursing and rehabilitation staff than did most of the surgeons. They tended to have longer contacts with the children and more contact with the families, and to discuss more the attitudes of the nurses than did the surgeons. None of them would have designated themselves as burn pediatricians. They presented themselves more as generalists, and they were much more open in discussing their own reactions to disfigurement. Discussion of life and death, whom to let live, where to "draw the line," or when to "pull the plug" was more easily initiated. But ours is a surgical service, where neither the pediatrician nor the nurses would make these decisions. One woman intern openly wept on the ward over a terribly burned child she thought should be allowed to die. He was kept alive, and her reaction was accepted as a sympathetic response that represented the feelings of many staff members. Such conduct in a male surgeon would have been an unforgettable occurrence.

PSYCHIATRISTS, PSYCHOLOGISTS, AND SOCIAL WORKERS

For most of the burn work, mental health specialists would be called in for particular cases (except for me—my office was in the Burns Institute). The original idea was to have trainees in psychiatry, psychology, and social work come over from Massachusetts General Hospital to the Burns Institute to participate in the manifold care, research, and teaching functions. However, it soon became clear that most psychiatrists, psychologists, and social workers did not want to work with burn patients. This was not unique to our location, because in many parts of the United States and in several other countries the same experience has been reported. This was buttressed by feelings that emotional problems are not a big concern while patients are in the hospital.

Nevertheless, the main reaction of mental health workers was one of unqualified horror. They felt that it was terrible work and that they would not be able to comprehend the complex technology of burn care that walled people off from approaching patients. Psychologists and social workers, particularly, felt inadequate amidst the apparatus. It appeared to have exactly the same effect on most psychiatrists, with the exception of the trainees who came through having been internists or pediatricians before becoming psychiatrists. One psychiatry resident, Dr. Nathaniel Hollister, had been a neurosurgeon and immediately set to work on a project to rationalize the use of drugs. There had been a tendency to handle pain and anxiety by polypharmacy. His status as a surgeon gave him a unique position as a doctor straddling both psychic and somatic care. The drug protocol that he helped to develop appears in Table 2 in Chapter 7.

Social workers were easier to reconcile with the work in that their tasks with the families were not much different from their work with families on a medical or surgical ward elsewhere.

Psychologists and psychiatrists expressed a strong feeling of futility: "I have nothing to offer. Their suffering is so much based on reality." While psychologists did do some testing, both for the investigation of body image changes after burns and for the general assessment of the children, who usually had many personality problems before and after their burn injuries, the number who were ready to continue work with the children was small but notable.

All the people who actually plunged into this work found it interesting and stressful, rewarding to both themselves and the patients, counter to their expectations. There were never sharp lines drawn about who should talk to the families or who should talk to the patient or about what would constitute a therapeutic consultation to the staff. Meetings for the ventilation of upsetting emotions or events were regularly scheduled with the professional staff, and meetings with practical nurses, burn technicians, and ancillary medical personnel were held whenever they seemed useful.

PHYSICIANS AND SURGEONS

Discussion of the reactions of the physicians and surgeons followed a format different from that for the nurses. Talks were more informal. Doctors, except for pediatricians who practiced family medicine, did not often come to the scheduled meetings on death, disfigurement, depression, or family problems. This was due in part to the long-standing differences in schedules and styles of practice of various specialists, with the surgeon going from early morning rounds to the operating room, and then to his private office or to the clinic. The discussions were usually casual corridor consultations or carried out over meals and coffee. The doctors were older than the rest of the staff and there seemed to be some of the traditional "officer versus enlisted man" split in that the doctors wanted to show themselves as globally competent. Merton [3] and Becker et al. [4] have delineated many of the important reasons for this, including the defenses of self-protection, maintenance of authority, personal imagery, *machismo*, and the style of medical practice. The majority of the staff both practiced and encouraged this type of separation, usually with some lip service to egalitarianism.

Reactions to Disfigurement

In the development of a professional attitude, reactions to disfigurement play a role. Sporadic responses to the way the burn patient appears occurred among doctors and medical students over time. When a group of medical students were asked about their responses to disfigurement they replied: "I'm shocked, and then I tell myself I shouldn't be and I shift to another gear where I control it." "I try and see if they can talk because that makes it seem better." "I try to imagine what it is like for them to live with it." A female student said, "I am morbidly curious about what they really are like"; an internist overhearing this said, "I just don't like disfigurement and I never have in twenty years of practice."

Another internist, with over forty years' experience, said he did not know how anybody could work with burn victims and thought it must be terrible. A surgeon said, "It bothered me at first; now it doesn't make a ripple in a clinical situation." A plastic surgeon said that he must develop a positive relationship with the person who is disfigured in order to continue the work. If this fails, "they disappear from my view." Other plastic surgeons agreed with this. Another, who had made a television film about a badly burned woman and had worked for many years with burns, said he no longer works with any child patients because it bothers him so much to think of what would happen to the children in the long run. He said the immediate reaction did not bother him. A tumor surgeon stated that he sees plenty of viscera in his regular work. He rarely sees facial disfigurement and finds it disturbing but manageable. He felt that a general surgeon has different issues to deal with. A surgeon said that he developed what he called a callous attitude, by which he actually increased tolerance. He said, "If I go to the operating room regularly it is not a problem, but if I stop going for a while I am shocked and upset when I first go back." He felt that there has to be "a continuing exposure to practice the emotional reactions."

All respondents appeared to describe the affects of familiarity as diverting them from the reaction to the patient. A plastic surgeon said he felt the main job of the psychiatrist in dealing with the disfigured is to learn to show attention to the mutilated people and to feel sympathy. He said that originally he had felt as shocked as everyone else but had trained himself not to have this reaction. A woman said she still feels horrified at seeing disfigured people, but feels obligated to suppress the reaction immediately and try to give them more attention and use a friendly manner.

A very senior plastic surgeon with forty years' experience pointed out the extreme concern about appearance he had heard expressed by blind people, who often worry about how other people see them. He brought this up in terms of blind people who are also disfigured. He described three groups that he sees for face-lifting: (1) Forty-year-old women who feel they cannot compete with other women in attractiveness and seem to respond well in surgery. (2) Women in their fifties who have grown-up children, are wealthy, and see this as part of improving their appearance. They also do well. (3) Fifty- to sixty-year-old women whose husbands are interested in other women and who do this to win them back. These patients generally are dissatisfied. He also pointed out that after a while most burn patients begin to focus on special things they want to have done, describing a patient who was obsessed with having one nostril repaired when she had widespread facial disfigurement.

Interaction with Patients

The dominant and dramatic aspect of care of the burn patient remains under the control of surgeons. Their work and their patterns of dealing with the patients and families have a continuing influence on the care of these patients. Kutner [5] pointed out almost twenty years ago that the surgeon occupies a position of high prestige among members of the medical profession and in the public's view, in spite of the contradictory and increasingly acrimonious complaints about surgical fees, malpractice, and bureaucratic practices being voiced around the world. In the burn center it is clearly the surgeon—whether the plastic surgeon, general surgeon, or orthopedic specialist—who is likely to have the greatest impact on the patient. As Kutner remarks, "The practice of surgery in the teaching hospital has two major goals: service to the patient and the training of future surgeons" [p. 386]. In an institute for specialized care of burn patients, where a variety of specialists are trained and where research is also conducted, this is absolutely a dominating feature.

Kutner feels "socio-psychological problems, the 'human' dimension of surgery, are comparatively peripheral to the mainstream of thought and activity in surgery" [p. 387]. In the highly technical setting of the burn center, extensive explanations are frequently not given to patients despite the fact that "many physicians feel that patients should know much more concerning their ailment" [p. 391]. Kutner notes that the lack of unanimity between nurses, medical personnel, and patients further decreases communication.

Our greatest boon has been the young surgeon's wish to be liked by the staff at large and by the patients in particular and his need to demonstrate his intellectual knowledge and his manual dexterity and courage in the operating room; sometimes this is referred to as "making ego tracks in the operating room logbook."

The way the surgeon behaves vis-à-vis the role the patient expects him to play is important, and this is affected by the belief system and ambitions of the physician who becomes a surgeon. Malt and Grillo [6] showed how knowledge, decisiveness, and confidence rank high in the minds of medical students. The striking style of the surgeons, both in training and in practice, incorporated these "manly" virtues— although altruism and honesty were not lacking—and there seemed to be a continuing need to prove them in a form that was different from that of anesthesiologists, pathologists, internists, pediatricians, and psychiatrists working with the same patients.

At the Burns Institute sometimes a person would be scheduled for reconstructive work without regard to the family or school vacations or jobs, and a squabble would ensue about having it rescheduled. Even if the family was upset, the surgeon would not be interested in talking with them because he felt he had already explained the situation. The surgeon properly is focused on the burn injury, the need for transplantation, the revision of scars, and the techniques involved in these problems. As Friedson noted, "Medical knowledge and procedures are themselves a function of the social character of medicine . . . with institutionally limited experience" [7, p. 277]. He pointed out that the specialist is most likely to see illness and the need for treatment rather than aspects of the patient that are healthy or tangential to his focus. For example, a child may have a retracted scar that merits surgical excision, but if he and his parents earnestly want to go on a camping trip to reestablish the sense of family closeness that has been damaged by long hospitalization, it may result in a fight with the surgeon about delaying the "needed" procedure. Except that they were all action-oriented and terribly busy, our surgeons were not all of one type. They varied from beginners who were anxious about their authority and the limits of their knowledge, uncomfortable talking to families, and concerned about not having their authority challenged, to very senior, authoritative, unthreatened men who knew and cared a lot about the family lives of their patients.

Patients see the surgeon in a variety of role types: anxiety-inducing, anxiety-relieving magical agent, omniscient protector, benevolent deceiver, indifferent apprentice, and doctor ideal. In our settings, it was always clear that the surgeon was the most powerful decision-maker. Power, in any system, as Stanton and Schwartz [8] observed long ago, is the locus of decision making. The pediatricians could qualify and the nurses could covertly alter, but the surgeon was the one who cut off the fingers, debrided the burns, executed the skin grafting, and carried out the skeletal traction, and thereby seemed to be the center of life-and-death decisions as well as the lesser ones about when a patient could go home.

Often the social problems of the patient with his disfigurement would come up at rounds. The most sympathetic surgeon might comment, briefly, "That's awful, but there is nothing I can do about it. Our job is to heal the wound." The narrow focus was necessary for them, but it upset others. It seems to be an inevitability of medical care and the stringencies of surgical work. For both psychiatrists and surgeons, it appears, however, that empathy for patients increases with experience, establishment of professional status, and gains in personal confidence. All the physicians in this work seemed to struggle over emotional acceptance of these patients, but the surgeons held no mourning rites. Pediatricians and internists would talk about the tragic death of a particular patient and then go to death rounds. Even the small disclosures of feeling were rare and abrupt with surgical specialists. The focus was always technique. The records of patients who died included the notation PI, EJ, or TE, meaning patient's illness, error of judgment, or technical error, as ways of rating how the surgeon had performed his duty. Staff members of all disciplines supported each other officially, and there was some sharing among all of the mental mechanisms needed—ventilation, repression, rationalization, and displacement, among the many—but the use of these mechanisms was influenced by sex and specialty.

BURN TECHNICIANS

The burn technicians were exclusively male and almost universally veterans of the war in Vietnam. They had been trained as military medical corpsmen and were given additional training in bacteriology, surgery, dressing care, and grafting. They harvested skin from cadavers and put this skin on patients.

There was a tide of resentment on the part of burn technicians at first when they found that they were under the authority of the nursing service, because many of them had been in positions of authority on their own in the military and had done many of the things that nurses

performed in the hospital, such as caring for transfusions and intra-
venous medications. They were not as comprehensively trained as the
nurses but sometimes took time to become cognizant of this and to
define roles in which they felt gratification and did not challenge the
nurses. Authority was not a great problem with female doctors, who
carried the authority of physicians and could discharge troublesome
children, send them to the operating room, or forbid visitors (which
was rarely done).

The burn "techs" joked and teased with the children and felt, as they
all articulated loudly and clearly in conferences, that this was a way of
showing appreciation and affection that these disfigured children would
never get from their schoolmates or peers or in the community. They
did not have the authority struggles with the adolescent boys, partly
because they were simply too big and tough, and they produced a
variety of flirtatious reactions from the girl patients, which the patients
giggled and gossiped about. However, some of the nurses were outraged
by what they felt was seductive behavior on the part of some of these
men and implied that some of it was conscious. Others felt that it was
unconscious. The issue was gradually resolved through the mediation
of formal staff conferences. Some of this kind of joshing and teasing
was allowed, but brash flirting and hints of dates were not. Everyone
felt that the presence of the men in the burn technician role lent a more
normal atmosphere to the ward and made dressing changes easier,
because they were bigger and stronger than the nurses and better able
to lift, turn, and move patients and equipment. The burn technician is
now a highly integrated and thoroughly esteemed part of the patient
care team.

SUBSPECIALISTS AND ANCILLARY PERSONNEL
Ward secretaries served both formal and unofficial roles, depending
on their personalities. Some spent a lot of time playing with the children, some disciplined the children by spontaneously taking charge
when they were rambunctious. By and large, the clerical staff kept to
its own friendly group through its separate scheduling and task assign-
ments, but there was a general casual overlap. Children and parents
developed ties to particular secretaries on a personal basis and kept in
touch over the years.

Although the physical therapists had many struggles to force the
children to work at their therapy, their anger toward uncooperative,
depressed, or recalcitrant children was less than that manifested toward
adults who were not "trying." Failure to eat and reactions to pain
troubled the nurses and remained perennial problems. Anesthesiologists,
as well as other members of the staff, were concerned about these

issues. The cooks had a special role and developed interest, along with the dietitians, in "saving" certain children by getting them to eat.

Any attempt to describe the caretakers must encompass the cleaning staff, teachers, clerical staff, and record librarians, who did not have much role definition in relation to the patients.

SHIFTING ROLES

One physical therapist became interested in establishing a teenage group to discuss the reactions of these patients to their experiences in the hospital. The other leader in this group was a student minister who was assigned to the Burns Institute to gain experience in pastoral counseling. He worked supportively with the children and then helped in running the group. He was supervised by a social worker and a psychiatrist, and it appeared that he was functioning largely in the role of social worker, though we all came to see the job of pastoral counseling more clearly through his efforts. He went on to become ordained and kept in touch with the staff. Pastoral counseling trainees at Massachusetts General Hospital visited but did not take an active role, though some priests and ministers did visit individual patients.

With the increasing establishment of a pattern of operations in the hospital and a clearer definition of roles, there also was some interest, on the part of the nurses in particular, to examine some of the social and psychological issues surrounding the families of injured children. Along the lines of most small hospital communication systems, informal data about these families were contributed by everyone working at the hospital. The receptionist who was offended by a mother who ordered her around, demanding that taxis be called and doctors summoned; the family that invaded the staff cafeteria and regularly commanded that food be brought—all were reported to the nursing and medical staff, and people became known for their overall pattern of behavior within the hospital. Mothers who could not control their children or who collapsed in the corridors and fathers who talked tough to their offspring were all noted, and often this knowledge shaped the way the staff responded to them. With the nurses' growing experience and the courses they took in nursing education, psychology, and group dynamics, there was a formal surge of interest in psychology after the institute had been running for five years. Courses at colleges and invited lecturers were requested.

THE NURSE INTERVIEWING PROJECT

Although the Burns Institute originally opened with a lot of talk about new nursing roles (and all of nursing is currently being stimulated by efforts to alter the profession by enlarging roles, e.g., nurse clinician and nurse practitioner), it did not utilize the services of the staff nurses in many unconventional ways. The nurses working with acutely ill patients did not feel they had time for any other activities, and this was true of the nurses managing patients for elective reconstructive surgery.

After the Burns Institute had been open for five years, we developed a project for interviewing adolescent patients. This derived directly from the freshly expressed interest of the nurses in finding out what the adolescents were thinking, in finding ways to educate them about what to expect when going back into the community, and teaching them how to behave. The emphasis on behaving was strong, because the surliness, smoking, flirting, and sneaking off the ward of this group were recurrent issues, and the staff hoped to find ways of setting down enforceable regulations for them. It evolved into a continuing project to learn about the psychology of adolescence and to train nurses in interviewing.

The project began with discussions of interviews, followed by video-taping of interviews between nurses and patients, which were then played back for teaching purposes. In some cases the children were then allowed to interview the nurses, with dramatically illuminating results. All the nurses had a more direct and natural style with the children and were more readily able to engage the children in discussions about their lives than students being formally trained in the mental health field. The surprise and embarrassment of mental health professionals on observing the beautiful first interviews of nurses should be emphasized. The nurses were more natural partly because they knew the patients more personally. The interviews were extended to include normal children and children with other medical problems, using videotape playback approaches or having one or two observers sit in.

In two ways these interviews helped considerably in managing the misbehaving adolescents. They interested the adolescents in what was going on, which helped diminish their boredom and rebelliousness. They also provided a forum for discussion with the staff, helping to diminish the anger and frustration of the staff over power issues, and provided a means of eliciting more information from the patients and thus of improving their management.

The nurses used the two behavior rating scales shown in Appendixes 2 and 3 (which were adapted from classroom use). They also prepared a written account of each case based on the following themes: reality sense, judgment, sense of future, self-control, relations with people, thought processes, overall coping, symptoms (e.g., emotional, de-pressed), independence, self-integration (having it "together"), and the nurse's impression of the kind of person the patient is. We have been aiming at a format that will parallel nursing-related experiences and will be much simpler than most psychiatric outlines but will give the "feel" of a child and provide information that will be helpful in managing his course in the hospital and planning for rehabilitation work after discharge.

THE PATIENTS' NEWSPAPER

One of the most interesting outgrowths of the nursing project was their spontaneous effort to start a publication with the children. The nurses began to collect drawings and written material, getting the patients involved in as much of the production as possible—typing, editing, criticizing. The newspaper was photocopied and given to staff, friends, and families.

Some sample material is given below. The first was written by a 17-year-old boy who had had repeated facial procedures over the five-year period we had known him.

The Whole Wide World

The whole wide world is terrible
The litter is unbearable
The bottles aren't returnable
The empty cans aren't burnable
The sonic boom's incredible
The tuna isn't edible
The offshore rigs are leakable
The slumlords are incurable
The smog is unendurable
The phosphates aren't dissolvable
The problems don't seem solvable
The mess is unforgivable
Let's face it, life's unlivable

A girl of 14 wrote: "Going to the operating room is like meeting up with that hidden Monster in the back of your mind . . . You're scared."

No effort was made to interpret these expressive efforts. However, the directness of the emotions seems striking in some, along with efforts to accommodate the feelings. The following are two such attempts, by a 14-year-old boy and a 13-year-old girl.

Inflicted with Pain

I was laying in bed suddenly I was
inflicted with pain
So I went to the Doc he said it's your
head your body's all right

So they sent me to a sanatarium because
I'm insane
So I got mad and raise patient raise
cain
So they tied me down so hard it fixed
my brain
Now I'm all right no more insane no
more raising cain
AND NO MORE INFLICTED WITH PAIN

> It's dark and quiet with the doors shut
> and all the lights off. You're laying in
> your bed sleeping when in the middle
> of the quiet you hear "BANG" and
> your door opens, all the lights go on;
> and you look up to see doctors and
> nurses looking down at you all round
> your bed. For a moment you are
> startled, but then you know it's only
> rounds and they are only trying to
> help you.

A 10-year-old hyperkinetic boy contributed the drawing shown in
Figure 13. This was one of the few light-hearted expressive efforts. At
the same time it is a remarkably accurate representation.

THE FUNCTIONING PATIENT CARE TEAM

Bezzeg and her associates [9] stressed that the child care worker who
functions as an integral part of the burn team by helping to maintain a
more peaceful relationship between the child and his environment will
insulate him from much unnecessary anxiety from a seemingly hostile
world around him. "The child care worker can offer to the child the
critical support and understanding needed throughout the long period
of hospitalization by helping create a more normal and child-centered
environment" [p. 624]. This is a worthy ideal, and completely in line
with the efforts of the many people working in burn units, but it is
far beyond the realities of most wards. The meaning of "child care
worker" changes with the institution and sometimes means recreation
therapist or auxiliary. Our team included recreation therapists, social
workers, psychologists, child psychiatrists, nurses, and practical nurses.
Schoolteachers and clergymen occasionally filled this role, but burn
technicians did not do this work nor did clerical staff or dietitians.
Only one female surgeon and a few pediatricians took on this supportive role, which we define as a person assigned to help the child with
his or her emotional cares. Our size permitted considerable flexibility,

Figure 13. Drawing that appeared in the patients' newspaper, done by a 10-year-old boy.

yet the roles were never perfectly delimited, and communication was not always clear when behavior was reported to the supervisory mental health workers. But overall it is a fine and satisfactory approach to giving humane care.

The amount of time needed for a group to shake down into a well-organized team runs to many months. Members of the disciplines work in a team, in which the informal sharing of information and support almost equal in quantity and value the programmed staff interactions and consultations. Growing into leadership roles and evolving a group composition that promotes good *informal* communication takes a long time. Ultimately, it is well worth it. Staff members have to learn to trust each other; a nurse has to lean how much to tell a frightened mother about the risk of her child dying; and the nurse has to know how much the team leader, the head nurse, and the doctors will back her in what she says. If they are to develop this trust, the team members must have the assurance that self-doubts confessed will not be used against them in the line of duty. Nurses need to be encouraged toward personal and professional development that does not intrude on the care of patients or totally disrupt the scheduling of ward rotations.

With all the staff, the disorder was condemned rather than the person, and an effort was made to be sympathetic to the patients and their families, though this was often rapidly followed by emotional distancing, which to families was unpleasant or disturbing and emotionally demanding. Over time, in all specialties, staff members did verbalize their feelings about their own body images and the social fate of patients, especially adolescents, and the role of disfigured persons became slowly but generally aired.

With the adult patients at Massachusetts General Hospital there seemed most commonly to be psychological concerns about excessive regression and depression. In the children's service the most common kinds of concern were uncooperativeness with procedures and teenage delinquencies. Regression was accepted with children, and depression was seen sympathetically but not as a disease. Delirium in adults and children stimulated the same reactions.

Emotional responses to patients are universal issues, and the handling of death is not unique. What is distinctive is the handling of disfigurement and the attitudes that the staff faces from the outside. Almost universally, our nurses reported that family members and friends asked them how they could tolerate the work. There was some praise for their courage in being able to "take it," but many times nurses reported that people were horrified by what they were doing instead of admiring. Outsiders often did not want to talk with them about it or ask questions, in contrast to the experience of nurses who worked in surgical or cardiac intensive care units, where there was a similar aura of intense and dramatic medical effort. Almost all the staff had to deal with the negative public attitudes. Although there was some admiration for the courage of the staff, there was little comment about how interesting, absorbing, or exciting the work may be. Some of this reaction applied also to the teachers, recreation therapists, practical nurses, burn technicians, social workers, and physical therapists. "They all groan and say, 'How can you do that?' or 'Isn't that terribly depressing?' " Part of the problem was that the stigma of burns also included the caretakers, and thus horror was admixed with admiration.

Becker et al. [4] pointed out that physicians can become major moral entrepreneurs by seeking to influence public opinion. This was a major theme of activities of most of the staff. Nurses, doctors, and other representatives from the hospital spoke to the public about the dangers of fires and particularly about clothing flammability; interviews for television, newspapers, and periodicals were given. Articles were written for medical and psychiatric journals. In addition, testimony and advice were given to the state legislature and to city, state, and national organizations. It became a psychological focus for all the staff to know that they were participating in *prevention*. The Burns Institute recently hired a director of burn prevention to help in public education and to coordinate the hospital's efforts with the state legislature and other groups. Doctors campaign, properly, against fire hazards, they testify, and they write. However, they tend to feel that if the end product is a disfigured face, there is little the physician can offer. Like the general public, he will probably view this person as lost. He will accept the disappearance of facially handicapped people from view and turn his efforts to other issues, where there is a better return on his efforts (economic as well as clinical). It is not remarkable that nurses like handsome men and physicians like feminine pulchritude. The separation between personal aesthetics and professional perspective is harder to maintain in the care of the disfigured. Added to this is the failure of the professions to overcome the disfigurements, which leads to feelings of impotence. But the major part is the enormous, imperious force of the culture, which will accept kidney transplants and cardiac pacemakers, which can be kept camouflaged under clothing, but which turns from the disfigured in public.

The whole atmosphere was influenced by newspaper articles of home disasters that led to hospitalization for burn care. The children of well-known public figures were admitted, and eminent visitors came. Bozo the clown visited, as did Colonel Sanders and numerous sports figures, especially hockey stars. The group morale grew over the years, and contacts with other burn centers and with professional delegations of international repute all added to the sense we were doing important work. Laboratory workers in the research division had some contacts with the patients, albeit slight ones. A common staff reaction was a heightened fear of fire. We all bought fire extinguishers, checked our wiring, and looked at our fabrics for fireproofing.

The special nature of the ward also showed in other ways. When one staff member was in a bad mood or became upset about a patient, this was telegraphed to all; it did not become dissipated as it would have in a larger, general hospital setting. On the other hand, staff members were quicker to rally to support each other. Overall, the evolution of distinct roles was tempered by accommodation to individual quirks; a particular surgeon might support a social worker following a difficult family, or the psychologist and the nurses might join together to get a pediatrician to visit a school to help with a troublesome transition, or the head nurse might get the psychiatrist to see a parent about whom she felt concern.

Conflict and disagreement have never been absent, but most of the ill will is defused in well-developed channels and informal interactions. Most important of all, a general philosophy has evolved that is shared and *practiced* by the staff to maintain contacts, to press referrals, to pursue further surgery and education, and to constantly prod patients and their families into greater social participation on whatever level is possible.

REFERENCES

1. Yankelovich, D. *The New Morality Profile of American Youth in the Seventies.* McGraw-Hill, New York, 1974.
2. Hay, D., and Oken, D. The psychological stresses of intensive care unit nursing. *Psychosom. Med.* 34:109–118, 1972.
3. Merton, R. *The Student Physician: Introductory Studies in the Sociology of Medical Education.* Harvard University Press, Cambridge, Mass., 1967.
4. Becker, H. S., et al. *Boys in White: Student Culture in Medical School.* University of Chicago Press, Chicago, 1961.
5. Kutner, B. Surgeons and Their Patients: A Study in Social Perception. In E. G. Jaco (Ed.), *Patients, Physicians, and Illness.* Free Press, New York, 1958. Pp. 384–397.
6. Malt, R. A., and Grillo, H. C. Prospective intern's views of the model surgeon. *J. Med. Educ.* 44:141–144, 1969.
7. Friedson, E. *Profession of Medicine: A Study of the Sociology of Applied Knowledge.* Dodd, Mead, New York, 1971.
8. Stanton, A., and Schwartz, M. *The Mental Hospital.* Basic Books, New York, 1954.
9. Bezzeg, E., et al. The role of the child care worker in the treatment of severely burned children. *Pediatrics* 50(4):617–624, 1972.

APPENDIX 1
Nurse Interviews: The Changing Role and Image of Nursing

INTERVIEW 1: Nurse Sharpe

Q. *How long have you been in nursing?*
A. Three and one-half years.

Q. *In what settings? Doing what kind of nursing?*
A. General Hospital in London, then a psychiatric hospital, and now here. I really have had no experience with burned children, just one child but only for a couple of days.

Q. *How did you happen to come to the Shriners Burns Institute?*
A. I saw an ad in the newspaper and I wanted to nurse children.

Q. *Was working with burned children an important factor?*
A. At the time I don't think it really registered. When I saw the ad I didn't really think of it. It was a specialized field and I did want it. I didn't really think of it until I started working and I became very interested.

Q. *Do you expect any particular problems? What kind? How do you expect to be affected by these problems?*
A. I think in dressing changes and the way the child will react. I think it will worry me personally. I'm just not used to hurting people and it bothers me. I think maybe I won't be able to cope with it, but when it comes right down to it, I think I'll react differently.

Q. *What satisfactions or gratifications do you expect?*
A. Seeing the child get better. I'm just so happy to see the children get well, and when I see them happy, my day is happy too.

Q. *In regard specifically to families of patients, what do you anticipate?*
A. I think knowing the families will be interesting and I think it will help the patient.

Q. *What would you consider a "good" mother in terms of your relationship with her in the hospital?*
A. Certainly someone you can communicate with and say things to who will not take it the wrong way.

Q. *What would you consider a "bad" mother?*
A. We have another patient who has a completely different setup at home, Margaret. Her parents come in very rarely. I think a mother who doesn't really care is "bad." One who has guilt feelings or can't communicate with her child. A mother who complains all the time and is very demanding. One who does not appreciate what is being done and goes against hospital rules.

Q. *What makes rooming in helpful? When is it not a good idea?*
A. I don't agree with it except maybe in the acute stage if the mother really wants
to be here. I really haven't had enough experience to make up my mind. Perhaps
rooming in would be good if the mother lived far away. I think the child's age
would make a difference and if the child had never been away from home. I think
the degree of the illness is the main factor.

Q. *How much or in what way should a nurse be involved in parent-child interaction (other than necessary)?*
A. I don't think she should get too involved if this is what is going on at home,
unless there are other patients near and the patient is not in a private room. I do
think it's important for the father to be around. I think a lot of children need a
man around them. Michael C.'s father, as an example, is very loving and affectionate
but also very firm, and Michael acts much better when his father is here with him.

Q. *What do you anticipate in terms of staff relationships? What is important?
Where do you feel difficulties will be and have been in the past?*
A. At the moment they seem very good. I think in a small hospital it's very easy to
have good relationships with the staff. I like the idea of team nurse and team conferences. Everybody here is friendly with everyone no matter what department you
work in. I am sure that if I had any problems I would not hesitate to talk to some-
body about it. When I worked in large hospitals in the past there sometimes seemed
to be a gap between doctors and nurses, but here we all talk to each other and
know each other's capabilities.

Q. *What is your opinion in regard to wearing uniforms versus street clothes?*
A. I prefer a uniform because I wouldn't want to ruin my own clothes. I think
the pink gowns look nice, and they are taken care of for us. I think street clothes
or colored uniforms are good because patients don't consider you the strict old
nurse. I'd be surprised if patients didn't react to them.

Q. *Do you prefer being called by your first name or your last name?*
A. I'm used to being called Nurse Sharpe because that's how it is in England. I
think it's better for the children to call you by your first name, and I like to hear
them call me Helen. Up to now I have been introducing myself as Miss Sharpe out
of habit.

Q. *Does it bother you that both patient and nurse are in constant view because of
the setting of the ward?*
A. I'm used to it so I do like it, especially for children. You can always watch them.

Q. *It is said that children who have been patients in the Burns Institute enjoy
coming back to the hospital, despite the painful and stressful experience they have
had. Why do you think this is?*
A. I think in lots of cases pain is forgotten. They make friends and look forward to
seeing them.

Q. *What has been the reaction of other people when you tell them you work here?*
A. It's usually, "Oh my goodness, isn't that awful depressing?" But most people

are very interested in the burn aspect itself and they also seem interested in finding out about what the Shriners are.

INTERVIEW 2:   Nurse Vorenberg

Q. *How long have you been in nursing?*
A. Three years.

Q. *In what settings? Doing what kind of nursing?*
A. As an operating room nurse.

Q. *Have you had any previous experience with burn patients?*
A. A little bit as a student at Children's Hospital [in Boston], doing dressings a couple of times, but that's been it. The fact of working with burned children did frighten me a little bit because of the care.

Q. *How did you happen to come to the Shriners Burns Institute?*
A. Mainly because it offered the kind of nursing that I was taught as a student, which I haven't seen since I graduated. It involves a little more individual care and also provides involvement in different parts of the hospital. I became so frustrated in the operating room with the lack of vocal communication. Usually in a larger hospital you haven't got the time to do anything but give physical care, and here you can sit down and talk to the doctors and other staff members and discuss things.

Q. *Do you expect any particular problems? What kind? How do you expect to be affected by these problems?*
A. Often I find myself becoming more frustrated than I thought I would. I just forgot what it was like to try to get medication into a child that was screaming and crying, and the more frustrated the nurse gets the worse the patient gets—it's just a big cycle. I have a tendency to withdraw and rather than getting it out of my system I hold things back and just let it build up. Then, rather than talk to someone, I bring the problems home with me and make them seem worse sometimes than they really are.

Q. *What satisfactions or gratifications do you expect?*
A. I guess learning while working and being able to build up relationships with different people, and also watching the children get better and finally go home.

Q. *In regard specifically to families of patients, what do you anticipate?*
A. Well, I've heard that the staff is planning group discussions with the parents, which I think would be good, but on the other hand I've found that some people don't feel comfortable in a group and will not participate. I think the family should be involved at all times so that if something did happen to a patient, a death, they would not be totally shocked because they have known what has been going on. They would feel that they have got some place to go for help.

Q. *What would you consider a "good" mother in terms of your relationship with her in the hospital?*
A. I think to describe a good mother you would have to use Michael C.'s father as an example. He is very firm with him but gives him a tremendous amount of affection so that Michael is not afraid of him, and he tells Michael that he doesn't want him to say "I can't" or "I won't," he at least wants him to try to do what the nurses tell him. I think a "good" mother is one who accepts and tries to help in the situation.

Q. *What would you consider a "bad" mother?*
A. I think a mother who is not willing to listen, regardless of the circumstances. A mother who doesn't want to be there for the dressings. I think a mother who gives negative support to the child, for instance, "You have to do what the nurses say or you're bad." I think it should be said in a positive way. Also mothers who don't come in at all to see the child and just seem totally uninterested.

Q. *What makes rooming in helpful? When is it not a good idea?*
A. I'm not particularly in favor of rooming in. I think it would be good for an infant if it were breast feeding and there were no other children at home, because I think an infant needs a special kind of closeness that only a mother can give. Among older children, if, say, two mothers were able to room in on a ward of 10 children, it would cause a lot of resentment. I don't think it's good for the mother to be in a hospital 24 hours a day—she has her husband to keep in mind.

Q. *How much or in what way should a nurse be involved in parent-child interaction (other than necessary)?*
A. I think the nurse should step in to something like the example you gave but I think that in a case like this you would have to start working with your psychiatric team. I think maybe the nurse could first talk to the patient and find out why he acts this way. I guess you would have to watch out for personality conflicts.

Q. *Do you think fathers should be involved?*
A. Yes, I think it's important especially for a teenage boy. I think he's able to relate better and the patient will feel better with a man.

Q. *What do you anticipate in terms of staff relationships? What is important? Where do you feel difficulties will be and have been in the past?*
A. Well, we have been having team conferences, which are helpful to all. One thing I do like is that there is no head nurse. I think it's an ideal place for a nurse to work because she is able to think, learn, and function, which she doesn't have the chance to do in a big hospital. I think that in the past, nurses, doctors, and social workers have never really had a chance to sit down and talk, and here they make it a point to discuss and share their experiences.

Q. *What is your opinion in regard to wearing uniforms versus street clothes?*
A. I think in a medical-surgical situation like this a uniform is better. I don't like the white uniform and cap; I never have because you have the Florence Nightingale, starry-eyed look. I think if you can wear street clothes it breaks down the first barrier. I think that if you are having a session with parents, you should wear street

clothes because then you become a person and not an authority. I think that a nurse does need to be able to identify herself and I think the colored gowns are good.

Q. *Do you prefer being called by your first name or your last name?*
A. I think it's the choice of the patient. When I introduce myself I usually use "Gussie Vorenberg." The only time I object to being called by my first name is when I am treating a man my own age, because there is a sexual attraction and it's hard to keep a patient-nurse relationship. I think it's much easier for the kids to call me Gussie.

Q. *Does it bother you that both patient and nurse are in constant view because of the setting of the ward?*
A. I don't think there are any drawbacks because I think the kids feel secure knowing that there is someone there all the time. I think the only time you would run into trouble would be when a girl and boy about 15 or 16 were near each other.

Q. *It is said that children who have been patients in the Burns Institute enjoy coming back to the hospital, despite the painful and stressful experience they have had. Why do you think this is?*
A. I don't think it's wrong for them to enjoy coming back to the hospital because they make friends here and they do get love and affection. I think that they know that they will have pain but I think they also realize that it won't be forever. They know that if they are in the play area they can play and they don't have to be fearful of pain.

Q. *What was the reaction of people when you said you were going to work here?*
A. Most of them thought it was really wonderful. I know my first reaction to burn patients when I saw them on the street was, "Oh, God."

INTERVIEW 3: Nurse Antonelli

Q. *How long have you been in nursing?*
A. Ten years.

Q. *In what setting? Doing what kind of nursing?*
A. In pediatrics for the past 10 years, both medical and surgical. Most of the work was at Massachusetts General Hospital.

Q. *Then you have had experience with burned children?*
A. Right.

Q. *Were you at Massachusetts General Hospital when the Shrine Service first started?*
A. Yes. I have also worked with burned adults.

Q. *How long would you say you worked on the Shrine Service?*
A. Five years.

Q. *Was working with burned children a particular factor in your choice, either for or against?*
A. It's something that made me think very hard. I've always liked working with burned children. I think *like* is a bad word, but the challenge of taking care of them was a prominent factor in my coming here. However, they do take a lot from you, which is a negative factor, and I'm not sure that a setting of just burned children is the best. In many ways I'm sure it's the best, but in other ways I'm not so sure. I wasn't sure if I did or did not want to work here, but you can only find out by trying.

Q. *Do you feel as if you were taking a chance?*
A. I feel like I'm a divided person because I love all my other pediatric patients and I do miss them, but of course I'm so busy I haven't really got that much time to miss them.

Q. *What satisfactions or gratifications do you expect?*
A. I think the work is very difficult because you do get attached to the burned children physically and emotionally. But I think you always feel that the time that you gave the patient and the family was worthwhile.

Q. *Do you thnk these patients have a deeper need?*
A. Yes, I think the patients do need more than any other kind of patient. Well, I think you always feel that you should do an extra good job to try to make things easier for them in the future.

Q. *You said that in some ways it's good to have just burned patients in a hospital and in some ways it's not. Would you explain that?*
A. I think it's good in that in any specialty you can learn more about it and be better in it than someone who is more diversified. For example, I think we do better with the children in preventing contraction because, partly we are aware and partly because we have more time and are not being called out on emergencies or for any other patient who ties you up in a different way so that you might have to drop what you are doing. We always have to respond to the emergency of the burn but it's all geared the same way. I think that's on the positive side. But, negatively, they can drain the people that care for them. I think it's good for the patient to see others with the same problems, but then again, you don't know if it's good for the patient to be constantly dwelling on burns and seeing them all the time. Like I said, you have to try it to find out.

Q. *Do you think they would get more general attention in quantity in a pediatric ward?*
A. I think the staff will give the medical attention, looking at the aspect of always being aware of the preventions and special things they need. But as far as the patient, not necessarily—they did get a lot of personal attention there.

Q. *In regard specifically to families of patients, what do you anticipate?*
A. I don't look at it as being much different than what I'm used to, except for the hope of trying to make it better for the parents. I'm used to having the parents around the ward, but if the patient isn't very sick or very far away from home, and

the parents do not have a lot of responsibilities, you see the patient's parents more. I think it's very important to think of the family as a unit and to care for all of them. They may sometimes feel guilty because the accident happened, and you need to help them adjust.

Q. *What would you consider a "good" mother in terms of your relationship with her in the hospital?*
A. An ideal mother would be one who would try to come here often, one with whom you could relate and establish an easy relationship, and one who would be able and willing to comprehend what we are trying to do for her child, why we are doing it, and how she could best help us.

Q. *What would you consider a "bad" mother?*
A. I suppose the mother who would be just the opposite. One who just doesn't care. I could understand one who could not go in and see the patient, but not one who didn't even care about it.

Q. *What makes rooming in helpful? When is it not a good idea?*
A. I think it can be helpful but it depends on the child and the mother and why they want to room in. I wouldn't advise blanket rooming in for everyone. Maybe if someone were from far away and didn't know anyone here and were very insecure, I think it might be good for the mother to room in. For a mother who is especially fearful, it would be helpful. Even if the mother spent just one night here it would be helpful for her to know that she is welcomed by us; then she may feel that she knows what goes on and that everyone is doing their best. Many times I feel that it will not be good for the child if the mother stays, but sometimes it would be good just for her own sake. Sometimes a mother feels much better just seeing how her child is going to act when she's not there and down the hall. She can see if he does cry or what exactly does go on.

Q. *Do you thnk that the age of the child makes a difference in rooming in or do other factors seem more important to you?*
A. I don't think I could put an age limit on it because every family is brought up so different. I think you have to look at both sides. I don't think a little baby would care as long as there were someone there to feed and love him, but it would mean a lot to the mother, whereas in the age group from 3 to 6 years it would mean a lot to the patient to have the mother there.

Q. *How much and in what way should a nurse be involved in parent-child interaction (other than necessary)?*
A. I think you do have to get involved even if you didn't want to. I don't think you can make anyone over in a day and actually that's not our job. Children acting up on a floor will influence the other children and, of course, make the nurses react. I think for the sake of all concerned you do have to be involved and set up some kind of rules of restriction.

Q. *What do you anticipate in terms of staff relationships here?*
A. Since it's such a small place, you become more aware of the staff and more involved with them, regardless of what department they are in. I think in nursing

you have an opportunity to know and understand people better than in a large hospital.

Q. *What have been difficulties in staff relationships that you have seen in the past?*
A. Areas of difficulty, I think, are that medical and nursing staff don't have—or make—enough time to spend with the parents or they don't have the understanding that they need at this time. Sometimes the doctors order conflicting procedures and it turns out that you don't know which to follow and you have to decide yourself what to do. I think it's important for the staff members to have good communication between each other.

Q. *What is your opinion in regard to wearing uniforms versus street clothes?*
A. I think there is a place for each depending on what you are doing. While taking care of an acute patient I wouldn't wear street clothes because I don't think it's the most efficient garb for me and I don't think it would be the most beneficial for the patient. You're a nurse no matter what you wear—white, pink, or print—and you have to be able to care for the patient no matter what you have on. I was talking to a mother the other day and she didn't object to the nurses' wearing street clothes, but she said that when she was on the floor many mothers came up to her thinking she was a nurse and this bothered her. Some parents accept this because they feel it's very relaxed and casual, but others, when they think of a nurse, think of a girl in white, and they can't accept street clothes. Some people don't observe a pin and a name pin so they can't identify the nurses. There are a lot of things to think about when considering this, but once the parents meet you and know you, I don't think it bothers them.

Q. *Do you think it makes much difference to the children?*
A. I think at the toddler age they seem to respond more to a person who is not in white and I suppose it could be partly due to their upbringing, if a nurse at some time made them afraid. No matter what color you're in, children know that you're the lady that's going to bring the medicine because they associate the keys around your neck with medicine. For the older children wearing a colored uniform is nice because it's a topic of conversation for them.

Q. *Do you prefer being called by your first name or your last name?*
A. I don't mind first names in the right place. I don't think I'd particularly like to hear them screaming "Carol" all over the ward; I think I'd prefer "Miss Antonelli." I think it depends on the relationship you have with certain people and their up-bringing. I always introduce myself to the patient and his family as Miss Antonelli.

Q. *Does it bother you that both patient and nurse are in constant view because of the ward setting?*
A. I think it has it advantages and disadvantages. In an open ward the child can see the nurse all the time and to some it gives a feeling of security to know that some-one is always there. Also they can see when you are busy with someone else and sometimes it makes them have a little patience and understanding that you are helping one of their friends in the next bed. This is especially true in an open ward for adults. A disadvantage is that if you do want to discuss a patient with another medical person it's very hard because the patient can hear. People tend to forget

that ears are always listening, and sometimes the patient will hear just a bit of the conversation and will start worrying about something that they don't have to worry about. Sometimes the patients need companionship, but if they are very sick they need the peace and quiet, and there tends to be a lot of tension in that kind of a ward. I think it might be better if there were cubicles so that an older child would not be disturbed by a crying baby and the baby would not be disturbed if the older child wanted to watch TV late at night.

Q. *It has been said that children who have been patients in the Burns Institute enjoy coming back to the hospital, despite the painful and stressful experience they have had. Why do you think this is?*
A. I think that they feel they have made friends here. I don't think that they would be saying I'm glad that I'm going back, it would be that they don't really mind it. I think for some who were over at Massachusetts General Hospital it will be hard because I think they prefer to be in the old setting, but for some it will be easy because they do know some of the nurses.

Q. *It has been said that children know that something good is being done for them even though they do have pain. Do you think they have this feeling?*
A. I think it depends on their age, and how many emotional problems they have. I don't think very young children would think along that line; I think all they know is that you're hurting them, and later on you love them, so they are willing to forgive you.

APPENDIX 2
Behavior Rating Scale

Patient's name _____   Age _____   Date _____

Recorder _____

Please rate each and every statement by putting an X in the appropriate square after the statement. The squares are numbered 1 to 5, and represent the degree to which you have noticed the described behavior. The bases for making a judgment are given below:

(1) You have not noticed this behavior at all.
(2) You have noticed the behavior to a slight degree.
(3) You have noticed the behavior to a considerable degree.
(4) You have noticed the behavior to a large degree.
(5) You have noticed the behavior to a very large degree.

Rating Scale

1	2	3	4	5

Vegetative-Autonomic
1. Hyperactive and restless
2. Erratic, flighty, or scattered behavior
3. Easily distracted; lacks continuity of effort and perseverance
4. Behavior goes in cycles
5. Quality of work may vary from day to day
6. Daydreaming alternating with hyperactivity
7. Explosive and unpredictable behavior
8. Cannot seem to control self (will speak out or jump out of seat)
9. Poor coordination in large-muscle activities (games, etc.)

Perceptual-Discriminative
10. Confusion in spelling and writing
11. Inclined to become confused in number processes; gives illogical responses
12. Reading is poor
13. Lacks a variety of responses; repeats himself in many situations
14. Upset by changes in routine
15. Confused in following directions
16. Confused and apprehensive about rightness of response; indecisive
17. Comments are often "off the track" or peculiar
18. Has difficulty reasoning things out logically with others

Social-Emotional
19. Demands much attention
20. Tends to be destructive, especially of the work of others
21. Many evidences of stubborn, uncooperative behavior
22. Often withdraws quickly from group activities

Social-Emotional

Rating Scale

	1	2	3	4	5

23. Constant difficulty with other children or adults, or both
24. Shallow feeling for others
25. Cries often and easily
26. Often more confused by punishment
27. Seems generally unhappy
28. Often tells bizarre stories

APPENDIX 3
Ward Adaptation Scale

Patient's name _____ Age _____

Please check the behavior description in each of the following sections that is *most* characteristic of the patient as you have observed him. Use other side for further comments.

Work habits
_____ Works well under own supervision
_____ Works moderately well with minimum of supervision
_____ Wastes time if not supervised
_____ Wastes time even when supervised
_____ Source of trouble if left unsupervised

Interest in education, therapy, procedures
_____ Sets up desirable personal objectives
_____ Does more than what is required
_____ Does only what is required
_____ Generally indifferent to school-work, etc.
_____ Outright disinterested in school-work, etc.

Participation in group activities
_____ Enters freely into group activities
_____ Needs to be encouraged before entering into activities
_____ Participation limited even when urged
_____ Refuses to participate in group activities

Cooperation
_____ Works well with others in all group activities
_____ Works well with others only if personally interested
_____ Prefers to let others do the work
_____ Interferes with effective group work

Social Adjustment
_____ Gets along very well with others
_____ Social relations limited to small group
_____ Insists on being center of attention
_____ Generally reserved and passive
_____ Immature social behavior
_____ Definitely antisocial or solitary, or both

Leadership
_____ Associates look to him for leadership
_____ Occasionally demonstrates ability to lead

Attitude toward those in authority
_____ Actively cooperates and is helpful
_____ Often uncooperative; cannot accept criticism

Responsibility

_____ Always carries out responsibility promptly
_____ Usually dependable; has good reasons for exceptions
_____ Needs occasionally to be urged
_____ Very likely to neglect responsibilities

Personal Appearance

_____ Always careful of appearance
_____ Occasionally careless of appearance
_____ Very careless of appearance
_____ Extremely fastidious or overly concerned

Observation of hospital standards and regulations

_____ Interested in mainenance and improvement of standards, rules, and
regulations
_____ Occasionally thoughtless; commits minor infractions
_____ Initiates violations and encourages others to do same
_____ Unwillingly conforms; reluctantly accepts

Care of hospital and personal property

_____ Makes personal effort to keep all materials and equipment in good condition
_____ Is sometimes careless in use of materials and equipment
_____ Is negligent and destructive of property of others
_____ Overly possessive; does not share willingly
_____ Shares with others; respects their property
_____ Too generous with possessions; buys friends

Temperament

_____ Generally friendly, happy, pleasant
_____ Quickly angers or shows temper
_____ Sensitive; feelings easily hurt
_____ Shows little emotion
_____ Excitable; too quickly reacts

9

The Burn Patient in the Family

It appears clear that for both adults and children, emotional disturbance and psychopathology in the family increase the chances of all accidents and burn injuries. The nature of these disturbances makes a considerable difference in the handling of the patient's problems, which can be both subtle and obvious. Normal, untroubled, intact households also have accidents. The nature and structure of any family are tested by a major burn with disfigurement. The time in the hospital, in which the family is separated from the burn patient, may be the least obvious time of familial disruption. Many troubled spouses will visit a burned husband or wife, and deeply upset and inadequate parents often appear unremarkable during hospitalization, manifesting their disturbance only after the patient's discharge. Nonetheless, according to most careful investigators, the existence of a burn victim in a family will alter the family functioning.

The work of Seligman, MacMillan, and Carroll [1], Martin, Lawrie, and Wilkinson [2], Wright and Fulwiler [3], Long and Cope [4], and others has brought proper emphasis to the influence of individual and family psychopathological problems in causing burn injuries in children, and a large body of literature on adult accidents confirms the import of this factor in grown-ups. This does not ignore the issue of true unmotivated accidents, random events in which the victim had no active participation of any kind, e.g., the person visiting a building that sustains an unexpected explosion. However, working on adult and pediatric burn wards impresses one with the numbers of motivated accidents, and the preponderance of depression, conflict, alcoholism, marital discord, work dissatisfaction, and acute tension preexisting most accidents. This observation may be due to my bias as a psychiatrist, who is called in to see only cases where there is suspected difficulty, or to the selection system of the Shriners Burns Institute, which chooses families from many parts of the country for its free care, but it seems to be confirmed by authors in Europe and North America.

FIRST IMPACT OF THE BURN INJURY

For both the normal, functioning family and the troubled family the burn catastrophe roughly follows an emotional course best described by Herschowitz [5]. He recounted a sequence that begins with *first impact*, a state of dazed shock accompanying the first exposure to the terrible news, which is likely to last for a few hours to a few days. This is followed by a period of *turmoil-recoil*, which continues for several weeks. The task of *emotional reconstruction* may run for months and, in our experience with disfigurement, may last for years, shading over into the phenomena of chronic sorrow described by Olshansky [6], wherein the family members never quite escape from or overcome the burden of tragedy they face. Herschowitz said:

In the impact phase, the individual is propelled by emergency fight-flight responses; caught between these, he may show frozen behavior. In the phase of recoil-turmoil, emotions include rage, anxiety, depression, guilt, and shame which may be expressed (by weeping, open anger, deliberate intoxication, etc.) or be concealed behind facades of over-control, detachment, and busy attention to other aspects of life. When the individual moves towards adjustment and reconstruction, his painful feelings become muted, and are gradually tempered with hope about his future [5, p. 36].

A particularly poignant example of what a mother felt during her son's hospitalization follows. It depicts many of the experiences of a parent with a severely burned child of three. The letter, edited, was written by a mother who did not tell many of her feelings and who was considered cooperative and understanding. It is a poignant document, which the staff has read with appreciation.

Letter from Willis's Mother
I cannot give exact suggestions for a handbook, because I would probably be too emotional, but I can tell what happened to me while we were still new there.
    It was the Sunday after Thanksgiving. We got to the Burn Unit [Shriners Burns Institute] somewhere around 7 P.M. (Willis and I; my husband went home to our

older son who had seen the accident and was frightened). The ambulance driver went to the Mass. General entrance and there was a good deal of confusion. I was told by the doctor at the Shore Hospital to be sure to see the plastic surgeon and not to settle for anyone else. At Mass. General they sent us through the tunnel to the Burn Unit. Willis was terrified. I kept trying to tell him it was okay, that everything would be okay. We went up to the third floor and the resident was there. I answered all the questions and asked where the plastic surgeon was. The surgical resident said the plastic surgeon would see Willis in the morning. I trusted him and fell in love with him as any mother would who was looking for the miracle that I wanted from him. He asked me to wait downstairs while he evaluated Willis. A nurse showed me to the lobby.

The woman at the desk asked what happened and I answered automatically. She got me a cup of tea. Another child's mother was there. She was extremely helpful to me. It may be a good idea to suggest to old parents to reach out to any new parent they may come across in the lobby. There is some desire to do this and if it is suggested, it will probably be done more freely. Simply say to the new parent "What," and try to be as supportive as possible when the answers come.

The woman at the desk asked if there was anyone that I could call. I said, "No." I really did not think there was. She asked me to think, maybe there was someone. I finally remembered my aunt who lives right in Boston. That receptionist must have called my aunt's apartment for a solid hour [before she answered] . . . . I am grateful to the receptionist for her persistence. My aunt and her friend came right to the hospital. She asked how much longer until we could have some kind of word and was told it would be quite some time. They took me across the way for supper. We told the receptionist where we were going.

We got back to the hospital and were told that it would be some time yet before we would hear anything. My aunt's friend left. The receptionist, my aunt and I all talked about what had happened. I went to the ladies' room and saw my face in the mirror. It was not me. It could not be me. The face in the mirror was covered with red splotches. I had never had them before. They turned out to be the beginning of psoriasis.

Finally, at about 1 A.M., we went upstairs. The nurse who took us up told us about the dirty floors and the strange things we would see. The resident surgeon told us about Willis's burns, chances and general health. He was "hopeful." Some x-rays were taken and the report was given. We had been sitting there for some time when he asked us why we did not go home. I told him that I would like to know how the x-rays were before I tried to go to sleep. He and the nurse had just read them and did not think to tell us. I do not know why they would not think of that, but they did not. I asked him to translate what they had been talking about and he told me that Willis had apparently not inhaled any fumes or smoke particles. I thanked him for allowing us to stay so late and for giving us the report.

The next day I was there quite early, and had to wait before going upstairs. I put on an apron when I got up there and went toward Willis. A nurse got quite upset at me for not putting on everything before going to the tent. She must have thought I was told what to wear the day before, but I was not. Then I made another big boo-boo and I opened the slit in the curtain too far. A nurse caught me again and made me feel very stupid. I was simply doing what the doctor had done the night before, when he needed to look closely at something, but I did not know anything about what to do and what not to do. A detailed description of what to expect and what to do should be included in the handbook, along with the instruction to parents to be sure that they ask someone on duty to assist them the first few times they go into the ward. I think that it should be made perfectly clear to all new parents that they should feel completely free to go to the nurse's desk and explain that they are new and do not want to do anything wrong and would like complete instruction before going too close to their child.

My husband came in the first afternoon and the resident came over to say hello. I asked if Willis would live and was told there are no guarantees but that his chances were good. I was told definitely that he would not be home for Christmas.

The days turned into weeks. All the time, I was doing more and more myself for Willis. I felt that it was important for us not to lose touch. One nurse told me I should leave during dressings because Willis would associate me with the pain. [That] knocked me off balance. I did leave, but I would not go downstairs. I asked her how long she would be and went to the Parents' lounge for that amount of time. I was afraid to go downstairs because they might forget to call me back up. That had happened before.

I am, luckily, a very uninhibited person.* I find that true as I run into more and more people who are so inhibited that they are not even alive. I knew my instincts and I knew to follow them. The head nurse and I had quite a discussion one day as to whether or not it was wise for me to help during dressings. I told her that I had been doing so all along, that I was saving someone else from doing the job, that every time I did what I was told, I only ended up regretting it, and that I was worried, as she was, not only of Willis's body, but also his life. I told her that I did not want to leave and the only way she could get me out would be to carry me. She said that I could stay, but she was concerned that some other parents might get the same idea and she asked me to be as discreet as I could whenever I helped with any of the procedures. I was. My main concern was, and is always, Willis.

Christmas and New Year's came and went. I knew, from being there during dressings, that Willis was nowhere near ready to go home. It had been six weeks though, and that was how long I was told it would take, at least, so I thought it was about time to ask what was what.

The surgical resident had left and my heart was broken. I asked the doctor who had taken over Willis's care how Willis was doing and he told me that Willis was not taking his grafts as well as could be expected. In fact, he was not taking grafts well at all. He explained to me how no one could tell how a burned child is going to [react to grafting] until it is done. I tried to understand and accept the fact that no one could predict the day Willis would go home.

I think that it really helped me to be involved in Willis's care. I got to know how careful everyone is and how everyone at the hospital really wanted to see Willis home. I am sure that it would be very easy for me to imagine that everyone at the hospital was conspiring against me and my son if I were sitting in the lobby most of the time.

I remember one day, in the beginning, I got there at the usual time and was told that there would be a delay. This, I was told, happens often, and I tried not to worry. I knew his right arm was burned all the way around. The burns were [of] varying degrees and the doctors were all worried about the arm. The doctors had always spoken optimistically about it, but suddenly, like a fire alarm, I became

---

*This actually contrasts with the author's conduct in the mothers' group, casework, and nursing relations during this time.

anxious. I was convinced that they were amputating his arm at the shoulder. I knew that before they did anything like that, they would tell me, but when you are sitting in the lobby, you have no real control over what you are thinking, especially when you are waiting to go upstairs and you do not know what is taking so long. I told this to the receptionist, and she called the ward to find out what was taking so long. They told her I could go up. When I got upstairs, I asked what had been going on and they said I could have come up long ago. That was when I learned to make a pest of myself with the receptionist and have her check upstairs often whenever I had to wait for any length of time.

I cannot remember the names of all the receptionists who were there when Willis was admitted, but they were equally helpful. But sometimes when I would ask them anything, the way I did, they seemed to be annoyed. The receptionist can do a lot for a parent's morale, if she is tuned in to people. She does not need to be a psychologist, but she should not simply be a switchboard operator.*

This may sound strange to some professionals at the Shriners, but I think a great resource is going down the drain. It was not too difficult for me to learn, slowly, how to care for Willis. I took stool specimens and urine samples. Parents' caring for their own children† not only saves money but also saves the child. I think that in some cases, it can mean the difference between life and death. Even if the child dies, it at least gives the parents the feeling that they did everything they could. I know that the child who is obviously going to die needs extra special care and tenderness, but there are some things that the parents can and should be allowed to do. The parents can be introduced to these things slowly and gently. Then the reality of the situation can begin to come more clearly into focus. It is very easy to let what the doctors say go in one ear and out the other and to go on dreaming, but when parents are involved in the actual care they cannot do that. There will always be the parent who really prefers to stay out of all of it. I do not mean for them to be forced into doing anything. We are all individuals. I think some people will be surprised at how cooperative and helpful most parents can be.

While Willis was sleeping, I would not leave for fear of not being called when he awoke. I would sit on a tall chair and read.

When Willis graduated from the tent, and was in a crib . . . I asked one of the residents for instructions on what precautions to take with Willis now. I knew that he came out of the tent too early because there was another emergency. I did not want to do anything wrong. He laughed and said to just wear an apron and a mask. He was a new resident and did not know that I was serious. I watched one of the nurses near Willis and did as she did. I asked if he couldn't sit in my lap and she helped me get comfortable with him.

That was the day Mike died. I was in the ward and they all knew that I would not interfere, so they did not ask me to leave. I am grateful for that. I saw how everyone there cares so much, even when there is no hope from the beginning. Tommy Z. asked me what all the noise was and I told him what was happening. Someone pulled the curtain and Willis, Tommy and I sat together while everyone did their

*Luck brought us one receptionist, a mother of nine, four of whose daughters had been nurses at various times in the Institute. Also, one son-in-law was a psychiatrist at Massachusetts General Hospital. She had an uncanny gift for knowing where to locate doctors when needed and when to call the floor about distraught parents at the reception desk.
†This continues to be done, modified by the obvious need to judge how technical the procedure is, how overwrought the parent is, and whether such "help" disrupts bacterial precautions, vital treatment, or nursing morale.

absolute best to try to save Mike. I knew Mike's mother was downstairs and when everything had quieted down, I went down to see if there was anything I could say to her, but she had left. I did write to her and we still exchange notes occasionally.

A few days after that, one of Willis's bandages slipped off his thigh and was around his ankle. If he had been in the tent, I would have known exactly what to do, but being out in the air, I was not sure. I looked for a nurse, but everyone was busy. I got the supplies I knew the nurse would need. Still everyone was busy, and meanwhile his burn was unbandaged. I had done dressings in the tent and I followed exact sterile procedures. Before I had the old dressing all off, the doctor who had laughed when I asked for instructions came running over to me shouting, *"What do you think you are doing?"* I told him what happened and what I was doing and reminded him that when I asked him for instructions, he thought I was kidding. He told me to get away and he started doing the dressing himself. He told me I could be bringing a germ to Willis from some other part of the hospital, that I could cause the graft to become infected and that I should not be allowed to have anything to do with Willis's dressings. I knew that I had done nothing wrong, yet that doctor made me feel I had just nearly caused a catastrophe.

Another day, when Willis was still in the crib in the open . . . it was getting close to nap time. A nurse came to Willis and asked me to leave. I told her that I would help her get Willis ready for bed and save someone else from having to help. She reluctantly allowed me to stay. She was tying Willis's right arm up and I told her she was doing it wrong. She reminded me that she was the nurse and that she knew what she was doing. I insisted that she was not doing it right, then she shouted at me, "This kid is crying, and it is upsetting me." I said, "This is *my* kid you are hurting and *you* are upset?" Then the . . . nurse who instructs the new nurses came over and asked what the problem was. I told her and she looked up Willis's record. I was right. I do not usually argue, otherwise. I could not get across to that nurse that she was wrong, that I had been there every day, that just because I have no RN does not make me an idiot. I do not remember seeing her again. Not that I missed her. I am sure Willis did not miss her either. She had that poor kid's arm up so high, I am surprised that the newly formed scar tissue did not open right up. I am glad I stayed to settle him for nap time that day, otherwise he probably would have been in that painful position until I was allowed back up.

Something else I do not want to forget about is the K-wire.* I was told about it and that Willis would be getting one sometime. I had seen them in other kids and, rationally, I knew what they were. I knew Willis was in the OR that morning. I came in at the regular time and checked to see if I could come up. I walked in and put on my sterile clothes. I went over to Willis, and there it was! I knew it was coming, but not today! I must have looked strange. I staggered over to the nurses' desk to sit on a tall chair. The head nurse saw me and asked what was wrong. I told her that I did not know about Willis's new part and she was surprised that no one had told me that it was done that day. . . .

The main thing that I did not like was that I had to be sort of on the sly with the other parents about what I was doing with Willis. I did not want to blow my special treatment. I felt it was extremely important for Willis not to feel abandoned.

I remember one day I asked him where Daddy was and he said, "All gone." I asked him where Bradley, his brother, was and he said, "All gone." I asked him

---

*Kirschner wire, used to transfix the whole limb in skeletal traction.

where Buff, our dog, was and he said, "All gone." I tried to explain to him that everyone was still at home, but he thought home was all gone too. He thought that what he had been through for the last few weeks was all that the future held in store for him, and I knew that he was depressed. I asked if Willis couldn't have the family albums in so that we could talk about home and I could get across to him that he would get better. I brought them in and out while he was in the tent [bacteria control unit]. There just was not the space to leave them on that side of the ward. When he got out of the tent, I brought them in to stay until he came home. I brought from home most of his toys, and he and his little black Ghanaian girlfriend had a ball looking at them.

One day the girl's father came in and his daughter would not look at him. The nurse told him that she was "mad" at him. Loosely translated, *mad* usually means *insane* in foreign languages. Being from another country, her father looked panicky. The nurse again said his daughter was "only mad at you," but that did not seem to help. With the look on that man's face, I could not keep my mouth closed. I told him that what the nurse was trying to say was that his daughter was "angry" with him for leaving her in such a place. He then picked her up and started talking to her in their own language and the visit went along well.

It looks to me that the thing that is needed more is communication between parents and staff, and acceptance by the staff that the parents are intelligent human beings.

A couple of other quick thoughts are a map of the tunnel should be included [in the handbook], and those tall chairs are great. If the chairs cannot be moved around the ward for reasons of germs, there should be one chair assigned for each tent. Try sitting next to those tents in a short chair for a couple of hours, or try standing, you will know how important those chairs are.

I hope this helps you and gives you some ideas.

TURMOIL-RECOIL

In terms of what happens to the family after the disfiguring injury, there appears to be a basic sequence of events for both adult and child patients. As a rule the relatives of adult and child patients are seen by the social service at the hospital; the children's families are also offered a parents' group they may attend weekly. Many of the parents of children do not feel that they are up to attending a group until their children are well along in their treatment or have already gone home. Frequent mention is made of isolation, loneliness, and a sense of incomprehension and helplessness; these feelings are partly due to the intrusion in their lives of medical technology, and partly due to the inner struggle over crisis management they were facing. They are concerned over the life or death of their relative, and over disfigurement, though this issue is covered to a surprising degree for most people who have heard about modern miracles of plastic surgery, which, they like to assume, will leave the patient as good as new. There also persists a picture of burns as similar to sunburn, affecting only the outermost skin. This is never said to them by professionals, but the notion does repeatedly crop up from friends and relatives and seems to be supported by mass literature and tabloids. They worry about finances, the cost of care, how to manage the rest of the family, and how to arm themselves for the long run. The groups, caseworkers, and other patients help them cope with these problems. After the patient's separation from the hospital, there are a few notable relatives who become active, both with the staff and outside the hospital, in fire prevention activities and in lobbying for flameproofing of clothing. A majority of relatives remain in contact with the medical care professionals, but they do not sustain long contact with other families of burned patients. This is also true of the patients; both adults and children seem to go their own ways and do not keep up long friendships with each other as far as we can ascertain. Some of the case histories presented earlier in this book showed the importance of keeping a close personal feeling about some member of the staff, or idealizing the physicians.

Anticipatory Mourning

An important, and even urgent, need of the relatives is to encompass the tragic events unfolding before them within some broad framework of meaning comprehensible in terms of their experience and beliefs. This search for meaning, stemming from an inability to tolerate a world in which disaster strikes a child without apparent rhyme or reason, takes various forms, such as seeking out some human or impersonal agency who could be blamed for the burn injury or placing it within the inscrutable significance of a religious scheme of things.

The process of anticipatory mourning, the gradual detachment of emotional investment from the patient, has been noted in most cases in which the course of illness was longer than three or four months, and results in a muting of the grief reaction so that the terminal phase and death of the child are often received with an attitude of philosophical resignation. However, there appears to be an inverse relationship between this process and unusually strong denial defenses; when the latter are present, the reaction to the death and to postmortem mourning is likely to be more distressing. But we also deal with anticipation of the loss of a complete functional person, the loss of hope for a husband's future or a child's career, and even the loss of hope that a wife or mother might be free from domestic chores at some future time.

After discharge begins the longest and ultimately the most draining part, which goes on for years, living with deviance. As Bott [7] indicated, there is a distinction between the ways people feel deviant and externally defined deviance. The world will define a physically disfigured person as deviant and handicapped. On the other hand, as

Poznanski [8] remarked, the visibility of a defect is crucial. She feels labeling someone as handicapped also stereotypes the attitudes of almost everyone—including parents.

The family of the burned person must bear his stigma and the feelings of guilt over what has happened, and the community is not likely to let them forget it. It is the long-term management of disfigurement that never releases the family. They share the financial loss, the constant extra work, the need to maintain medical care, but they cannot hide problems as well as can diabetics or cardiac patients. As Pless [9] commented about families, the relationship between the family and the patient's adjustment is a reciprocal balance that shifts back and forth. The ways in which the patient's adjustment is enhanced by the family members will depend on other family members and on the functioning of the family as a whole.

A particular problem we had in assessing the reactions of families was that we began to study them first by sending out questionnaires. To keep them from being too "psychiatric" and focused on problems, we used a variety of letters for eliciting information. We had the hospital schoolteacher and the recreation therapist write and the nurses telephone for information about how patients were getting along. The information from these sources was deceptively hopeful. Mothers would generally tell us that their children were doing all right in school and husbands would report that their wives were attending physical therapy sessions regularly when they were not. Apparently there was some unwillingness to open up to the recreation therapist and schoolteacher interviewers, which was in sharp contrast to the wealth of material revealed to the psychologists, psychiatrist, and nurses, whom they knew personally and to whom they came back for follow-up visits. Also, they were more informative with the research worker who visited homes to find out how the families were faring. We found out less from the 150 people responding to the questionnaire.

We moved rapidly to gather information in the beginning, on a wave of initial enthusiasm, first sending out the questionnaire devised by the psychiatrist, the psychologist, and the schoolteacher. Then the nurses eagerly began to phone people, and one of the research staff began to call and to make home visits with the psychiatrist and psychologist. This researcher had previously worked in sociology. At another time a sociologist began some of the work but was appalled by the disfigurement and dropped out quickly. The information that filtered in from clinic visits came by way of anecdotes reported by staff nurses. Only later, when the staff had a sense of the social evolution of burned children in their families, were more systematic ways of obtaining information established. For the first three years of operation we had several different patterns of social work deployment, using several part-time workers, and then full-time ones. It was (and still is) difficult to get case-workers for this type of activity, but the main difficulty was that the social workers had such heavy loads of social problems, dying children, destroyed homes, disturbed families, child abuse cases, insurance questions, newspaper interrogations, and the intrahospital communications that they could not participate very actively in this work until several years later, when the socioeconomic data gathering had become routine for pediatricians and social workers who could be conveniently added to the roster of investigative workers.

Some of the patterns of unresponsiveness are illustrated in the following two cases.

Case History: Guthrie M.

Guthrie, aged 47, had a history of financial failure, depression, alcoholism, and philandering. He had shifted to a career in refinishing jewelry and was working in his shop, carelessly handling highly inflammable solvents, when he tipped over a can and burned his neck, arms, and legs. In the hospital, he passed over his problems by indicating they were in the past. His wife had been planning to leave him prior to his accident, and had been having counseling in preparation for this. On her last visit to him in the hospital, she poured out her antipathy and despair over the marriage, but after they returned home her stated response to the efforts to find help for him was that things were going very well, that she was grateful for all the help she had received, and that his disfigurement was not marked. Actually, she had merely delayed her plans for divorce.

Case History: Elwynne H.

Elwynne was a 31-year-old housewife and mother of two children and had been unhappily married for eight years. She had burned her chest, back, right arm, and face while angrily handling an electrical appliance in the presence of flammable materials. Her 32-year-old husband felt, and stated repeatedly, that she had purposely harmed herself in order to gain sympathy from him. During her hospitalization she had had intensive help from an experienced caseworker, but after her release she did not follow through on any of the recommendations for further counseling regarding her marital problems. She was contacted several times to see how she was doing and she responded evasively. Some months later a photograph of her husband and son appeared in the local newspaper. When the researcher wrote her again about her situation, she reported that she was divorced from him, and that she had begun to look for psychiatric help.

Oftentimes the families will be genuinely grateful for the help they have received from the hospital, but once they have made a break with the institution, they would like to forget as much as possible of the whole tragic picture and seek whatever emotional help they want from other sources. There are others, of course, for whom it is merely more convenient to go elsewhere.

Because of these factors, we have pursued a fairly aggressive policy of trying to visit all the people we could to assess what was going on in their homes to determine the ways in which people coped with these problems.

EMOTIONAL RECONSTRUCTION

Some of the families were poor, limited, and only *partial* families, poor people worn down by multiple burdens, generally with no men in the home. The mother of Norma W., a 7-year-old with severe disfiguring burns on her face, neck, and chest, had been suggested for psychological evaluation by a plastic surgeon whom Norma had seen three years earlier in her local hospital and again at our Plastic Clinic. The following is a report of a home visit.

Case History: Norma W.

Mrs. W. lives in a shabby inner-city housing project. As I approached her door, I could hear voices within screaming at one another. When I rang the bell, the voices stopped, the door opened, and two black women stared out at me. After I introduced myself, one of the two, a short, chubby woman in her late twenties, said that she was Mrs. W. and that she had forgotten about our appointment, but invited me in anyway.

After the other woman left we sat down at the kitchen table. Mrs. W. explained that Norma had been burned at the age of four when she had turned on the stove accidentally, while climbing up on the kitchen counter. It was about 6 A.M. and her mother, younger brother, and sister were still asleep. Her cries awakened her mother, who rescued her. She gave no other details except to say that it took some time to get help because she did not have a telephone. Although there was little damage to the apartment, the police investigated the fire. Mr. W. had left the family sometime before the accident.

When I asked about Norma's hospitalization, Mrs. W. had little to say other than that the nurses spoiled her daughter and this made discipline difficult to maintain when she came home. She was able to visit the hospital only every other day because, she stated emphatically, her own family was of no help during this time. But later she did mention that her brother, who had been a medic in the army, had helped her change the dressings. Apparently the only person who supported her during this ordeal was a social worker, whom Mrs. W. feels was very understanding. She does not remember how long her daughter was hospitalized or how much subsequent surgery has been performed.

Mrs. W. thinks Norma looks much better now, but added that maybe I would not think so because I had not seen her before. She feels that her daughter acts like a normal child, playing and fighting with the other children in the housing project "just like they all do." She disciplines her exactly as she does her other children by spanking or taking away ice cream and television. She spends more money on

Norma's clothes than she does the others, buying the prettiest things she can find, to compensate for the scars. However, she does feel that her daughter is not nearly as bright as her younger children, who are both in the Head Start program. Although Norma has been in special classes for over a year, Mrs. W. did not speak in terms of retardation or emotional disturbance. She simply thinks that she is slow because of the accident.

She then said that she never thought anything like this would ever happen to her and that it was especially difficult because she had never known anyone who had had a similar accident. There were no other badly burned patients in the local hospital while Norma was there so there was no one she knew who understood what she was feeling. She cannot understand why nothing happens to her sister's children who are allowed to play around the stove and light cigarettes. And she added, "I resent my friend's children. She brings them over to play. Why should they be perfect when Norma is so scarred? It just isn't fair."

Then, with much feeling, she told me how much she hated taking Norma out in public. Groping for words, she said, "I felt—I can't think of the word—I guess you would call it 'shame'—I felt as if everyone was staring at me and thinking, 'Why wasn't she home when it happened?' " This was a surprising comment for two reasons. First, she had already told me that she was at home and, second, her thought was that people were staring at her and not at her daughter whose scars would, in reality, attract attention. She then mentioned that occasionally after people had noticed her daughter, they would come over and give her money. (Stevie R.'s mother had reported the same experience.) When I said that the mothers I knew felt angry when strangers stared at their children, she replied that she never felt that way, but if they ever came over and asked questions, she would "let them have it."

Then she sighed, "I don't feel that I'm to blame for what happened, but then maybe I'm to blame for the whole thing. My mother is snappy. She says it is all my fault—that if I had been awake it wouldn't have happened." Some of her neighbors had also begun warning her that her husband would come back and "get [her] because [she] let Norma get burned." When I asked if he did, she giggled and replied, "No." Then she said that she really blamed her husband for the accident, saying, "I know what I'm doing—I'm trying to find someone other than myself to blame. He blames me, so I blame him." When I asked how she felt he was to blame, she replied that if he had not left the family, he would have been home, and "two noses are better than one."

She sees herself as being very different from the way she was before the fire and guesses she will never again be the same. She feels nervous all the time. Before the accident she had been very thin, but afterwards began overeating because food made her feel better. She also has become a chain-smoker.

Finally, we talked about her future and she says she cannot wait for her children to grow up and become independent so she will not have to stay home. She hopes to go back to school (she dropped out in the ninth grade) and then get special training to become a keypunch operator.

This mother was unusual in our group in that she was so preoccupied with her own feelings, which she freely revealed, that she hardly mentioned her child. In fact, she only discussed her in response to my direct questions. Her comment "Why did this happen to me?" ignores the fact that the accident really happened to her daughter. And when I asked about Norma's hospitalization she responded in terms of how spoiled she had become, with no mention of the pain and suffering she had endured. Perhaps what seems most revealing is her feeling that strangers were staring at her rather than her very scarred daughter. She never seems sensitive to Norma's feelings. Her own guilt and shame are being reinforced by her mother and her neighbors. She appeared as someone so hung up on her own feelings that she had few emotional resources left to support her daughter.

A totally different kind of family response—and family setting—is the one depicted by the mother of Alfred W.

Case History: Alfred W.
Alfred had been a college student working on a project when the building he was in exploded, leaving him with dreadful scars after long hospitalization. He had been an outstanding student, and returned to his work, albeit with considerable anxiety, and more social limitation than his mother suggests, but her interview with the research worker gives much of the sense of her way of coping. It does, however, put the father in the shadows. He stood by, with little of her demonstrativeness and controllingness, but he was always available to his son, and continued his quiet career as a pharmacist. The interview took place six years after the accident, when the patient was 26 years of age but still dominating the family in his role as a graduate student in science.

Mrs. W. was not very warm when she greeted me, saying she was expecting someone a lot older. She invited me in and asked where I thought we should sit. All of the rooms were very dark. We agreed on the kitchen, where we then talked for over two hours.

Mrs. W. sees Alfred as a person who is fated to have bad things happen to him, things over which he has no control. She said that he was an only child and they had plenty of money "to grease his way, but it was not to be." The examples she gave to support this were that he had been a premature baby who needed special care during the early months. When he was in elementary school another child had tripped him and he had broken either an arm or a collarbone. In high school, a mistake by the principal resulted in Alfred's not winning a science award. Thus, she sees the explosion as one more incident in a series of bad things that have happened. She did not mention what anxiety she has about the future.

Because of his age Alfred was hospitalized in the burn ward of Massachusetts General Hospital. His mother's first words to her son in the hospital were "You are not alone—your father and I are here—we will not go home until you do." And she didn't. Mrs. W. did not return to their home in Rhode Island until they took Alfred home four months later. She says that the only way she got through this time was by blanking out the future and living just one day at a time. "I felt that each day Alfred lived was a bonus and I never thought beyond that." One day a nurse told her to prepare for the fact that her son faced years of surgery and she became very upset.

She said that she kept all her anxiety to herself so that Alfred would not see how worried she really was. Mr. W., however, was very upset every time he saw his son during the first month and often had to leave his room. She feels that her training as a registered nurse helped her in this regard. The only thing that broke down her defenses was when Alfred would thank her for something she had done for him. On several occasions when this occurred she had to rush out of his room so that he would not see her tears.

She knows that Alfred did not tell her all that he was going through, either. Each tried to spare the other's feelings. She mentioned that Alfred never took out his angry feelings on her as the psychiatrist had predicted. She emphasized that his innate great sense of humor sustained him at this time. He often made up jokes and puns, which the surgeon would pretend to be horrified by. Later, he was able to joke about the pictures of himself taken after the fire and to enjoy the surgeon's joke that he wanted them for his Christmas cards. He had many visitors and especially enjoyed seeing his friends from college, which was nearby. He kept up with some of his college work during this time.

Mrs. W. talked quite a bit about how much of the actual nursing care she did herself even though they had private duty nurses for much of the time. She was critical of the care her son was given in the hospital and often had to redo something that the nurses did improperly,* for example, cleaning Alfred after a bowel movement. She was given access to the kitchen and the linen closet and changed the sheets frequently. She was always prepared to give all this time because there were no other dependents at home.

Several times she mentioned one conflict she felt strongly. When the nursing care was not up to her standards, she wanted to complain to the doctors. Yet, she felt that if she did complain, the nurses would not take good care of Alfred. Therefore, most of the time she held back what she was feeling. On several occasions, however, she did talk to the doctors and one nurse did resign from the case.

When I asked if her religion had been any help during this period, she said her rabbi had visited several times and also had telephoned to see how Alfred was coming along. She grimaced as she recalled that he had assured her that he was praying for her son's recovery. Very cynically she said, "That made me feel just great—it really relieved me." She does not believe God had anything to do with Alfred's recovery, unless you call the surgeon "God." Then she said that perhaps God had been working through the doctor. She concluded, "Anyway, I guess you'd call me an agnostic—you can't prove anything either way."

Mrs. W. feels she has never been the same since the accident. When I asked how so, she said she has not been back to a hairdresser since then. She started washing her hair in her Boston hotel room so that she would not have to spend time in a beauty salon. She also said she was a great talker, had a large vocabulary, and loved to express herself, but that after the accident she was a lot quieter. She mentioned having a recurrent nightmare in which she sees Alfred in an explosion and says she still has this occasionally. She also takes medication for high blood pressure and has an incipient ulcer.

Although the parents had been told that their son would be hospitalized about eight months, he was actually released after four months because his mother was a trained nurse and could care for him at home. She emphasized that her care was so complete that it was unnecessary for the visiting nurse to stop in at all. Her husband came home daily at 3 o'clock to bath Alfred because he was adamant in not want-

---

*A perennial problem in any hospital is distinguishing valid complaints about staff performance from complaints caused by venting of personal animosity, sadness, or guilt. When the families are scientists, lawyers, academics, or medical professionals, there is special edginess in judging complaints.

ing Alfred's mother to see his body. She explained that he probably would not have minded a nurse who was a stranger, but he definitely did not want her. Mother and son began taking long walks in the public park near their home. To prepare for the outing, Mrs. W. filled her handbag with many heavy household items to defend them both in case they were accosted by a "pervert." This apparently never happened.

Soon after he was released from the hospital Alfred insisted on going back to the laboratory where the accident had occurred to see how it had been restored. He has no fear of fire.

Mrs. W. commented on her son's convalescence: "Alfred turned out instead of in." His college friends came down each weekend, bringing him the school newspaper and the latest gossip so he kept in touch with his school life. Usually they played cards, listened to records, and just talked. When he was an outpatient at Massachusetts General Hospital Alfred visited the burned children in the Shriners Burns Institute—would take along stacks of comicbooks and read to them. He would also talk with adult burn patients in the intensive care unit. After he returned to college in Boston for his undergraduate degree he did volunteer work with young boys at the Y.M.C.A. His fellow students and teachers brought him books and tapes of lectures, gave special help in tutoring, and a matrix of academic support and encouragement all the way.

At present Alfred is completing work toward his Ph.D. He shares an apartment, which his mother completely furnished ("down to the monogrammed glassware"), with another graduate student who has an eye disfigurement. He has friends, including some close relationships with a few faculty members, and enjoys music and books. He does not drink or smoke. He drives a car that his mother gave him. He has made at least one trip to Europe by himself to attend scientific seminars and while there rented a car and went sightseeing on his own. He has done some university teaching, but his mother discouraged this because he did not need the money. At the beginning of the interview she showed me Alfred's grade report containing five or six grades of 5.0 (the highest marks possible). She explained that she always opens his mail because there might be something she has to do for him.

When I asked if Alfred enjoyed parties, Mrs. W. replied that he does go out on dates occasionally, blind dates. He always insists that the girl be told ahead of time that he has been burned. She feels that this is the area in which the accident has the worst consequences. "Think how important beautiful skin is to a girl," she mused. She can now understand and sympathize with middle-aged women who want cosmetic surgery because she believes our society puts a high value on beauty. She said, "Alfred is like an iceberg—his worst scars are covered."

When the family is in Florida, Alfred puts on bathing trunks and swims in public beaches. I got the feeling that she wished he would not do this, although she did not express this in words. She admits her eyesight is failing and that at a distance his face does not look so bad to her. Sometimes she forgets and stares at him to see how he really looks. Recently when this happened Alfred noticed her and asked her to stop. Mrs. W. seems better able to accept the situation because she keeps the rooms dark and does not wear glasses. She consults her own doctor a great deal so perhaps it is significant that she is neglecting her eyesight.

I said that mothers of burned children were sometimes bothered when strangers stared. She said very forcefully that this does not surprise her at all because there was a great deal of cruelty in the world. Then she stood up and went over to a shelf, and took an antacid pill for her incipient ulcer. For the next ten minutes she talked about the fate of the Jews in concentration camps, and the people in Bangladesh and Northern Ireland. Thus, she responded to my statement about people staring only in an indirect way.

Mrs. W. wishes Alfred had had more reconstructive surgery than he has, and there is tension between them on this issue. Several years ago he had a chance to go out to the University of California at Berkeley to study and his mother developed hysterics, which she implied were partly feigned, in order to keep him here because she knows that if he ever left this area he would never again bother with surgery. She encouraged her husband, to whom Alfred has never said no, to join her in dissuading their son from making this move, and they were eventually successful. Alfred handles all his appointments now with his surgeon; in this, she said, "Alfred is the master of his own faith [sic]." When Mrs. W. recently suggested to her son that he ask to have a keloid removed from his chin, he refused. With some exasperation she said to me, "How do you tell your son he looks horrible?" She is very aware that if she pushes the idea of more reconstructive surgery too much Alfred will run away from her, and the thought that he would stop coming home bothers her more than the way he looks. Alfred is very close to his father but they are not demonstrative with one another. However, he is affectionate with her and she often reminds him that he is never too old to kiss his mother. So, again, she keeps back the intensity of her feelings that a lot more could and should be done to improve his looks. She reiterated that if reconstructive surgery were left up to Alfred, he would not bother with it.

When I asked what she saw her son doing five years from now, she replied that he would probably leave college for a short time after he earns his degree to gain experience elsewhere, but that he would eventually return to teach and do research. With much feeling she said, "They shouldn't take him back just because they feel sorry for him. They really do owe him something." Again she expressed her feeling that Alfred is entitled to anything he wants after what he has been through and this includes anything connected with the university as well. Apparently he could have sued the laboratory where the explosion occurred, but their lawyer indicated they would also have to involve the university and several of his favorite instructors, so it was Alfred's decision not to sue. At this point she mentioned how opposed she had been to Alfred's taking this job in the first place because of the potential danger, and how both husband and son had persuaded her to let him do it. This is no doubt distorted, because danger of an explosion seemed quite remote from anyone's mind.

As I was leaving, I noticed a large photograph of Alfred taken at the time of his bar mitzvah and another, smaller picture of him with a girl taken at his junior prom. He had been an exceptionally good-looking young man—a fact his mother never mentioned. She pointed out several letters from his surgeon on the mantle.

When I thanked Mrs. W., she said that this was the most she had ever talked to anyone about this ordeal; she tries not to think about it and all the other tragedies in her family. She said it was all so painful that she put it in the past and lived in the present. Having said all this, she invited me to come back any time I wanted to talk.

The clarity of detail in the entire interview made the accident seem to have happened last week, not almost seven years ago. The reality of the whole situation is still very close to his mother. It is the core of her life.

Mrs. W. shows the extreme focus of her life on this boy, a phenomenon that we have seen in several families with disfigured children. Of course, it occurs with other types of handicapping in offspring.

Overattachment to the child has been termed *hyperedophilia.* This does not clarify the family configuration, which may be more guilt, depression, and covert frustration with the child than heightened affection. Holt [10] described the mothers of retarded children who had their normal children adopted in order to give their whole time to the retarded child. Unquestionably, for some of the time, the healthy children are pushed aside by the press of circumstances, and have to make do with whatever neighbor, grandparents, cousin, or friend will help out in getting the meals and making their home and school arrangements while every effort is focused on going to the hospital and visiting the burn victim. Teachers have even come forward to offer foster homes.

BLAME PLACING AND GUILT

Inevitably there is the problem of making some sense out of the tragedy and its aftermath, and also dealing with the question of who is responsible for what happened. This sense of blameworthiness runs through most of the people who were present at the accident as well as to the family members, whether there is a reasonable basis for culpability or not. Bystanders feel they should have done more. Peers wonder why they escaped and whether they were cowardly or could have done more to rescue the victims; families feel all of these reactions as well. The owners of factories that exploded or manufacturers have never come to us. They have appeared as the enemy in insurance struggles and fights over new legislation and fire regulations. Universities or philanthropic institutions in which accidents have occurred have often been much more helpful and accommodating, offering money and coming to help. But it is with the family members that the most poignant guilt feelings linger. In diseases of uncertain origin, mothers ponder what they did wrong with their children. The mothers of retarded children feel they have produced something defective because of some unconsciously expressed defect in themselves, regardless of what the genetic counselors tell them. Even when a disease has a very specific cause unrelated to the parents there is sense of blame. However, in the mothers of children who have been burned, there are several very common and prominent areas for dealing with blame and guilt. They ask about whether they were supervising the children properly, whether it was a little girl reaching over a burning stove or an adolescent climbing into a storage area that was locked. They are concerned about their absent husbands, wondering whether they should have checked the household wiring more carefully, who left matches around the house, or even if their marital problems lie at the bottom of the lack of supervision that surrounded the injury. In the parents' group that meets at the Burns Institute, mothers will join in helping to suppress this culpability and talk about how it was a true random event, an accident about which nothing could be done. But the theme recurs. Fathers come less to the group, and while they speak of some of the same issues, the separated father asking if his absence was not contributory, the theme is not as prominent as it is with mothers.

Gardner [11] found in a study of parents with diseased children that some of them do suffer guilt because of unconscious hostility toward their children, but that others suffer a feeling that what has happened is their fault and that they merit punishment. He concluded that much of the sense of fault in these people is due to a struggle to gain some control over the calamity, to manage the uncontrollable. He feels, quite reasonably, that unconscious hostility is not an adequate explanation for a sense that seems to involve almost all parents, and that the feelings of helplessness in the face of catastrophe are universal. His view is that involving families in the care of their children is far more useful than confronting them with conflicted impulses. Certainly this has been the finding of our group.

However, guilt can be conscious and logical. It can be a quite lucid sense of having been irresponsible, having shown poor care, or having been inattentive at an important moment, and this guilt is not to be excluded from the list of causes of these problems. The endemic parental sense of having failed one's children is not precisely the guilt parents have when children are burned. It is more prevalent when there is a visible residue of parental failure! The parents of the retarded have developed elaborate systems for helping each other, for campaigning to remove the stigma of retardation. But the stigma of physical damage is not subject to the same kind of control. Work on fire prevention is one way of expiation; hard work with the child is another. No parent who cares can escape some of the unhappiness that goes with burn disfigurement. The new group APBIC (Association for the Prevention of Burn Injuries in Children) is an important beginning. Time, measured in years, is required to come to grips with it, and often the parents feel that the child is a living reproach to them for what they have done or failed to do.

When one child survives and another dies, parents will grieve for the departed in a more or less normal way, but the burden of guilt is naturally heavier. The survivor has many of the feelings described by concentration camp survivors, who ponder why they were spared, and who idealize others who died and seemed more worthy.

Case History: William S.
William was 12 years old and with his family at a picnic. His father was pouring fire starter fluid and William ran past him, jostling his arm unintentionally, and set his sister Patricia on fire, burning her face, chest, and arms. She retained grisly scars that permanently disfigured her, and required long and repeated hospitalizations and multiple operations on her nostrils, eyelids, lips, and cheeks, as well as releases of the scar contractures under her arms. For 18 months after the accident William had nightmares and was obsessed with his guilt. His sister formally and repeatedly forgave him, as did his parents and the nuns at his parochial school. He was seen a number of times for psychiatric help with his oppressive sense of guilt. Over the succeeding years he did resolve most of this and was reported to be playing with his sister, and teasing and joking in a generally normal manner. Patricia was a sanguine and cooperative child, whose adolescence showed the very common social withdrawal and fear of encountering negative reactions from people, in spite of a uniformly protective attitude from her parents and brother, and the nuns at the school. Later she began to be more independent, without help from her parents, who became preoccupied in unrelated marital problems.

Case History: Jimmy S.
Jimmy, who at the age of 12 had sustained bad facial disfigurement, and had ropy scar overgrowth on his chin and cheeks, had nightmares and was preoccupied for years about his sister who had died in the fire, and who had been a "better person." He discussed her with his family, the nurses, the social worker, his psychiatrist, the physical therapist, and anyone with whom he maintained any relationship, requiring reassurances for years. His sister reappeared in dreams, where he rescued her from her fate, and not until he was well into adolescence did he seem to have some distance from this event.

An atmosphere of reassurance helps, but guilt feelings are so ingrained in our social styles that they cannot be avoided. What appears to perpetuate the issue of guilt is the problem of insurance, the question of finding out what the cause of the fire was, and *who did it*. In the most benign actuarial approach there is still the need to have a defined cause, and in the disturbed families, so much involved in burn injuries, the need to blame each other covertly or consciously may be intense. What has developed in our experience at the Burns Institute has been a series of changing and edited stories that serve to cover the parents while their sense of culpability festers below. Sometimes only when the insurance issue is settled and the police, fire investigators, and the rest have long disappeared from the scene will the families tell all. Very commonly they lie from the outset. Often they are vague, and deny painful and dangerous memories. Most often, they are encouraged by repeated questioning to standardize their stories into a compromise report, which exculpates them and which gives an approximate story of how the child has been injured. For adults in an industrial accident there is often a wish to exclude any possibility that the worker was at fault. Later a need is felt by many families of both adult and child burn victims to stress the incapacitation in order to maintain insurance benefits, or to evade returning to work before the patient feels ready. We have not seen this shade over into the compensation neurosis pattern in its fully developed form, but the ingredients are all there. With children, the parents more generally want to get them back to school and do not give distorted pictures of their incapacitation, though many parents are fearful of putting too much strain on their children. Another factor intrinsically involved in all of the family reactions is the problem of shame.

SHAME
Even the origin of the verb *shame* in the Indo-European *bas scham* or [*s*] *kam* means "to hide or cover" in a basic sense of covering up, also seen in the Latin origin of "shirt" or "chemise" as *camiso*. It goes right to the issue of having one's defects and guilt exposed, which is exactly the feeling we have in mind when we speak of the shame that relatives experience over being seen with their disfigured kin. Traditionally, we have distinguished *guilt* as a feeling of having done wrong and *shame* as a sense of being exposed, which is one of the most salient features of adolescent behavior. The teenage daughter of a disfigured man is likely to avoid bringing friends home, for this and other reasons. Again, the most widely examined group here is the retarded, whose siblings have been offered groups to help them deal with their mutual problems.

Children under 4 or 5 years of age demonstrate more concern over deformity of the extremities and trunk than the face. Facial deformity does not become a major personal issue until the child begins school and body areas that are covered by clothing are deemphasized. Other children at this age do not disguise their reactions to deformity and can frequently be cruel in their treatment of the child who is different. The depressive withdrawal exhibited by deformed children of this age seems most related to such hostile rejection by other children. Between the ages of 6 and 11, deformed hands are more a personal, practical handicap to the child than are other areas of the body. None of these observations are without exceptions.

Once the disfigurement begins to be evident, many of the feelings of shame come up with siblings that are analogous to feelings in families with a retarded member whose behavior is not disguised. Outsiders exhibit curiosity, excitement, horror, and some cruelty toward the victim and the siblings struggle with the sense of shame about having an imperfect relative or one they cannot be proud of. Rarely, we have heard of children disparaging their disfigured kin to evade the stigma, but usually they are loyal and tense, silent and guilty about what they feel because they sense no way out of it. Big brothers often fight or threaten children who tease. If they have been involved in the fire, they have more complicated conflicts to manage.

Adult burn victims we have interviewed, who have lived with these problems, see them in a negative light, and while their feelings are tempered by time and experience, they do not report an enlarged tolerance and sense of being broadened by the experience. Rather, they continue to see this as a chore, a burden, and nothing to be proud of. The shame can be normalized; experience with other families, hospital staff, experiential groups, other mothers, and teachers over time does improve the reaction. However, the public is not a great help with its stares and shock responses. The occasional response, as in the case of Norma W., to whom strangers gave money, is not really helpful. Some people will be overly helpful and compliant for specific social tasks, such as giving directions to a couple where one is handicapped or disfigured, partly out of sympathy but partly to get rid of them quickly.

STIGMA AND PHOBIA

In general child psychiatry practice the problem of phobia is endemic, and phobias are generally agreed in definition to be unwarranted fears of nondangerous situations or activities. The phobic individual may fear illness, crowds, blushing, heights, or appearing on a stage. As it is expressed, the fear is more of an internal danger rather than an external one, and is actually anxiety about some feared event or experience that is not likely to occur. The common fears of crowds and going out in public must be seen differently for the disfigured person.

Unlike the phobic person, the disfigured person will receive undue attention from the public, he will be stared at, and people will not be comfortable with him. Practical effects are such that some disfigured people will harden themselves to these experiences and continue to go out, but as they are real experiences and invariably painful, the facially damaged person is kept by society from receiving an unequivocal clean bill of health. His parents cannot be convinced that a little shoving into the public is mandatory, and making the parents responsible or pressing the school to encourage the disfigured child is not always successful because the parents feel they have been stigmatized as well and the school personnel often suffer from horror and fear in dealing with these situations. Also, these parents' energies have often been so depleted in dealing with the long illness that they need to be given help rather than exhorted to work even harder with their children, especially when they and their children feel very much damaged and stigmatized. Parents of facially handicapped children often find it easy to give in to the child's wish to hide and evade, which is not a true phobia. These patients may act like phobic individuals when exposed to a new social challenge, but it is objectively painful.

The ideal mother produces ideal children, and this means usually well-scrubbed and physically attractive offspring. Mothers of congenitally handicapped children seem to share the feeling that their own imperfections caused them to have a damaged child. They may project the blame on their own mothers for insufficient love and care during their growing years, or they may blame their husbands or their older children for exhausting their resources by excessive demands. However, all these projections serve only to mitigate the overriding feeling that their own imperfection caused the damage.

These mothers also seem to share the fantasy that their child was born unfinished, and they work on the child's rehabilitation to achieve the creation of a complete child. The successful care that she is able to give her handicapped child mitigates the mother's guilt and increases her dwindling self-esteem. The denial of the permanence of the damage and the fantasy of restitution seem to give her the strength to handle her grief and to pursue her active efforts toward the child's rehabilitation.

Indeed, the very presence of the child with his defect is a constant source of narcissistic hurt to the mother, and her unresolved grief has many and continued manifestations throughout the child's growing years. Mothers tend to react with acute anxiety and feelings of loss whenever they have to face still another proof of their child's being different.

The mother's unresolved grief and her devaluation of herself and the child, combined with her positive feelings and investment in the child's care and rehabilitation, create a relationship characterized by marked ambivalence, resulting in varying degrees of overprotection of the child. Wives and husbands as well as children of those who have been disfigured will often meet the needs of their relatives by denying some of his suffering and anxiety. They will often assume a rather blank expression to cover hurt and impotent rage or sadness, saying, "It doesn't matter," or more often saying nothing.

The role of denial in maintaining adjustment to serious disfigurement is an important one and it serves many useful functions for all members of the family. It is not to be uniformly punctured. The patient and his relatives all need the opportunity to ignore the problem from time to time; denial systems of families vary enormously, and it often gives them strength to face situations where they cannot ignore the disfigurement and its problems.

SOCIAL SHIFTS OF FAMILIES

Some studies have attempted to use parents and other observers to gauge the social participation of facially disfigured children and adolescents. Schmitt arrived at two overall conclusions:

The first is that the behavioral topography and depth of involvement in life experience of primary school age children is neither necessarily nor overwhelmingly affected by the presence of acquired facial disfigurement.

Second, by and large, the disfigured group is more prone to seek more limited experience in informal settings closer to home. The nondisfigured group is the more adventurous, roaming further from home, and exploring more facets of the community horizon [12, p. 89].

Schmitt's first conclusion pertaining to primary school age children is not so readily applicable to teenagers. As discussed earlier, disfigured female and male teenagers appear to adopt different community adjustment styles. Schmitt's second conclusion is easily applied to disfigured male teenagers but not to females. These similarities and differences between Schmitt's findings and our observations suggest that either (1) a shift to community adjustment style occurs as the disfigured child moves from the primary school age to adolescence, or (2) these differences are already present during primary school age but were not detected because of small sample sizes in Schmitt's study. The issue requires more study.

Further data are needed to determine how stigma and denial fit into the long-term behavior of burned children; and judgments of how families help or hinder are needed.

Case History: The A. Family

Linda, Hal, and Adele A. were three children whose family had moved from Baghdad to the southern United States, where their parents had opened a grocery store. The father was an old-fashioned autocrat, strong, hardworking, and affectionately undemonstrative. On an unusually cold day, a space heater exploded, seriously burning the three children and leaving them all with major facial disfigurement. In the hospital the children varied in their responses. In a determined effort to be manly that he never abandoned, Hal always acted tough and aggressive. He was expected to help in the family store and, in fact, did return to this role in spite of his disfigurement. The family went from wild and dramatic mourning in the hospital to apparent disregard of any problem whenever they could at home. The denial of his problem helped Hal to work in the store and master his disfigurement. The family usually acted as a group, as if there was nothing wrong when they were together, combining denial in action with a confederation for mutual support.

Tizard and Grad [13] showed in regard to the mentally handicapped that large, poor, incapacitated families do not always exhibit incapacity to manage handicapped children, and they stressed the need for professionals to see this. Schwartz [14] indicated that for many families with a handicapped member there is a crisis of *means*, simply having to struggle to get that person what he needs and for everyone to get by. For the well-to-do family there is a crisis of *ends*, in that the handicapped person is not seen as having the same goals as the undamaged members of the family; more appropriate goals are sought, and the families redirect their efforts toward careers or training that seem more appropriate for the patient.

While there is no consistency in the studies he reviewed, Fisher [15] noted that mothers with handicapped children have been shown to be influenced by this fact. For example, Howell [16] found that such mothers do have lower self-esteem than mothers of well children. Dow [17] demonstrated that parents of disabled children are best able to adjust to the whole problem by a general de-emphasis of the importance of physique in the world.

One particularly interesting finding that emerged from Fisher's study was that the parents of the deformed children manifested a significant positive correlation between the way they rated their children's bodies and their own. The analogous correlation for the control parents was not significant. Centers and Centers [18] speculated that difference represented a greater emotional involvement and identification with the child's body in the instance of the parent with the deformed child than was true in the case of the control parent with his child. It was proposed that special involvement of a parent with the body of his deformed child prevents him from clearly distinguishing it from his own.

Fisher thought it pertinent that Jabin [19] detected (in a population of high school students) low but significant positive correlations between body concern, as measured by the hypochondriasis scale of the Minnesota Multiphasic Personality Inventory, and anxious, negative attitudes toward the disabled.

All the families and the individuals involved need advice about surgical care, the prognosis, and the problems they will face. They need to know about dressings, the spacing of surgical procedures, when the patient can return to work or school, and when they can feel that active treatment will come to an end. They can use a lot of help regarding family reactions to the handicapped and disfigured, the physical stresses they will face, and the financial problems entailed in the overall problem. Among other things, they need sustained help and understanding of the chronic stress that they will face as a group and individually. The unremitting strains of dealing with these multifaceted problems are not comprehended by the families for a long time, and they need friends and professional workers to help them evolve styles of coping.

MOURNING

Among all the problems these families have to cope with is the process of grieving for the "lost" person, for with disfigurement there is a loss of the image of what the patient was and might have been. This involves all of the traditional feelings of separation about someone who has gone, but is complicated by the fact that the person remains, in an altered form.

McDaniel [20] and Wright [21] pointed out that the psychological value of mourning is yet to be confirmed. What they were focusing on was the frequently made assumption that once a handicapped person has gone through the grief period and assimilated the loss of total competence and ideal body image entailed in his handicap, he can make a better adjustment. This sounds very neat, but it is clear that it is not proved. Quite the contrary, many patients indicate clearly that they never get over their mourning, and while it is not so intense for all of them, the idea of chronic grief described by Olshansky [6] seems more appropriate. Again we see the combination of denial, shame, and grief determining the way people cope.

The mourning reaction has been characterized most clearly and concisely by Wright [21]. Serious illness or disability is accompanied by a constriction of psychological awareness and experience "down to the skin" and is expressed by despair, depression, and emotional withdrawal. Any change (new situation) is brought immediately and sharply into predominant focus and unimpaired capabilities are ignored during mourning. Preoccupation with the loss is primary and all else is secondary, this being caused by the desire to maintain the self-concept and body image intact. There is also a "requirement of mourning" that demands that the patient show proper respect for his loss and for the gravity of his situation. Any other response is considered to be inappropriate behavior according to the values of society. The gradual abatement of mourning occurs following the reconstruction of the body image and self-concept to accommodate changes and the reestablishment of a sense of personal worth.

In an extensive survey of reactions to chronic illness, Pless [9] reported that in the work of Farber and Ryckman [22] there is a series of stages that, much modified, might be applied to the burn victim:

1. Attempts are made to handle the deviance within existing family arrangements.
2. Distortion of family coalitions occur, leading to the assignment of the deviant role to the burn victim.
3. There follows a revision of age and sex roles for all family members.
4. This is followed by a changed association with individuals and groups outside the family, e.g., doctors, clinics, helping friends.
5. The question arises of whether to keep the patient as a *real* or functional person in the family, or to treat him as an object (as by hospitalizing him).

Elsewhere Pless found that fathers played a more important role in the child-rearing processes of families with handicapped children, but he noted disagreement in various studies about whether parents used approaches that were similar to those used with their other children in bringing up handicapped children. He found that some parents appeared quite realistic in their expectations about the future of their handicapped children. However, Wright [21] reported distinct differences in ways of handling the children. We found in our experience that disfigured children were sharply demarcated in terms of parents' ways of responding. This seemed true for adult patients' relatives as well. Spock and Lerrigo [23] and Kvaraceus and Hayes [24] stressed the need for hope and emotional strength in the parents with handicapped children. They are hard responses to urge people to manifest. Spock and Lerrigo [23] pointed out the need of relatives to get away from the problems from time to time. They gave the example of a veteran who would like to forget his handicap—"forgetting about it is the best thing, but how are you going to forget when everybody keeps reminding you of it?" This applies to both families and individuals.

ISOLATION OF AFFECT

An alternative to forgetting or being pressed to acknowledge illness and defect has been described by Chodoff, Friedman, and Hamburg [25], who call it *isolation of affect:* Parents look as though they were observing events occurring to others: seeming cool and aloof to others. This approach often makes relatives easier to *train* in dressing changes and physical therapy when they are called on to participate. A semi-professional style is assumed, which has its positive values in getting on with the work of rehabilitation. It also diverts relatives from their sorrow. Wives and mothers in particular, including some who had medical experience, have told us of consciously forcing themselves into this frame of mind and of hardening themselves to the task. They also comment that this attitude was a counterbalance to the falling apart emotionally of their disfigured spouse or child. One mother's letter shows her thoughts and style in suggestions to the social worker on how the hospital might improve care:

Letter from a Mother
Evening or weekend group sessions to involve parents who cannot make the Wednesday afternoon meetings are important. A pen pal program should be suggested to children and parents. It should be stressed that children will be physically weak when they go home. Parents should not expect them to be up to par. Do not expect complete recovery upon returning home. It takes years to gain back all physical strength. The scars never disappear completely. The biggest thing we can all do for our children is give them the emotional support they need and impress upon them that it is not what you look like that really counts, but what you are and those who think otherwise are not worth our time.

Honesty and understanding to children who tease burned children usually helps them to realize that the burned child is just a child, not a freak. If unburned children do not know what is wrong, they will be afraid and will tease, more as misunderstood self-protection than as cruelty. One little girl thought that Warren was contagious. She had had it explained before, but when she touched him, she was afraid she would catch it. I wouldn't want to catch it either! She had forgotten the explanation. They need to be reminded occasionally. Once the teaser realizes that burns happen to everyone and the burned person is still a person, the fear is gone and the teasing stops.

With most of the families we have seen there has been little problem in accepting help from professionally trained medical helpers, physical therapists, surgeons, pediatricians, and family doctors. Some people did eschew psychological help from social workers or psychiatrists and clinical psychologists, while accepting emotional help more readily from those providing medical care. This led us to elaborate some approaches to indirect support that are described in Chapter 10. The parents' group has always been a combination of professional and nonprofessional bridges to individual relatives.

In each area of family and neighborhood relations, the relatives need to reexamine their ways of interacting. They must determine how much they can expect their neighbors to shy off or to stimulate the patient socially. Brothers and sisters of adult and child patients vary in their ability to maintain a normal level of relatedness, and grandparents and in-laws have not been major positive influences in most of our cases. Finances take on special meaning. Relatives are stressed by the horrendous and mounting bills for medical care, whether they have insurance or not. Yet they yearn to let a husband have his drink, or a color television if he is going to sit at home endlessly, or to buy lots of toys for their disfigured child. This rarely does harm except to the exchequer, and ultimately realities inhibit this approach through special indulgences.

Husbands and wives do not readily bring up sexual problems related to disfigurement, but this is one more area of readjustment. Spouses note the loss of facial expression, and how they learn anew to gauge expressions. One husband, who took scrupulous care of his wife, said, "I feel like vomiting when I think of sex with her."

Relations with doctors are critical, whether long-standing or of short duration. The relational styles of families with their doctors are infinitely varied, but generally are based on clear subordination-authority rules, with the patients negotiating what they do and do not want done and arranging the timing of different procedures. Doctors are, of necessity, somewhat glorified, as a source of hope and place of security, but often there is some jealousy between a wife and a husband over the attachment to the doctor, who is seen as so grand in contrast to the spouse. For the man-to-man relationship there seems to develop the camaraderie of people who have been through a war together, which is supported by all the family members. This extends to adolescents as well. These positive relations are enormously useful in maintaining the follow-through of surgical procedures that may seem endless. In spite of careful presentation and repeated instruction, families do not understand a lot of the technical details in the beginning, and later, as the problems move into the chronic stage, the need to hope for better cosmetic results makes everyone distort what the doctor has told him. Like patients who come for elective cosmetic surgery in their desire for improvement, the disfigured patients and their families tend to ignore and repress the possible hazards of operations.

Families seem to exult when they find a doctor with whom they can relate, and if this is reciprocal, it simplifies all the problems of arranging referrals for other specialized work or consulting about unrelated illnesses. However, it need not be elaborated on here that there are problems for all patients with complex medical problems trying to navigate through the multitudes of people and organizational and bureaucratic intricacies of modern health care systems. Kidney failure and leukemia cases are other clear examples.

The general patterns are clear, that more effective people in terms of psychological normality and family intactness handled problems better. Woodward and Jackson [26] pointed out the high incidence of psychiatric disturbance in children after burn injuries, and subsequent reports on burned childrens' mothers from around the world indicate how many are overwhelmed, at least temporarily, by the catastrophe. With adult patients we are still unable to determine precise figures, but the same issues—how people can support each other, combine aggression, share feelings, and teach others to make an overall pattern of coping—remain the salient themes. What has come to be most helpful is simply looking at an overall pattern of family adjustment, at the unique qualities in the social structure to focus on how to be helpful.

If one follows the schema offered by Ackerman [27], a family serves several distinct purposes:

1. Provision of food, shelter, protection, and material necessities,
2. Provision of social togetherness and an affectionate matrix,
3. Opportunities for personal identity tied to family identity,
4. Patterning of sexual roles,
5. Training toward social roles and social responsibility, and
6. Cultivation of learning and the support and initiation of creativity in family members.

However, as Poznanski [8] indicated, the tremendous amount of work, time, effort, and money focused on the burn victim or other handicapped family member is likely to make a marked shift in the overall functioning of the household on a permanent basis, impairing or altering all of these functions. Necessities may be scarcer; affection is transformed into concern for the handicapped; identity becomes *spoiled identity* for all; sexual roles for the disfigured are distorted, as is social behavior; and the energies for learning and creativity are depleted. These factors have to be individualized for useful professional intervention.

REFERENCES

1. Seligman, R., MacMillan, B. G., and Carroll, S. The burned child: A neglected area of psychiatry. *Am. J. Psychiatry* 128:52–57, 1971.
2. Martin, H. L., Lawrie, J. H., and Wilkinson, A. W. The family of the fatally burned child. *Lancet* 2:628–629, 1968.
3. Wright, L., and Fulwiler, R. Long range emotional sequelae of burns: Effects on children and their mothers. *Pediatr. Res.* 8:931–934, 1974.
4. Long, R., and Cope, O. Emotional problems of burned children. *N. Engl. J. Med.* 264:1121–1127, 1961.
5. Herschowitz, R. G. Crisis theory, a formulation. *Psychiatr. Ann.* (12):36, Dec. 1973.
6. Olshansky, S. Personal communication, 1975.
7. Bott, E. Normals and Ideology: The Normal Family. In N. W. Bell and E. F. Vogel (Eds.), *The Family*. Free Press, Glencoe, Ill., 1960.
8. Poznanski, E. O. Emotional issues in raising handicapped children. *Rehabil. Lit.* 34(11):322, 1973.

9. Pless, B. Adjustment of Chronically Ill and Disabled Children, A Selective and Critical Review of the Literature. Report from Department of Preventive Medicine and Community Health, University of Rochester Medical School. Unpublished.

10. Holt, K. S. The Impact of Mentally Retarded Children upon Their Families. M.D. thesis, University of Manchester, England, 1957.

11. Gardner, R. A. The guilt reaction of parents of children with severe physical disease. *Am. J. Psychiatry* 126:636–644, 1969.

12. Schmitt, R. C. Some ecological variables of community adjustment in a group of facially disfigured burned children. Ph.D. thesis, University of Houston, 1971.

13. Tizard, J, and Grad, S. *The Mentally Handicapped and Their Families.* Oxford University Press, London, 1961.

14. Schwartz, C. G. Strategies and Tactics of Mothers of Mentally Retarded Children for Dealing with the Medical Care System. In N. R. Bernstein (Ed.), *Diminished People: Problems and Care of the Mentally Retarded.* Little, Brown, Boston, 1970.

15. Fisher, S. H. *Body Experience in Fantasy and Behavior.* Appleton-Century-Crofts, New York, 1970.

16. Howell, M. C. *Some Effects of Chronic Illness on Children and Their Mothers.* Ph.D. thesis, University of Minnesota, 1962.

17. Dow, T. E. Social class and reaction to physical disability. *Psychol. Rep.* 17:39–62, 1965.

18. Centers, L., and Centers, R. Body cathexis of parents of normal and malformed children for progeny and self. *J. Consult. Psychol.* 27(4):319–323, 1963.

19. Jabin, N. *Attitudes Toward the Physically Disabled as Related to Selected Personality Variables.* Ph.D. thesis, New York University, 1965.

20. McDaniel, J. W. *Physical Disability and Human Behavior.* Pergamon, New York, 1969.

21. Wright, B. A. *Physical Disability: A Psychological Approach.* Harper & Row, New York, 1960.

22. Farber, B., and Ryckman, D. B. Effects of severe mentally retarded children on family relationships. *Ment. Retard. Abstr.* 2:1–17, 1965.

23. Spock, B. M., and Lerrigo, M. O. *Caring for Your Disabled Child.* Macmillan, New York, 1965.

24. Kvaraceus, W., and Hayes, E. N. (Eds.). *If Your Child Is Handicapped.* Sargent, Porter, Boston, 1969.

25. Chodoff, P., Friedman, S. R., and Hamburg, D. A. Stress, defenses, and coping behavior. Observations in parents of children with malignant disease. *Am. J. Psychiatry* 120:743–749, 1964.

26. Woodward, J., and Jackson, D. Emotional reactions in burned children and their mothers. *Br. J. Plast. Surg.* 13:316–324, 1961.

27. Ackerman, N. W. *The Psychodynamics of Family Life.* Basic Books, New York, 1958.

10
Routes to Rehabilitation

After detailing in some extensiveness the special characteristics of facially disfigured people, it is difficult to go along with classic authorities, such as Wright [1], who say that there is no substantial indication that persons with an impaired physique differ as a group in their general or overall adjustment. It has been our premise that facial disfigurement represents such a major social and individual handicap as to distinguish it from other impairments. Rehabilitation specialists also say there is no clear evidence of an association between the type of physical disability and particular personality characteristics, a point with which we generally agree. Nevertheless, we find that the people who do best in handling these catastrophic issues are those who have the least depression, the most assertiveness, and the best ability to compensate for their sense of damage and inferiority. The problem lies in the task we set ourselves. In what ways can we offer direction toward the public or toward individuals and families that will be most helpful in rescuing facially disfigured people from despair and lives spent in isolation or hiding?

Garrett and Levine [2] emphasized that rehabilitation is essentially an issue of managing social problems that have a medical focus, and that the psychological goal is to view a person as a whole interacting with the environment through time and space. Nonetheless, it is very much still as written in Leviticus: "None . . . who has a blemish may approach to offer the bread of his God. . . . a man blind or lame, or one who has a mutilated face . . . may not profane my sanctuaries" [3]. I have observed in earlier chapters how advantageous good appearance is in most aspects of social life and individual functioning. Authorities on all kinds of handicapping point out that patients seek to live normal lives and that most of the people planning for them arrogantly plan for them to have low expectations with restricted opportunities for the fulfillment of social and sexual needs. I cannot offer any easy slogans for altering the perspectives of the public or the deeply imbedded reaction patterns, or even the structure of language that connects disfigurement with negative personal connotations. Rather, what I would like to offer is a series of emphases on different facets of the problem that will lead to better help within realistic limits for the many facially mutilated people who struggle in our society. This always means locating the person beneath the disfigurement by bringing the *social body image* of the handicapped into sustained contact with others.

TEACHING PROFESSIONAL TOUGH-MINDEDNESS

Educational efforts must follow several different directions, and be sustained over long periods of time. Health professionals need to be educated and drilled. There are textbooks on rehabilitation but they are not read by many surgeons, pediatricians, psychiatrists, social workers, or psychologists. The concentration of medicine on acute care needs to be altered toward a greater emphasis on the lives of the patients and a proper attention on narrow techniques for focal defects. This change needs to be spread through the different faculties by interested people. Many highly intelligent specialists can recite all the correct phrases. They know the lyrics, but they cannot carry the tune when it comes to implementation; and the burgeoning medical care system leaves less and less time and space for this type of humanistic focus.

This approach must begin with curriculum changes that expose professionals to the best, not the worst, ways of handling disfigured and mutilated patients. Rosemary Dybwad [4], a long-time worker with stigmatized people, has stressed, "You cannot legislate attitudes, but you can force people into contact, so that when they mingle they can begin to feel differently." Part of the problem is the way professionals are trained to think of their goals and to judge themselves and their competence in terms of focused and categorized problems and results so that they can finish their tasks decisively.

The professional does not like the idea that he cannot cure certain conditions. The problem is endemic to all of medicine and is one reason why chronic diseases and rehabilitation services have generally been underfunded in this country. There is much more money proportionately for immediate care. The burn situation is typical. A badly burned person may have treatment that costs a minimum of $150 a day for several months, but then there will be inadequate money to help with rehabilitation. The results of intensive care and an outstanding technical medical treatment may be vitiated by the lack of rehabilitation counseling, guidance, and support during transition back to the community. An example is the selective withdrawal of professional people as they feel their own job is done. Frequently the trauma surgeon withdraws after the patient's life has been secured. If the patient is a child, the pediatrician may feel it is largely a surgical and rehabilitation matter, or he may focus only on the fluid-electrolyte balance problems that obtain during the early phase of care. Some surgeons express a sense of failure about results with burns. What kind of a life will this disfigured child have? This is probably a more common undercurrent than is acknowledged. Most surgeons say it is simply a hard job to deal with this or "It's not my job—I can only do what I can about the wound, and then it's up to someone else."

The anxiety of dealing with incurability, as Kessler [5] has pointed up, is part of the burden of many physicians faced with large, complicated social and psychological problems related to physical disease. Care that is so specialized sets up a system that makes for easy extrusion of a particular disfigured patient. The rejection is never explicit, but the patient is shunted from one specialist to another. As the surgeons withdraw, or the patients and their families become discouraged, there appears to be a mutual change in the patient's course. He has to surrender the contact with the surgeon that, however intermittent, does symbolize hope in that what the surgeon does will lead to improvement and a change in appearance. This exclusion tends to leave the rehabilitation workers without support, the visiting nurses without an overall program, and the physical therapists with a diminishing role. In the successful cases described in earlier chapters, there is a striking feature of continuing contact with important medical, nursing, and physical medicine personnel. This initiation, development, and continuity of relationship is a crucial factor in successful readjustment after disfiguring burn injury. It shows hope for some improvement, albeit a limited one. The relationships of these patients endured for years. As mentioned in the first chapters the marginal status of the disfigured, and prejudices about appearance, need to be energetically opposed.

This does not mean that every physical therapist has to plan for a decade of Christmas cards and personal social contacts, but it does mean that every member of the staff should be systematically trained to keep open certain contacts wherever they are tolerable to enhance the patient's social participation. Nurses cannot be forced to like *all* patients, but neither should they avoid some semisocial contacts with patients, exchange of postcards, visits on the ward, or friendly chats, which can be so crucial to these patients. This is an aspect that is largely muted through professionalization, and as Etzioni [6] has pointed out, one style of nursing, in particular technical nursing, leads to further separation and splitting of human contact from the job. More and more as nursing becomes intensive care work, and struggles to professionalize itself and to achieve higher status, nurses follow the surgical model, frequently at the expense of patients who need personalized attention. There should be training for the staff so that they see these relationships, and so that they can tolerate them and not be overwhelmed by patients' bottomless needs.

The issue of toleration comes up because facially disfigured people often remain embittered and angry and they characteristically are more likely to express their bitterness and anger to the people who are closer to them and who appear "safe." The family will hear more than the professionals. The nurses and physical therapists will hear more than the pediatrician, and the pediatrician will hear more than the surgeon, who is most feared and who remains, also, the most powerful symbol of changing the situation.

UPGRADING ATTITUDES ABOUT REHABILITATION
The concern of professionals should be focused on making clear to the patients that something can be done in rehabilitation. Unless the rehabilitation program is given explicit status by the medical staff, it is very much more likely to fail. There is a general tendency to hand over the patient in a most casual way so that the patient feels that he is being downgraded. Social class differences sometimes come into the picture. Lower class patients may be more attractive to the nursing and medical staff if they assume a grateful and dependent role and do not ask many questions. Middle-class patients, who are obviously critical, more overtly demanding, less passive, more articulate, and less inhibited about complaining may be less acceptable as objects of the kind regard of the staff. They are hardest to treat charitably. Some authors talk of social class difference in attitudes toward the physically disabled; however, this does not appear to be very clear. It is much more apparent that educated people will find cliches to cover their attitudes and be more adroit in ducking out of situations requiring contact with the disfigured, but they are no less likely to be bothered by them and

no more able to be helpful than others unless given special instruction.

It is also true that professional literature on rehabilitation is well-intentioned, idealistic, and quite often abstract. Herman [7], for example, sees a healthy adaptation as one in which the individual accepts the reality of his situation and strikes resolutely in goal-directed, positive activities toward conquering his problems. This is too visionary and optimistic in terms of our disfigured patients, and rather too brisk about how people can bounce right back toward coping with their problems.

The time perspective is the most obvious thing to change in professional training. It is not difficult to convey that patients must deal with their initial trauma, with its shock and pain, and the grief and sadness that go with facing their disfigurements, and readjust to their altered vocational, social, and familial roles. However, professionals work under time pressures, and careers marked by seminars, semesters, and academic schedules tend to make them much more brisk about the pace of a patient's recovery than is realistic. They need to see how long it takes people to make these painful readjustments, and how precarious are the best human adaptations. Though the job is now enlarging, rehabilitation counselors have most often focused on vocational goals and the problems overlapping with them. The overall rehabilitation goal has been that of a salvage operation, as described by Roth in his book *Rehabilitation for the Unwanted* [8], where there is some hope of restoring as much as possible after the damage has been done. This gets into the web of compensation problems, where the costs of care, insurance claims, litigations, and lawyers all make complex additions to the rehabilitation scene, and to the patient's presentations of his feelings. In this regard, Gair [9] stressed that professionals should not give the patient cause to distrust the motives of people helping him. He also stressed that rehabilitation is long in duration and costly, and that it will remain costly because of the large numbers of people involved, which intensifies litigation and the struggles to get more money. He noted the pressure on the patient to edit his tale along lines that will yield more monetary support. Leaders in rehabilitation have generally been clear about these complexities, as exemplified by Rusk, who pointed out how important it is to get direct information from the patient about what his goals are and whether they are consistent with rehabilitation; "to fully understand the patient's motivation we must know his total personality and situation with the conscious and unconscious meanings of his disability to him" [10, p. 230]. And this takes time. There is some basis for arguing that in the long run this time will yield up better results in motivating patients to follow through on their rehabilitation programs, both socially and medically, but there is also the categorical problem that certain issues need more attention and that in order to meet the overall needs of the patients we must keep seeking ways of deploying professional time in more humane directions. When surgeons and medical and psychiatric workers really go after the attitudes of patients and push them to try over and over in social, vocational, and educational situations with a sustained interest, in more than a routine manner, it *can* yield attitude changes.

PUSHING

Samuel Johnson wrote that it was important for a man to be pushing but it was important not to be obvious in appearing this way. So it is with families. If they are always ranting about how to get on, this becomes hollow rhetoric and not very useful. But without the sense of support shown in some of the cases in preceding chapters, it is not likely that the patients would have done as well. Sometimes it is remarked that pushing these patients sets them up for great social disasters. This, of course, can occur, but it is so sure that they will face social disaster unless they get out and try, that it is worth the risks. In addition, persons who are disfigured do not take the encouragement of their relatives or their advice any more reliably than any other persons.

DEALING WITH SCHOOLS

School systems are currently so burdened with overwhelming issues that it is not readily feasible to involve them with still another group of children's needs beyond the categories of handicapped and learning disabled, which currently receive inadequate professional attention within the school system. In our first efforts with the schools after the opening of the Burns Institute in 1968, we were appalled by some of the stories we heard about the reactions of schoolmates toward disfigured children, and then, perhaps the most shocking kind of reports (all substantiated), that teachers were not only unable to manage their own responses to the scars, but would actually taunt the patients at times. Let one example suffice: James was a 14-year-old who had sustained facial and neck burns in a house fire. He returned to school, where he had always been a marginal student. When he was called on in class and failed to answer a question, the teacher asked, "What's the matter? Did they also burn your brains out?"

If there is one group that should be educable, it should be the staffs of schools. At the college level, the varieties of institutions seem to be so individualized and complex that it is hard to make suggestions, other

than to advise the immediate faculty members what to expect. It is
more feasible to enlist friends in class to help and support the returning
student. In high schools and grammar schools the overall pictures seem
similar. Although many teachers have a strong sense of obligation to
help handicapped children, they have all the conventional negative
societal attitudes accumulated about disfigurement. They must cope
with their own fearfulness while in full view of their students, and they
must also cope with the fearfulness of children in their class. Vengeful-
ness, teasing, and scapegoating are common in the classroom situation
when a handicapped child is not given the clear support of the teacher.
The faculty has to be taken into the clinic's plans and the family plan
for dealing with the patient. The teachers themselves need to be
drilled about reactions to physical peculiarities so they can surmount
their subjective fantasies about the horrors of deformity and popular
superstition about evil and disfigurement, and then *show* greater comfort and humane feeling to the disfigured. More than brittle false
nearness is needed. They need to hear about rehabilitation, and to be
given information they can pass on to the class about how the child is a
person, and how treatment is continuing. This hopeful attitude will
help all involved. The social body image of the patient needs to be taken
into the group spirit in class. The child needs to be part of the group,
and actively seen as a person of future promise and hope rather than an
object to be borne. In all situations the facially disfigured should be
urged to *talk*. The important feature is to convey the same kind of
hopeful and forward-looking attitude that helps in the medical care
setting. This hope does not depend on any specific act or belief, but on
an assumed attitude that there are things forthcoming, and that there is
reason to look positively to the future; this carries over to the young
patient a sense that he is still worthwhile and that he can be helped.

Often it has been useful to (1) to have the nurse go to the school or
have teachers come to the hospital to see what the patient looks like,
(2) to send clear reports about what the patient can and cannot do
physically, including some general statements about managing the child,
because this provides wording which the teacher can paraphrase for her
own use, and (3) in selected cases, to send photographs of the patient
from the hospital to the teacher, which she can choose to show to the
children in class. This last method has to be used discriminately because
it can be a double-edged blade. Sometimes pictures dehumanize the
patient and make the appearance even more frightful; sometimes the
photographs minimize because they do not show the true color contrasts that are so important in demarcating a disfigurement. In most

cases we have found that a photograph will take the disfigurement out of the realm of individual imagining and will define more clearly what the child looks like, even though this can be frightening.

A crucial factor in making the collaboration between the medical care system and the school system actually function is that of ongoing communication. The school needs to know that it can call the hospital, and that there are particular people who can be reached. In the burn hospital it is most commonly the schoolteacher, but our play ladies and visiting teachers know a lot about the explicit school-related problems of these students, and we draw them into the picture as much as possible. Sometimes the problem is focused on the nondisfigured aspect, e.g., the accompanying contracture of a hand or questions about how far to push the child. The advice as well as the positive thrust that the physical therapists need and exemplify in their approaches are helpful to get these children to do more. It has been useful for some teachers to see this so that they can forcefully engage disfigured children and make a breakthrough into a more personal relationship with the person who resides behind the mask of scar tissue. This is a continuing struggle against the castration anxiety provoked by the facially marred. They make many onlookers apprehensive about their own bodies, fearful of person damage; this is best countered by dealing actively with the actual person to dissipate these fantasies and feelings. Because parents are so commonly downcast and inarticulate about what to do, help must also reach out to the family.

FAMILY SUCCORANCE

Many opportunities occur in dealing with the families of the disfigured, for counselors, nurses, physical therapists, doctors, social workers, and other professionals to intervene briefly and help guide the whole family system. Wives and husbands, parents and siblings all face the disasters, and need long periods of time to make something meaningful out of the experience. Patterns of response are multiple, and months and years pass before the problem is worked out. Quinby and Bernstein [11] have examined some of the patterns that families follow, and so many of the families are disturbed that often the efforts involve the same kind of social support system that is described in caring for multi-problem families *without* a handicapped child. The drain of needing to keep actively supporting such partial families in the hope that they will be able to pick themselves up and ultimately function like intact families defeats this vain and exhausting goal.

If the medical team can decide who will try to be the long-term supports, and let the others simply react to people they like in a friendly and encouraging manner, it may lead to the best deployment of staff. It is the *long-term* contact that is vital. With our patients longitudinal care has often come through the plastic surgeon's office or the plastic surgery clinic, where the family can expect to return for a decade. The secretaries or the nurses may be the jolly supporters, but there must be a blend of friendliness and an espoused plan. The implications of surgery are always ameliorative, and it is this emphasis on going ahead that has seemed so important for our patients young and old. After a while the patients begin to tell what they want to have done. This is negotiated between the relatives and the doctor in terms of whether a nasal flap or an ear is to be worked on, and it is very important in maintaining the idea of hope. It is of interest that chronic reconstructive patients, even those who have seen many of the possible complications of surgery, including infections of wounds, grafts that do not take, and anesthesia complications, are like patients who have totally elective cosmetic surgery, such as mammary augmentation, in that they are much more relieved of anxiety by their relationship with the doctor and nurse than by medications, and that they show repression and denial of most complications and hazards in the surgical work planned for the future. This can sometimes lead to legal problems with cosmetic patients who abruptly sue because the results are unsatisfactory, but this has not been our experience. All lawsuits brought to our attention have related to the original fire or explosion and who was at fault.

Overall, what does occur is an education of the family in the intricacies of plastic surgical and other medical care. This approach plays a major role in educating the family about the course of their struggles and subsequent treatments that are part of learning to live with any chronic problem. Our experience has varied with different families in terms of how much they wanted to know, and how much this could help them. We advise meetings with the whole family and with key members individually, be it a mother, husband, or grandmother. No precise rule can be made other than to be alert for this person and his needs in order to engage him as actively as possible in dealing with the patient.

In addition to individual approaches, we have found that as they do in other conditions, group meetings for relatives have considerable usefulness. A number of burn units have ward groups in which the patients participate, as well as relatives' groups. Mothers' groups have helped with the children. There are many combinations of these run by the doctor and focused on medical information and group support, with nurses helping to discuss activities of daily life and review matters of dressing changes and specific procedures. Groups have been run by psychiatrists, psychologists, vocational counselors or physical therapists, and clergymen. In groups, families can work through their own feelings about loss and grief and helplessness, talk over their struggles in dealing with the disfigured person, and ventilate their attitudes toward the caretakers, be they nurses, lawyers, or teachers. They can also express some of their hostility about people in their community who make it difficult for the patients to adapt. Group members teach each other— they can make suggestions about school, job, and church; and fellow relatives can often be much more direct in dealing with other relatives of the disfigured in confronting hostility or acting out. These groups can be hospital-based or home-based, but they serve as enormously useful ways of helping families to cope.

SOCIAL ACTION

As so many of our patients have been involved in burns from flammable fabrics, many staff members as well as parents have been active on local, state, and federal levels to try to improve fabric standards, and to improve fire prevention. These involvements have varied from passive participation on the part of depressed parents who want to divert themselves, to more intense participation, and finally to desperate, rabid, and almost fanatical participation, which seems to be a compulsive effort on the part of the individual to turn away from his own problems by throwing himself into a different level and direction of thought and feeling. One is put in mind of the classification of coping mechanisms described by Dimsdale [12], which includes focusing on something good, finding a purpose in survival, and removing oneself intellectually, through religious beliefs, intellectualization, humor, or a changed time focus. There is a similar group of mechanisms in some of our families. We have always felt that the social benefits were unquestionable, and that the individuals needed these defenses so intensely that we have encouraged their activities, only gradually trying to redirect some of their attentions back toward the emotional needs of the disfigured person.

In and out of the hospital, self-expression groups for children have been helpful in our experience. In all of this, we have tended to stress activities. Because of the large diversity among families in education, stability of the family, and social class, we have not been able to find one activity pattern that is most helpful. But several principles may be seen clearly. There are activity patterns that are important to each individual. Personal relations are crucial and disfigured people should be encouraged to maintain them by any means possible. For many people, religious support is enormously supportive. Yet problems exist in getting clergymen to handle the disfigured; they are often very upset, as are other individuals. In our experience this has led patients to turn away from religious support because they felt that their counselors were acting in a different way than they preached. Wright [1] and other rehabilitation experts describe the broadening understanding and philosophical tolerance of a person who has mastered a defect or a handicap. This has remained a noble goal, usually beyond our patients. The striking observation has been the bitterness, the hurt, and the narrowing of focus, even in people who handle disfigurement well. Although some individuals may talk philosophically, one sees much more a determined suppression of this type of intellectual examination of the issue.

Reich [13] depicted the self-conscious person (actually only one type) as one who inherently strove for a high level of praiseworthiness in himself, then felt a failure at this and became angry at the world, but turned this anger inward toward himself and felt frustration and animus toward himself when placed in public situations where he would be superficially judged. There are other types of self-conscious persons who do not follow this pattern, e.g., the retarded individual who fears realistically that he will show a major defect in his behavior and who then wishes to hide it by inhibited behavior. However, his rage toward himself and his internalization of it appear to follow the same general order. Disfigured people and their relatives share this sometimes.

Families with disfigured offspring have some of the same problems. To some extent, all mothers have apprehension about the birth of their children and fear that there will be some defect in the newborn. When they have a child with a defect or a handicap, there is a profound period of depression and their self-esteem is injured. With conventional people there is a wish to send out photographs of the well-scrubbed and happy-seeming family at Christmas or on other occasions. With unconventional or idiosyncratic types of families there is an assumption that the family is capable of such a performance, but scorns it to choose a more special type of behavior: casual slovenliness, children in dirty clothes—a protobohemian, neo-hippy, pseudo-graduate-student style. But such families appear no happier when they have injured or handicapped children; in fact, their narcissistic stance seems to be *more* shattered. It is important to the hippy family or individual that his appearance is *chosen* and can be altered upon a wish to do so.

When families can share these feelings they are mutually supportive. In some families, as with cancer patients, crucial topics may be taboo, and there are parents who in very feeling ways say they cannot talk to the child about the facial burn because they all become inexpressibly upset. Many of the communications, as Rusk [10] has noted, are nonverbal, and many of the relatives have to learn to read expressions differently owing to the facial distortions produced by the scarring. The overall rules are as simple as the specifics are varied if the patient's family accept him when it is an enormous help in getting on with the next steps, moving out into the community, back to a job, and school and life lived in relation to others. If the family closes up, or closes off the patient, or is paralyzed by his presence and hopeless about him, it forecloses many of his avenues of adaptation. Everything that can be done to keep them all communicating and pushing the patient will be helpful.

SEXUALITY

I do not know of any agency or rehabilitation group that gives much attention to providing clinical help with sexuality for the handicapped in general, much less the facially disfigured. Derek Burleson, of the Sex Information Council of the United States, urged recently that handicapped people be viewed not as a problem but as a human potential: "They are not castaways on a desert island. They are brought up in a sexually oriented society, only with less chance for adolescent experience in preparation for life. But they can be deprived and neuterized by overprotective parents or professionals" [14, p. 44]. Again, the banner of permissiveness may be waved easily but not necessarily in a useful way. For the most part, the disfigured adolescent has such a wretched time socially that he or she cannot be shoved into parties and dating without careful preparation. Parents need to discuss what is sexually tolerable to them. They need to be clear about giving license to the disfigured adolescent to masturbate, if this becomes an issue. There have been isolated episodes of disfigured girls being promiscuous or engaging in prostitution, but these are rarities. Mostly we hear of sexual inhibition in the community, with some sex play in the hospital between adolescents who are similarly disfigured and who seem more accepting. This goes right back to basic attitudes about who is an acceptable sexual object, and how dehumanized people can be made to seem when they are facially deformed. Margaret Mead remarked, "We treat sex like constipation, and feel we should not deprive people in institutions or prisons" [15, p. 22].

Actually, there is exactly the opposite attitude for many deviant groups like the retarded for whom there is fear of sexuality, and there is no question that the prisoner is punished partly by making sure he is deprived sexually. The problem of homosexuality in prison is related here, as it is in many custodial institutions. Our experience has been in active medical and surgical hospitals, and we have seen exclusively heterosexual experimentation. But no doubt other sexual patterns exist. Sexual information needs to be brought up for all the younger people. For married people, facial disfigurement *may* be no problem, though many associated lesions may make the sexual act unappealing. The partner may be repelled by kissing scar tissue. One husband evaded sexual contact with his wife. In spite of serious efforts at discussion, he could not improve this attitude, which was clearly communicated to his wife, even though he verbally denied it when confronted. Generally, talking about these "forbidden" topics does help.

If the patient can talk to the social worker, the nurse, or any of the professionals, he has an opportunity for gaining new information or ventilating his feelings. This must remain a function of all of the people who work with these families, trying to get them to the right person for help when a problem comes up. Sex must be viewed as a valid and nonshameful topic for the disfigured.

PSYCHOLOGICAL REINFORCEMENT: MAINTENANCE OF MORALE AND HOPE

It is clear that the matrix in which all these issues can be best worked on is a healthy family. Among the crucial dimensions of a sound family life is a set of communication patterns that are clear in meaning, but that are spontaneous and flexible in picking up subjects when there are interruptions and that permit people to talk in their own special words about disturbing and tender subjects. In addition, the whole family has some quality of caring, and warm feelings predominate over hostility. A similar pattern can be seen in the relationships between the staff "family" and these patients; here, there is a slightly more formalized series of relationships and the affective ties are diluted, but the sense of friendliness, affection, and reliability remain. For the people who have been through the worst with the patients, there is a closeness that often lasts for years, just as children will rely on their parents as sources of strength and will aggrandize their parental qualities to gain security.

There is a definite element of this in the ways patients and their families idolize their clinics, doctors, and nurses, partly in response to actual help and valid assets, but also to enlarge the sense of power and security. This is why so many successfully treated burn cases, whether disfigured or not, will tell how they have been at "one of the best centers in the country." This gets tied to a series of hopes and wishes that combine fantasies and reality. A great hospital is more likely to invent new kinds of prostheses and to develop new procedures through research, e.g., new types of skin transplants and better methods for storing skin for grafts. (The latter actually occurred at our center to the pleasure of all who knew about it, staff and patients.) This mixes optimism and magical thinking; people know that the best is being done. The psychology of reconstructive and plastic surgery epitomizes this; the scrupulous giving of information to our patients by the cosmetic and plastic surgeons was quite accurate, as attested to by social and professional visitors. Yet the tremendous need for the patients and their families to maintain hope and to avoid the day of reckoning, when they would have to accept that little more could be done, led to distortions of what was told by the doctors, so that the families could always hope for more physical improvement than was possible.

These advances in medical science shade into the active public relations and advertising approaches to life, which talk of "self-image modification" or "self-image surgery" and tell how to alter your looks to change your life. They have the positive aspect of supporting morale and keeping people trying, while implying unfeasible goals. In order to keep from depression, people have to look forward and not backward: There needs to be some challenge, as well as some goal lying ahead. This is another part of the doctor-patient relationship and explains some of the motivation of doctors who, unless they become imbued with visionary zeal, as did the plastic surgeon turned mental healer, Maxwell Maltz [16], withdraw from the treatment and care of the disfigured when they no longer see a future. There has to be a series of balances, but the sum of the different forces in these equilibriums must press the patient toward better coping. As Nietzsche [17] wrote, "Man is the only animal who can make promises." This involves possibilities for both hope and deception, false promises and encouragement. The ingredients and their combination are crucial.

FOCUSING ON THE INDIVIDUAL PATIENT

In examining the forces for adjustment in coping with burns, we have used the diagram reproduced earlier in this book in slightly modified form (see Table 1), emphasizing environmental resources and the temperament of the individual. Some patients have shown an ability to deal with their problems that does not seem to come clearly from the experiences of their background. They seem to have some innate qualities that fit into what Thomas, Chess, and Birch [18] have construed to be the biological bases of personality and temperament. Without making a detailed examination of these qualities, suffice it to say that individual features, such as intellectual level, are crucial in the type of adaptation that a patient will make. The quality of his moods will determine his interpersonal style and the ways in which he can use

interest and affection from others, but it will also determine how
people react to him. In addition, the patient's attention span, rhythmicity of reactions and affects may or may not fit in with the medical
routines or the family style. Persistence, adaptability to change, and
the intensity with which the patient reacts to change (new surgical
procedures and the shifts from hospital to school or work) all enter
into how he will make out with his handicap.

The people who make it into what E. M. Forster [19] called the
aristocracy of the considerate and the plucky are those who live with
their problems and do not surrender to them. Olshansky [20] has
referred to the overall quality as the "strength to endure," and Chedekel
[21] has stressed the common denominator of "persistence" in his
review of the people who have adapted well in the follow-ups cited in
this book. What we are moving toward may sound like some form of
simple-minded activism. If this be the case, we will accept the charge,
leaning a little on Aristotle's dictum that the aim of man is action. For
those patients who have achieved through more platonic intellectual
mode, we have felt that intellectual *action* was essentially the issue, and
that the common feature was the effort to make more of the person's
potentials in all spheres. This is in accord with Rollo May's view [22]
that having intentions to reach out to the world and cope with it relates
intensity of life to the intensity of experience and the aliveness of the
person. In practice it means pressing every caretaking person to talk
out his own attitudes toward disfigurement in a systematic way so he
can be ready to *talk* to these patients to reach out to their *person need*
at all ages and help them, urge them, support them to use all their inner
resources to keep striving. It must be individualized: hobbies, sports,
studies, jobs—all need to be culled from the special interests of the
patient by *talking*.

This does not contradict the importance of supporting influences of
family, friends, and caretaking people. Studies in the prediction of
success at rehabilitation indicate that economic support from the
family improves the prognosis for rehabilitation. This is related to all
of the things that families can do for a handicapped person, if they
have financial wherewithal. There are, of course, corroborating data
about how much more feasible it is for middle-class and educated
people to manage in the medical care system than it is for poor, less
well educated people, and it is clear from our case material that social
stability seemed to correlate directly with good economic status, which
provided all the factors listed under "Environmental Resources" in
Table 1. None of these factors either absolutely determines outcome
or precludes the need for direct work with the patient himself.

I have been describing the family and medical contexts as open systems for interaction. The patient may be viewed as the center of these open systems, in which we have a determined goal of more active coping for him based on the assumption that this directly correlates with better life adjustment and with personal growth. The question of philosophy overlaps and is, in fact, another way of restating the same issue. If a person seems to cope, to manage his problems, to show good nature, we say he has a good philosophical attitude or has achieved maturity and growth through his handling of the problem. It becomes a kind of circular discussion. If our standards for good adjustment include the ability to work, the ability to sustain relationships with other people, and the availability of some energy to follow these activities, then what we mean by growth and maturity should be encouraged wherever possible. For the disfigured person, this may mean answering a telephone where he cannot be seen, it may mean night work as a janitor, it may mean boldly facing the world as a salesman; there is no one pattern. The work ethic in rehabilitation applies to the assiduous, determined tolerance of pain and dedication to the goal through hard work at physical medicine and repeated surgery. If this attitude can be harnessed toward the goal of getting out into greater social activity, reaching out toward people, and pursuing people, it may be crucial.

Communication Skills

Because so much of the disfigured person's trouble lies in his diminished repertoire for communication with facial expression, and the habitual restriction of bodily activities in dealing with people, retraining can be an important modality for help. Patients need to be instructed in the manner of Carl M., described in Chapter 5, who stressed how he learned to speak out boldly so that strangers can see that he speaks and be distracted from the dehumanizing appearance of his disfigurement. Katherine M., described in Chapter 4, in the mobile use of her eyes, her brow, and the way she sits near people and speaks up immediately, also has developed a repertoire for engaging people that transcends her disfigurement. The decision to become socially outgoing involves learning to sit without curling up, to grasp hope without hiding and constricting, learning to move expressively, and relearning body language. Disfigured persons cannot sit too close because this overwhelms people who do not know them, but they can focus on tactics for engaging them in conversation. It would be grandiose to assume that simply by giving instruction to people on how to sit and how to gesture we would be able to alter the whole social context, much less the individual's personality pattern, sense of shyness and despair, and all of the intense feelings that do not change readily for physically normal people who are shy about their social performance and strive to feel more socially competent. There are several points to be borne in mind. Basically we are trying to provide a new frame for relating to others. The situation is so clearly altered from the conventional one that new rules apply. It is more analogous to the experience with neurotics in the military service who perform as well as anyone else under dangerous conditions, but return to their neurotic patterns as soon as the situation permits. Similarly, neurotics may do quite well in hospital situations. However, the basic issue seems to be that much neurotic defensiveness is overridden by the urgent need to face a grim and threatening world. The disfigured patient finds it physically exhausting to keep up his guard and not to overreact or miss any chances to relate normally. He must always be vigilant.

Erikson [23] follows Anna Freud in citing that children who come to feel loved become more beautiful, as if some energy from the inner psychic economy transforms the whole appearance of a person and heightens his *"tonus of living."* It refers to the whole picture of joy that transmutes the appearance of a loved person, and also involves the greater tolerance of the loving observers for conduct that is unattractive, which they can accept as cute because of their lovingness. The observer of the damaged face may be a nonloving total stranger or a tortured relative who is grieving for the patient. Nonetheless, if an affectively positive, friendly mood can be established, the humane basis of the interaction is underscored, and the man behind the face becomes more visible and his scars are at least less disfiguring, even if he does not abruptly appear handsome. The maneuvers that can be taught, about where to sit, about giving cues with the voice, using one's hands to gesture, and finding jokes or standard lines to open a conversation, can help the individual to establish more comforting and comfortable inter-action. This is the kind of work that Davis spoke of in his papers on the strained interactions of the visibly handicapped. He noted that the potential of the handicap to inundate the social situation and wreck the chance for social exchange can be avoided if two people can "break through . . . draining away some of the stifling burden of unspoken awareness" [24, p. 12] by having a broader base of conventional rela-tionship to stand on while conversing. For some handicaps this means that the disfigurement is no longer seen. For most it is merely miti-gated, but this can be enough.

Even in this special situation, we are speaking about activation of the patient to achieve something in the world of social participation, to avoid hopelessness, and to avoid withdrawing from the situation, which would mean returning to a helpless and passive state. Activation here means drawing recognition as a significant *person* rather than as a damaged *thing*. We must strive to see that these patients do not resign hope of winning social recognition. This does not mean that they can expect to win social praise for their appearance. Kardiner and Ovesey pointed out that being a member of a despised or feared group is damaging to self-esteem, and is an enormous impediment to opportunity in life. "Depressed self-esteem almost always remains a private matter. But self hatred is a stronger feeling and generally requires some form of projection to attempt to stay its damaging effects" [25, p. 364–65]. For some disfigured people there is a kind of hatred of the mutilated state and of other patients, and a great deal of energy can go to waste in bitterness, complaining, and self-loathing. Handicapped people commonly exhaust their emotional and physical energies in struggles to cope, and accomplish this largely by restriction of their life space rather than through an expanded awareness or sensitivity to others—except that they are always aware of a possible reaction to their own appearance. Just as the normal person is bound to reality by his work and the demands on him, the disfigured person is bound to hope for a better reality by the focus on medical care. As long as surgery is pursued, there is an element of hope, because the professionals feel more secure in the role of technique-oriented relations and, most of all, because of the reality that the better the results, the easier will be the chore for the patient. Along this line, there is a place for vocational counseling for the disfigured, balancing the patient's desires with the realities of his strengths and the possibilities available for him in industry. Krusen et al. [26] advise us to avoid half-truths and overenthusiasm. These are usually caused more by the guilt and apprehension of the counselor than the needs of the patient himself.

Cosmetics

Most health care professionals, as well as patients, have been subjected to the maxims of our society that solutions that are superficial or merely cosmetic are not really helpful. This attitude has hampered efforts to help patients with devices they might use to cover some lesions and make others less obvious. The extent of this kind of help varies with the lesion and the willingness of the patient to try. Wigs should be encouraged, but they need to be of appropriate quality to avoid an air of added grotesqueness. Some patients may be encouraged to have artificial ears attached, and some may be advised to have multiple reconstructive procedures done on their ears. These matters need to be negotiated with the patient. The staff member should offer his own preference in a noncoercive way and be willing to have it ignored, very much like the parent of an adolescent, who needs to have a clear opinion that the adolescent wants to hear but will not accept. The disfigured patient need not be an adolescent chronologically, but his frequent changes of mood and his struggles between the poles of dependence and independence will all give him some of this interpersonal style, which should be taken into consideration in negotiating treatment plans. Sometimes the patients *do* know best.

Clarinda G., a 14-year-old black girl, was brought to the hospital for reconstructive therapy. With good intentions, effort was made to bring in a beautician who covered lesions with makeup. He came to see Clarinda and put on a heavy layer of pancake makeup. It covered much of her scarring with a thick coating, but made her skin many shades lighter. The staff, all white, was focused on covering the scars and was not sensitive to the child's unwillingness to accept the change of color. Later, when she was given a chance to put on the makeup herself, she altered it to suit her own sensibilities, with a more acceptable result overall.

Linda D., aged 11, had help from the same beautician. The result was again quite satisfactory to staff observers, but these onlookers later reported that only when Linda had taken over the application herself and could modify it to suit herself did she find it worthwhile.

Group Approaches

Patients need a variety of choices to find a place for themselves. Family groups are best for some patients, and patients' groups for others. Some adolescents can go to an adult group, and some younger patients can function only within a group of their own peers. As many types of group endeavor should be mounted as are feasible in terms of staff time and interest. Counselors, recreation therapists, teachers, psychologists, clergymen, nurses, psychiatrists, social workers, pediatricians, surgeons, volunteers, and physical therapists have done this work profitably and in different ways in many burn centers.

If the group leaders can be flexible in their approaches, patients will take what they need. They can be educative, didactic, exploratory, supportive, experiential, analytical, or inspirational. If there is true interest and sincere feeling for the patients, there is little likelihood of harm, and considerable potential for helping people to manage and to share their feelings in productive ways.

Associated with this is the possibility of either a team approach or a special viewpoint. Undoubtedly, each has its advantages, but while the group leaders are activating patients and going after their strengths, the patients and their families will find favorites and divine differences in emphasis and perspective. How many times have the pediatrician and the surgeon who both agree on what is to be done explained the problem in ways that make the family feel that conflicting viewpoints are at issue? How often does the nurse, in passing, answer a question with correct information, but in language different from that of the social workers, so that the patient's spouse is alarmed by the data? These situations are not always avoided. Patients and their families get to know the doctors in the long run, and it is in the long run that the rehabilitation has to be planned. Wives get to know when the surgeons are harried and not to be questioned. They learn to work around the secretary to delay surgery, or sometimes to have extenuating letters sent to the insurance company or compensation board; nurses are implored to call the school when the pediatrician will not. In most cases, tolerance of this and a good-natured awareness that it is adaptive behavior will make it bearable for the staff and they will not feel that they are being made fools of and manipulated, an attitude that does not augur well for long-term care.

Group meetings on the part of the staff are essential for keeping these issues in perspective and making sure that communications do not get wildly distorted. These meetings do not require much time once the staff know each other. They can consist of brief, informal comments on the cases coming up for review. But such an informal communication system can save the staff a lot of unnecessary tension and ill feeling that will work to the detriment of the patients. Group meetings focused on staff feelings have proved useful in our hospital, whether they involve the psychologist, psychiatrist, social worker, nurse clinician, or pediatrician as leader. It is also clear that there will be differences in personalities as well as in the action styles of different specialists, which will change the direction of the overall team approach. In places where the emphasis is on aggressive surgery, more will be done. In those where other modalities are favored, they will prevail. It is also true that *hard* and *soft* lines may vary from doctor to doctor. While the psychiatrist is commonly expected to be the soft-liner, in contrast to the surgeon, we have experienced a number of situations in which the surgeon wanted to be more cautious and gingerly with the patient's feelings, while the psychiatrist was plumping for a tougher approach. These are some of the benign complexities that make this work interesting. Where the staff is open about disagreements and has an understanding of basic goodwill, the disagreements will not be a problem, but covertly maintained disagreements can frighten and annoy patients and their families even when the wording of the staff is skillful—the affects have to be right, and then there is leeway for minor linguistical differences.

Hypnosis and Behavior Therapy Techniques

Devices such as hypnosis may be quite useful in turning corners in rehabilitation. Patients who are fighting physical therapy can be given suggestions that will get them back to working on their medical regimen. Children who are fighting against their fears of going back to school can sometimes be helped to make this transition with hypnotic suggestions. If the staff agrees that this is worth trying, it can be distinctly positive. If the staff opposes this, either because they find it is not "honest" to use suggestion, or they oppose the manipulation of patients, or they simply see it as a theatrical maneuver, it may not be helpful. Contrasts in technique and theory should always be made clear to the patients and their families, as well as the staff, as an opportunity for learning, by showing alternatives and being as open as possible about being eclectic and individualized. It has always been part of good patient care.

Behavior therapy techniques, behavior modification, operant conditioning, and other types of therapy to alter behavior based on learning theory are being tried in more and more varied ways in clinical settings, and both provide an opportunity for investigating which types of problems are most responsive to these techniques, and finding out which procedures are most suited to particular patients, and also expose some of the strong and adverse opinions of different clinicians about what approaches are felt to be the most acceptable. Counterconditioning, positive reconditioning, and experimental extinction may be some of the tactics used to deal with behavior problems of the disfigured, to get them to go out in public, to teach them new social skills. Theoretical differences between most social workers, clinical psychologists, and psychiatrists are great, but not insurmountable. Behavior modifiers deal with the negativism and depression of patients without looking at their subjective states but rather viewing them as "habits" and trying to handle them in terms of reinforcement contingencies.

The best reconciliation of these viewpoints in terms of rehabilitation will not come from theoretical arguments but rather from the advice that both experienced teachers of behavior modification and other mental health workers agree on, as well as from asking the patient what he wants to change and using this in the formulation of a program. In dealing with a variety of approaches, the worst hazard seems to be chaos or open friction that frightens or drives away the patient. We are enjoined to be varied and experimental in combining different methods, but we should also be cautious about trying to do too many things simultaneously—lining up physical therapy, psychotherapy, counseling, an educational program, and more surgery in tandem will obviously not work. Some coordination is necessary, which simply means keeping all the co-workers informed through the chart, by telephone, or by mail.

THE ORDER OF TACTICS, STRATEGIES, AND DEFENSES

Efforts in dealing with the disfigured depend on better exchange of information. That is now a commonplace dictum—but it is often difficult to implement. Patients need to know where to turn, and they need to know what will happen if they follow particular guidelines. People working with them, in their turn, need to be in touch with the family system, the job situation, the public and community attitudes, and the educational system so that there is some reasonableness in the planning. One cannot give simple answers to problems of facial disfigurement. We need to forge sincere interdisciplinary efforts to remake the lives of these patients so that we are realistic Pygmalions rather than messianic dreamers or dispellers of hard truths. In dealing with these problems we have had to recast many of our psychological formulations.

Some of the mechanisms that might be considered neurotic for physically unremarkable patients came to appear more adaptive for our group, such as the extensive use of denial in those who functioned rather well. The use of extensive denial in fantasy, and sometimes by word, saves the energies needed to confront other issues. The whole range of "neurotic" styles and defenses—counterphobia, repression, displacement, reaction formation, and protection—are all frequently useful in the dire circumstances in which these patients find themselves.

The enormity of facial disfigurement shifts and alters the overall personality pattern and methods of adaptation. The people who work with these patients need to make large shifts in their own perceptions in order to put together the special patterns of professional and humane intervention that will yield the most gratifying lives for these patients. The approach needs to have an experimental and venturesome quality; the goals must be long-term and not require perfect results or continually smooth relations with grateful subjects.

Societal attitudes about deviance and people who look damaged can be modified only a little, but determined professionalism coupled with humane feeling can yield great increments in improved living for many people who would otherwise be lost to society and whose lives would be largely lost to them.

REFERENCES

1. Wright, B. A. *Physical Disability: A Psychological Approach.* Harper & Row, New York, 1960.

2. Garrett, J. F., and Levine, E. S. (Eds.) *Psychological Practices with the Physically Disabled.* Columbia University Press, New York, 1967.
3. Lev. 21:17–23.
4. Dybwad, R. Personal communication, 1974.
5. Kessler, J. *Psychopathology of Childhood.* Prentice-Hall, Englewood Cliffs, N.J., 1966.
6. Etzioni, A. (Ed.) *The Semiprofessionals and Their Organizations.* Free Press, New York, 1969.
7. Herman, C. Psychiatric Rehabilitation of the Psychically Disabled, the Mentally Retarded and the Psychiatrically Impaired. In F. Krusen, F. Kottke, and P. Ellwood (Eds.), *The Handbook of Physical Medicine and Rehabilitation.* Saunders, Philadelphia, 1971.
8. Roth, J., and Eddy, E. M. *Rehabilitation for the Unwanted.* Chicago: Aldine, 1967.
9. Gair, H. A. The Injured, His Lawyer and Rehabilitation. In *Proceedings of Conference on Rehabilitation Concepts*, University of Pennsylvania, Philadelphia, October 17–18, 1962. American Mutual Insurers Alliance, Chicago, 1962.
10. Rusk, H. *Rehabilitation Medicine.* Mosby, St. Louis, 1964.
11. Van Quinby, S., and Bernstein, N. R. How children live after disfiguring burns. *Psychiatry Med.* 2:146–159, 1971.
12. Dimsdale, J. E. The coping behavior of Nazi concentration camp survivors. *Am. J. Psychiatry* 131:792–797, 1974.
13. Reich, A. Pathological Forms of Self-Esteem Regulation. In R. S. Eissler et al. (Eds.), *Psychoanalytic Study of the Child.* International Universities Press, New York. 15:215–234, 1960.
14. Burleson, D. L. Handicapped Aim for Normal Lives. Sex Information Council of the United States. *New York Times*, October 14, 1973.
15. Mead, M. Interview in *Practical Psychology*, May–June 1974.
16. Maltz, M. *Psychocybernetics.* Prentice-Hall, Englewood Cliffs, N.J., 1960.
17. Nietzsche, F. *Portable Nietzsche.* Viking, New York, 1954.
18. Thomas, A., Chess, S., and Birch, H. *Temperament and Behavior Disorders in Children.* New York University, New York, 1968.
19. Forster, E. M. *Two Cheers for Democracy.* Harcourt Brace, New York, 1946.
20. Olshansky, S. Personal communication, 1973.
21. Chedekel, D. Personal communication, 1975.
22. May, R. *Love and Will.* Dell, New York, 1964.
23. Erikson, E. H. *Insight and Responsibility, Lectures on the Ethical Implications of Psychoanalytic Insight.* Norton, New York, 1964.
24. Davis, F. Deviance, disavowal: The management of strained interaction by the visibly handicapped. *Soc. Prob.* 132(9):120–132, Winter 1961.
25. Kardiner, A., and Ovesey, L. *The Mark of Oppression. Explorations in the Personality of the American Negro.* World, New York, 1962.
26. Krusen, F. H., et al. *Handbook of Physical Medicine and Rehabilitation* (2nd ed.). Saunders, Philadelphia, 1971.

Index

DATE DUE